Terror, Religion,
and Liberal Thought

THE COLUMBIA SERIES ON RELIGION AND POLITICS

THE COLUMBIA SERIES ON RELIGION AND POLITICS,
edited by Gastón Espinosa (Claremont McKenna College) and
Chester Gillis (Georgetown University), addresses the growing demand
for scholarship on the intersection of religion and politics in a world
in which religion attempts to influence politics and politics regularly
must consider the effects of religion. The series examines the influence
religion exercises in public life on areas including politics,
environmental policy, social policy, law, church-state relations,
foreign policy, race, class, gender, and culture. Written by experts
in a variety of fields, the series explores the historical and contemporary
intersection of religion and politics in the United States and globally.

Mark Hulsether,
Religion, Culture, and Politics in the Twentieth-Century United States

Gastón Espinosa, ed.,
*Religion and the American Presidency: George Washington to
George W. Bush with Commentary and Primary Sources*

Gary Dorrien,
Economy, Difference, Empire: Essays on Social Ethics and Politics

John M. Owen IV and J. Judd Owen, eds.,
Religion, the Enlightenment, and the New Global Order

TERROR, RELIGION, AND

LIBERAL THOUGHT

Richard B. Miller

COLUMBIA UNIVERSITY PRESS
NEW YORK

Columbia University Press
Publishers Since 1893
New York   Chichester, West Sussex
Copyright © 2010 Columbia University Press

Library of Congress Cataloging-in-Publication Data
Miller, Richard Brian, 1953–
Terror, religion, and liberal thought / Richard B. Miller.
    p.   cm. — (The Columbia series on religion and politics)
Includes bibliographical references and index.
ISBN 978-0-231-15098-9 (cloth : alk. paper) —
ISBN 978-0-231-52186-4 (ebook)
   1. Violence—Religious aspects. 2. Terrorism—Religious aspects.
3. Political violence. 4. Liberalism. 5. Human rights. 6. War—Religious
aspects. 7. Toleration—Religious aspects. I. Title II. Series.
BL65.V55M56   2010
201'.763325—dc22
                                          2010022780

Columbia University Press books are printed on permanent
and durable acid-free paper.
This book is printed on paper with recycled content.
Printed in the United States of America

c 10 9 8 7 6 5 4 3 2 1

References to Internet Web sites (URLs) were accurate at the
time of writing. Neither the author nor Columbia University Press
is responsible for URLs that may have expired or changed since
the manuscript was prepared.

To my students

CONTENTS

ACKNOWLEDGMENTS

I have been reflecting about social criticism and religious violence since the terrorist attacks of 9/11, and my debts to those who have joined me in that intellectual project are vast. Sections of this book have benefited greatly from close readings by Byron Bangert, Jae Chung, David Cockerham, Cheryl Cottine, Jennifer Girod, Connie Furey, Oz Kenshur, Mark King, Nancy Levene, Terence Martin Jr., Ann Mongoven, Douglas Ottati, William Schweiker, Melissa Seymour, Faraz Sheikh, Lisa Sideris, David Smith, Aaron Stalnaker, Charles Wilson, and Mark Wilson. John Kelsay, Gabriel Palmer-Fernandez, and John Reeder provided input to improve my argument and steer me clear of several mistakes.

Portions of this book took shape from various academic presentations. In January 2002, I gave a paper on "Terrorism and Its Aftermath" at the annual meeting of the Society of Christian Ethics, out of which I drafted parts of appendix II. In June 2002, I presented a paper on "Terrorism and Casuistry" at the invitation of the Catholic Theological Society of America, providing the seeds for chapter 3. In November 2002, I presented a draft of chapter 2 at the annual meeting of the American Academy of Religion. In March 2006, I presented what became parts of chapters 3 and 4 at St. Olaf College. Many thanks to the audiences at these sessions for their comments and input.

Colleagues in the Department of Religious Studies and at the Poynter Center for the Study of Ethics and American Institutions at Indiana University have provided intellectual community and engagement that are enviable by any measure. Thanks to David Haberman and David Brakke for generous support in their capacities as departmental chair, and to Carol Bland, Karen Boeyink, Robert Crouch, Ken Pimple, Glenda Murray, Brian Schrag, and Chera Steimel for their collegiality and dedicated work at the Poynter Center. I owe a special debt of thanks to Glenda Murray for her editorial advice as this project unfolded and to Cheryl Cottine for providing invaluable assistance by checking my references. I also wish to thank Stacy Miller, Scott Seabold, and Mary Elizabeth Mitchell for hosting my visit to New York City in the wake of the 9/11 attacks. A summer faculty fellowship from the College of Arts and Sciences and a research fellowship from the College of Arts and Humanities Institute at Indiana University provided support to move this project forward. Wendy Lochner at Columbia University Press and Chester Gillis and Gastón Espinosa, the coeditors of the Columbia Series in Religion and Politics, offered key advice for advancing this project and seeing to its completion. To all of these friends and colleagues I am deeply grateful.

Parts of chapter 5 were published in an earlier form in Richard B. Miller, "On Identity, Rights, and Multicultural Justice," *Annual of the Society of Christian Ethics* 19 (1999): 261–83, and they appear here thanks to the editors' permission.

As always, I owe an incalculable debt to Barbara Klinger and Matt Miller for their tireless good cheer and affectionate support.

Terror, Religion,
and Liberal Thought

1

THE PROBLEM OF RELIGIOUS VIOLENCE

FROM INCOMPREHENSION TO INDIGNATION

Reports of religious violence are often met with incomprehension. For many of us, violent religious zealots seem fanatical to the extreme, fueled by ethnic, tribal, racist, or national antipathies that border on the pathological. Whether such persons act within regimes of toleration or in illiberal contexts, they seek to impose their visions with brute force and fail to grasp the benefits of peaceful coexistence wrought by respect for individual rights, pluralism, and religious liberty.[1] For citizens who enjoy such benefits, appeals to religion to authorize indiscriminate killing and seething intolerance are abominable, beyond understanding. The fact that individuals find personal meaning and sense of community in cultures intent on death and destruction seems incongruous if not unfathomable.

Our bafflement, however, may be shortsighted. Even a cursory understanding of history would remind us that religion's power to inspire violence is hardly new. Today that power is manifest in regions far removed from each other by creed, race, economy, and local tradition—ranging across cities and villages in Western Europe, North and sub-Saharan Africa, the Middle East and the Gulf States, Central and South Asia, the Malaysian Archipelago, East Asia, and North America. In 2009, the U.S. State Department produced a list of forty-five terrorist groups around the world, over half of which cite religion as their motivation.[2] Those numbers increase appreciably if we include domestic militant Christian organizations. Religious groups responsible for carrying out recent acts of death and destruction include members or associates of al Qaeda, renowned for destroying the World Trade Center, bombing the train systems in Madrid and Mumbai, attacking hotels and embassies in North and sub-Saharan Africa, and sponsoring suicide bombing missions across a swath of territory ranging from Morocco to Bali; Aum Shinrikyo, a militant offshoot of Japanese Buddhism that plotted to release nerve gas into the Tokyo subway system; Sudan's Islamic regime, which is carrying out a genocidal war against non-Arab ethnic minorities in Darfur; Sikh nationalists fighting Hindus in the Punjab; Hindu and Muslim militants battling over control of Kashmir; members of the Islamic Resistance Movement (Hamas) in Palestine; Christian white supremacists and antiabortion activists in the United States; and Zionist militants who attacked one of their own leaders in addition to Muslims in the West Bank.[3] Whether conceived in churches, synagogues, mosques, or temples—or in government offices, training camps, or underground cells—violence as a sacred duty is a ubiquitous feature of the global landscape.

How to think normatively about religious violence and terrorism is the subject matter of this book.[4] To that end, I will focus in particular on the events surrounding the terrorist attacks of 9/11. I will do so in large part because, among the recent acts of religious terrorism in the United States and elsewhere, 9/11 raises moral questions about human rights, respect for persons, and the limits of toleration with vivid clarity. For many persons, 9/11 iconically represents not only religious violence but also the globalization of violence—its easy exportation and disregard for borders. More philosophically, 9/11 puts in stark relief questions about the moral challenges of coexistence in an increasingly pluralistic public culture, questions concerning religious authorizations of violence, human rights, and the basis and limits of tolerating the intolerant. These matters are the source of ongoing concerns in liberal democracies, brought on by cases and controversies regarding persons who challenge the limits of our respect for differences and alert us to the demands of justice to ourselves and to innocent persons more generally.

The attacks on 9/11 thus invite us to reflect on basic norms and values according to which liberal democracies organize public life around a vision of citizenship and coexistence—norms regarding personal security, the assignment of respect for persons, and the grounds and bases for religious and other forms of toleration. Such norms provide a deep moral structure to the democratic beliefs and practices that violent religious zealots mock. Drawing sustenance from that structure, citizens can speak with clarity and confidence about the moral stakes involved in defense of themselves and their democratic institutions.

As a work that addresses questions about liberal democratic norms and values in the wake of 9/11, this book is an exercise of liberal social criticism. By "social criticism" I mean intellectual work that enables us to assess customs, practices, and policies that shape the direction of institutions and aspirations of public culture. Social criticism has as its object the moral quality of society and the res publica. Yet the adjective is also reflexive; it reminds us that social criticism is a social activity, contributing to our shared reflections on public life.[5] Social *criticism*, of course, does not aim solely at identifying moral problems or social evils; it can be laudatory or aspirational, calling us to our higher natures. *Liberal* social criticism modifies its subject matter by designating certain commitments. By "liberal" I mean two things. First, I mean a basic philosophical view of moral anthropology and, in particular, the value of freedom and deliberation. As Will Kymlicka puts it in his liberal defense of multicultural politics: "We lead our life from the inside, in accordance with our beliefs about what gives value to life," and we have an interest in questioning and revising those beliefs in light of whatever information we acquire.[6] Liberalism is premised in part on our interest in freely developing and critically revising our desires and wants against a background of meaningful options. As John Rawls writes, individuals "do not view themselves as inevitably tied to the pursuit of the particular conception of the good and its final ends which they espouse at any given time." Rather, they are "capable of revising and changing this conception."[7] Liberals thus assign value to autonomy or "moral subjectivity," understood as our capacity to self-critically evaluate our immediate, first-order desires in order to determine whether they are indeed desirable and worthy of our attachment. Second, by "liberal" I mean to designate general values underlying modern, liberal democratic societies: the presumption of individual liberty; respect for persons and, with that, the tolerance of different loyalties, communities, and convictions; a commitment to equality; an account of the limited authority of the state; and the organization of political life premised on popular sovereignty.

One of my aims in these pages is to offer reasons for speaking confidently in defense of liberal principles and practices in response to religiously authorized calumny and terroristic activities. I offer my thoughts as an act of resistance against what Michael Walzer calls the "culture of excuse and apology" surrounding terrorist action.[8] That is not a culture in which terrorism is openly defended, but one in which the rationales come from oblique and indirect angles. Typically such rationales assume the form of excusing terrorism, including religious terrorism, by assimilating it into a broader critique of political inequality, Western imperialism, or American foreign policy—as if violent zealots were themselves advocating liberal and egalitarian causes. Such views demand a direct counterposition. Writing soon after 9/11, Walzer put the point forcefully:

> Secular and religious intellectuals, scholars, preachers, and publicists, not necessarily in any organized way, but with some sense of shared commitment, have to set about delegitimizing the culture of excuse and apology, probing the religious and nationalist sources of terror, calling upon the best in Islamic civilization against the worst, defending the separation of religion and politics in all civilizations. . . . For all their inner-directedness, their fanatical commitment and literal-minded faith, terrorists do rely

on, and the terrorist organizations rely even more on, a friendly environment—and this friendly environment is a cultural/intellectual/political creation. We have to work to transform the environment, so that wherever terrorists go, they will encounter hostility and rejection.[9]

The easy conscience of terrorism, itself a formidable foe, scarcely materializes in a cultural vacuum. Although intellectual work is no substitute for politics and the powerful resistance it affords, social critics proceed on the premise that ideas can do real work. Without the practice of social criticism in public culture, the opportunities for excusing the inexcusable are left dangerously wide open.

Yet my purposes go beyond addressing the serious challenges of religious terrorism in the wake of 9/11. The questions I pose and the answers I offer aim to address enduring normative matters surrounding human dignity, religion, and terrorism—the ethics of political religion and violence more generally. In this sense, 9/11 will serve as a crystalline case about which I will address fundamental ethical questions regarding rights, respect, recognition, and toleration. That is to say, the arguments I develop are relevant to moral judgments and practical reasoning about religious terrorism beyond the particular challenges posed by the atrocity of 9/11. I will thus take as my point of departure several questions: On what basis may victims and their sympathizers avow a grievance against religiously authorized terrorism? In particular, how are we to think normatively about radical Islam and its disturbing relationship with religious intolerance and violence? More generally, how are we to think about the aspirations and claims of political religions whose beliefs chafe against what are presumed to be settled liberal norms and practices? Can liberal social critics speak normatively in ways that are sensitive to cultural and religious differences? Underlying these questions is a host of others regarding what it means to respect human rights, questions raised by the liberal democratic commitment to religious toleration and, today, by broader concerns regarding respect and recognition in multicultural politics. Those concerns might lead us to be unclear or uncertain about the grounds for moral indignation in response to violence and injustice, even while we feel our outrage so strongly.

Indignation is one theme that weaves through the pages that follow—sometimes explicitly, sometimes inchoately.[10] That theme stands in tandem with the theme of toleration and its limits. Toleration is a central tenet in liberal political doctrine, indignation less so. Perhaps we think that one idea excludes the other—that to be indignant toward someone is to be intolerant of him or her. But that impression can be deceptive. It is rather the case that these ideas are conceptually linked: our indignation moves us toward the limits of tolerance and alerts us to basic standards according to which we (and others) rightly expect to be treated. Given that fact, we do well to reflect on what it means to feel aggrieved in response to 9/11 and other acts of injustice.

The British philosopher Peter Strawson invited readers to consider feelings such as indignation in an influential essay devoted to the free will–determinism debate and the idea of moral responsibility. Although my interests here do not align with that particular discussion, I want to sharpen my focus in light of Strawson's ideas and terminology. Strawson asks his readers to consider what he called "morally reactive attitudes" that arise in our responses to experiencing or seeing another person's conduct or attitude of indifference or malice.[11] Our reactions that flow from witnessing indifference or malice are directed at the perpetrator's intentions or attitudes. Strawson identifies three reactive attitudes in response to malice or indifference. A person who is wronged typically has a reactive attitude of *resentment*. A third party witness to wrongdoing typically has the reactive attitude of *indignation*, which Strawson construes as a "vicarious analogue" of resentment felt on behalf of the wronged party. And the agent of wrongdoing, upon reflecting on the wrong he or she committed, has the self-reactive attitude of *guilt*.[12] For Strawson, to hold a person morally responsible for wrongdoing exhibits our propensity toward the morally reactive attitude of disapproval. Strawson uses his idea of morally reactive attitudes to argue that denying individuals moral responsibility for their wrongdoing is tantamount to demanding that other members of the interpersonal community forego having morally reactive attitudes toward them.

Strawson's aim is to show that philosophical debates about whether determinism threatens moral responsibility are idle. On his account, it would be psychologically impossible to stop holding persons accountable because it would be psychologically impossible to stop having certain kinds of emotional responses to them. Our everyday practices presuppose the existence of certain deep emotive states. Viewing moral responsibility as part of a larger life-world, Strawson invites his readers to grasp the interpersonal expectations that express and give structure to our morally reactive attitudes and to see how they are deeply woven into the conventions of everyday life.

Strawson does not set out to provide bases that underlie *justified* reactive feelings of resentment, indignation, or guilt. That is to say, he does not have us think about the *moral* wrong to which the reaction of indignation is appropriate. Strawson's argument is addressed chiefly to metaphysicians, not moral philosophers. But if we are to have confidence in our moral feelings, I propose, we need more than the conventionalist account suggested by Strawson's discussion. Our grievances presuppose a moral world about which we can argue and provide reasons. In the pages that follow I will offer one set of reasons that lie at the heart of justified feelings of indignation, namely, the idea of human dignity and the respect that it deserves. My account will attend to the notions of resentment and indignation on the premise that both can be justified responses to another's malice or culpable indifference.

For the purposes of simplicity, I will conflate such feelings under the general category of *indignation*. Our indignation is justifiably aroused when matters of basic human dignity are violated by others' acts of malice or indifference. Later I will say more about those ideas and indicate the relevance of human dignity and equal respect for thinking about feelings of indignation and the limits of toleration. Both ideas, indignation and toleration, are wedded to the idea of equal respect for persons—or so I will argue. That argument will have us focus on what it means to expect respect from others (a self-regarding claim) and what it means to assign respect to others (an other-regarding claim).

But I am getting ahead of myself. Here my point is introductory and general: without a grasp on moral reasons that support our indignation in response to 9/11 and events like it, we are left with only our incomprehension and a desire for some explanatory account of religious zealotry and violence.[13] Without moral reasons, our emotions will lack voice and confidence, and our commitment to toleration may find itself tethered to benign indifference as a *modus vivendi* rather than to principles of justice and respect.

So we have two grounds for thinking about indignation, both of which—oddly enough—are connected to the idea of toleration. At one level, indignation points to the limits of tolerance: our moral reactions reveal where we draw lines regarding acceptable and unacceptable behavior. At another level, *reasons* for our indignation include grounds that help make sense of our toleration and why we draw limits where we do. Reasons enable us to say why and on what terms we can meaningfully conceive of coexistence in a world of diverse beliefs and worldviews. Indignation and toleration, rather than operating in different conceptual spheres, indeed shed light on each other.

I will address these and related matters in the pages that follow. The attacks of 9/11 pose questions not only about the strangeness but about the wrongfulness of religious terrorism. I will comment on our incomprehension in passing. It is the immorality of the atrocity itself on which I wish to focus our attention, and I will do so with an eye to basic liberal values—especially those concerning toleration, respect, and recognition—on which democratic citizens often unreflectively rely.

SETTING THE STAGE

To help set the stage for our discussion, it may help to recall the following statements and events. Three years before 9/11, five leaders of the World Islamic Front, including Osama bin Laden, issued a fatwa variously translated as a *Jihad against Jews and*

Crusaders or *Declaration on Armed Struggle against Jews and Crusaders* that stated:

> The ruling to kill the Americans and their allies—civilian and military—is an individual duty for every Muslim who can do it in any country in which it is possible to do it, in order to liberate the al-Aqse Mosque and the holy mosque (Mecca) from their grip, and in order for their armies to move out of all the lands of Islam, defeated and unable to threaten any Muslim. This is in accordance with the words of Almighty Allah, "and fight the pagans all together as they fight you all together," and "fight them until there is no more tumult or oppression, and there prevail justice and faith in Allah."[14]

Bin Laden's fatwa was fueled by his dissatisfaction with the policies of his own government of Saudi Arabia and, in particular, its policy of permitting U.S. presence in that country. He was also aggrieved about allied sanctions against Baghdad and the continued military activity over Iraq's no-fly zones in the wake of the first Gulf War.[15] The *Declaration* thus advocated the use of violence to force an American withdrawal from the region. Bin Laden found American presence to be not only a defilement but also a form of ongoing aggression against Muslims and Muslim territory. With those concerns in the background, he and his associates write: "We . . . call on Muslim ulema, leaders, youths, and soldiers to launch the raid on Satan's U.S. troops and the devil's supporters allying with them, and to displace those who are behind them so that they may learn a lesson."[16]

These and related statements against the "neo-Crusader-Jewish alliance"[17] suggest antipathy that draws from religious conviction. Bin Laden encourages killing in the name of religion: "As for the fighting to repulse [an enemy], it is aimed at defending sanctity and religion, and it is a duty as agreed [by the ulema]. Nothing is more sacred than belief except repulsing an enemy who is attacking religion and life."[18] Ayman al Zawahiri, second in command at al Qaeda and bin Laden's long-time associate, described the 9/11 attacks as an opening salvo against Christian and Jewish "infidels."[19]

Soon after 9/11, bin Laden, with al Zawahiri at his side, praised the perpetrators as martyrs. After claiming that "here is America struck by Allah the Almighty in one of her vital organs," he went on to say that, "Allah has blessed a group of vanguard Muslims, the forefront of Islam, to destroy America. May Allah bless them and allot them a supreme place in heaven."[20] Indeed, bin Laden and al Zawahiri's religiously grounded antipathy is comprehensive. It draws on religion both as a *warrant* for carrying out violence (Islamic tradition) and to name the appropriate *targets* of that violence (Jews, Christians, pagans).[21]

Islamic beliefs and ritual protocols likewise inform the handwritten document, sometimes called the "Last Night" document, found in the luggage of Mohammed Atta after the 9/11 attacks. Atta admonished his fellow hijackers to view the last night before the attacks as one of spiritual preparation in which they were to pray, read, and reflect on the Qur'an and concentrate on God's promise of victory and paradise. Echoing the preparations necessary for worship or pilgrimage, Atta instructed his fellow operatives to shave and make ablutions required for a state of ritual purity before departing for the airport, after which they were to make supplications to Allah. Atta's admonition to "Strike for God's sake" was followed by an exemplary story of Ali ibn Abi Talib, the cousin and son-in-law of the Prophet and renowned as a devout and disciplined fighter. The hijackers were also instructed to treat their first victims as sacrificial beasts, whose throats were to be cut in ritual fashion, should Allah so decree. Toward the conclusion of his instructions, Atta writes: "When the hour of reality approaches, the zero hour, [unclear] and wholeheartedly welcome death for the sake of God. And always remembering God. Either end your life while praying, seconds before the target, or make your last words: 'There is no God but God, Muhammad is His messenger.' "[22] As Bruce Lincoln observes, the key for Atta was to weld "practice to discourse: providing each grubby, banal, or lethal act with authoritative speech that ennobles and redefines it not just as a moral necessity, but also a sacred duty."[23]

In response to these statements and events, President George W. Bush went to great lengths to distinguish terrorism[24] from Islam in the weeks and months after 9/11, remarking that "the face of terror is not the true faith of Islam."[25] While visiting mosques, conferring with Islamic clerics, and speaking out against harming Muslim citizens, Bush denounced those who scapegoated Muslims and those who might be mistaken for Muslims. British Prime Minister Tony Blair, in an interview with the Arabic newspaper *al-Hayat*, similarly stated: "There is nothing in Islam which excuses such an all-encompassing massacre of innocent people, nor is there anything in the teachings of Islam that allows the killing of civilians, of women and children, of those who are not engaged in war or fighting."[26] One aim of these statements was to defuse a highly prejudicial picture of Islam as religiously intolerant, politically regressive, indiscriminately violent, and virulently anti-Western.

Bush's and Blair's statements echo a concern for justice and a regard for respect, equality, and recognition in democratic public culture. Their comments speak to challenges posed by al Qaeda and radical Islam, a wing of Muslim belief and practice led by Osama bin Laden and his lieutenants that, in the words of John L. Esposito, "not only declares jihad against governments in the Muslim world and attacks Western representatives and institutions in the region but now makes America and the West a primary target."[27] Conflating Muslim terrorism with Islam tout court creates a false picture of Muslim piety and undermines grounds for civic trust and equal respect. Muslims and non-Muslims alike possess fuller resources for properly imagining Islam than provided by the self-styled practitioners of what Esposito calls "jihad international."[28] In this vein, the Pakistani journalist Ahmed Rashid writes, "The Taliban, like so many Islamic fundamentalist groups today, divest Islam of all its legacies except theology—Islamic philosophy, science, arts, aesthetics, and mysticism are ignored. Thus the rich diversity of Islam and the essential message of the Koran—to build a civil society that is just and equitable in which rulers are responsible for their citizens—is forgotten."[29] In the wake of 9/11, Muslims rightly expect continued assurances of nondiscrimination, respect, and recognition that take into account a full picture of their tradition.

At the same time, a firewall between faith and ethics can lend the impression of innocence regarding Islam no less than other political religions. In the wake of 9/11, one mood toward Islam and religion more generally has been notably apologetic, underwriting a priority of religion to ethics.[30] By "priority of religion to ethics" I mean the idea that religious conviction is not only immune from social criticism but sets the terms for moral norms and practices. Rendering religion prior to ethics in that way crowds out concerns about religion's more general social and political responsibilities—responsibilities that religious adherents might disregard in the name of faith. But such worries cannot be long suppressed. Echoing this concern about innocence, religion, and the ethics of belief, the editors of the *New York Review of Books* have bluntly asked, "How Aggressive is Islam?"[31]

In the pages that follow I will not seek to answer that question in any comprehensive sense; I am not sure that anyone can. As I stated earlier, I want to articulate and defend liberal norms and values for assessing Islamic terrorism with an eye to thinking about respect, recognition, toleration, and the relationship between religion and ethics more broadly. My aim is not to focus on religion to *explain* the conduct of Islamic radicals or other religious zealots who carry out terrorist acts. My purposes are normative and evaluative, not causal and explanatory. That is to say, I will be thinking throughout this book in light of moral concepts and categories that shape liberal social criticism about right and good conduct. I will set out in the next chapter to examine recent efforts to help us think about the relationship between Islam and terrorism and show how such efforts differ from vigorous non-Muslim social criticism of Islamic extremism. I want to defend the superiority of the latter approach to social criticism, drawing on a liberal theory of human rights along with an account of moral disagreement and the values that underlie the practice of religious toleration.

At stake are two related concerns: first, whether (and on what basis) we may evaluate actions justified on terms that invoke religious warrants; second, how and on what terms those aggrieved by Islamic and other forms of terrorism may justifiably feel indignation. Attention to the moral basis of indignation is important, of course, because it provides the foundation for confidently expressing one's grievances and acting appropriately in response. In the aftermath of 9/11, the United States and Britain, along with several allies, deployed military force in Afghanistan and, later, Iraq; rounded up, interrogated, and detained numerous terrorist suspects for prolonged periods of time; and increased intelligence efforts around the globe to thwart the danger posed by Muslim extremists. Those policy decisions presumed a moral grievance that invites thoughtful analysis in the wake of the terrorist attacks.

In the chapters that follow, I will argue that Muslim extremism is unjust when it violates the rights of life and security, basic human rights that I will defend in liberal terms. Central to that argument is the idea that all persons have inherent dignity by virtue of our moral subjectivity, our capacity to deliberate about, establish, and revise our ideas of the good life. The value of dignity lies at the heart of each person's entitlement to respect. I will supplement that claim by arguing that the grounds for believing in such rights connect with a liberal understanding of respect for differences and religious toleration. On this view, we can say that Muslim extremists should respect human rights, all else being equal, even if they do not endorse specific practices or beliefs those rights function to protect. We can also say that individuals who seek recognition in a multicultural world must first satisfy baseline conditions regarding respect for other persons. We will thereby understand how respect and recognition take their bearings from a key normative concern in this book, namely, the idea of equal liberty.

Defending these ideas will involve identifying and developing core norms in moral theory, in particular, respect for persons and human rights. They will also involve sharpening the distinction between *respecting* and *endorsing* that builds on Stephen L. Darwall's analysis of respect and John Rawls's account of the "burdens of judgment" in his explanation of liberal toleration and moral disagreement.[32] Darwall and Rawls enable us to understand the moral grounds that support the norm of respect for persons along with the idea that understandable reasons exist for intractable moral disagreement. They also help us grasp the idea that such disagreement should not prevent differing parties from respecting each other along with basic rights and claims of justice.

The fallout of this line of argument is twofold. First, it provides a basis for an ethics of belief that holds religions (and other comprehensive doctrines) morally accountable on grounds that are independent of any single religious belief or practice.[33] Understanding human rights in terms that are independent of any particular religious provenance enables us to draw on rights as an idiom of radical critique. Second, it presumes that recognition of others, properly understood, has limits. Persons who fail to respect rights are not due the kind of sentiments or attitudes that recognition typically requires. Violations of human rights are morally wrong and deserve to be condemned, however much those violations claim the aura of religious authority, and however much recognition of cultural or religious difference is important to the formation or authentication of another's identity. Or so I will argue.

Readers familiar with liberal thought will likely feel disquiet or at least a sense of irony about the critical interrogation that I will pursue here. Liberals are typically associated with defending religious toleration in the wake of theological and civil conflict. The European wars of religion are central to any understanding of the cultural context in which liberal doctrine and modern political philosophy arose.[34] Posing questions about religions' duties and the limits of toleration seems to chafe against basic liberal intuitions. But religious toleration is not unconditional. Establishing the qualifications—drawing the limits—requires us to probe values that underlie the ethics of toleration, inviting us to consider the norm of respect for human dignity and equal liberty. To be sure, probing the terms of criticism and the norms of toleration is scarcely new to liberal democratic theory. Yet that task has acquired added urgency given new patterns of global interaction, religious activism, and political conflict in the aftermath of 9/11.

BETWEEN APOLOGETICS AND ETHNOCENTRISM

Liberal social criticism today is mindful, indeed anxious, about being either apologetic or chauvinistic. Stated differently, liberal social critics are careful to avoid offering what Charles Taylor calls "favorable judgment on demand," on the one hand, and ethnocentric judgment, on the other.[35] These tendencies mark two reference points, the Scylla and Charybdis, of liberal social criticism in diverse, multicultural contexts today. The first is a romantic tendency that reflexively valorizes others because they are different. On this view, the experience of difference is expansive: it bids us to look outwardly, to discover how (say) the non-Eurocentric imagination has found noble and creative expressions, often under adverse political and social circumstances. The second is a chauvinistic tendency that reflexively dismisses others for the same reason: because they are different. On this view, the experience of difference is contractive. It bids us to look inwardly, to champion the insights of (say) the Eurocentric imagination and its contributions to Western history and culture. These two tendencies have set the terms for much of the culture wars today, expressing broad sentiments about how identity, including civic identity, is to be properly formed and how pluralism is to be negotiated. More abstractly, they presuppose that no encounter with others can be value-neutral, that judgment is an unavoidable feature of any interpretation. Yet both of them operate on the same terms, namely, the "us-them" comparison, and they beg the obvious question about how to defend the yardstick on which any such comparative evaluations are premised.

I want to navigate between these two reference points by describing and defending what it means to respect others along with baseline terms for assigning recognition and esteem to cultural practices and traditions. Against apologetic temptations, considerations of respect may require us to inject a disconcerting note into discussions of religion in a context that is sensitive about diversity insofar as those considerations require us to step back and ask normative questions about *others'* respect for human dignity. Against ethnocentric temptations, my argument will require social critics first to assign "benefit-of-the-doubt respect" to others in cross-cultural commentary. That requirement of respect introduces a normative check on tendencies to privilege one's own way of being in cross-cultural exchanges and comparisons. The norm of respect for persons will thus enable us to mediate, self-reflexively, between habits that incline toward exoticizing otherness, on the one hand, and chauvinistically dismissing it, on the other.

Typically, in liberal social criticism and cross-cultural dialogue, anxieties about making imperialistic judgments preoccupy us. I am aware of those worries but do not see them as imposing an insuperable obstacle to the inquiry that lies ahead. There is an equally troubling danger to avoid, namely, safeguarding piety from social criticism. Such problems, of course, are not unrelated: our worries about avoiding ethnocentrism often incline us in an apologetic direction. Ellen Willis correctly identified these tendencies when she observed soon after the 9/11 attacks, "We are especially eager to absolve religion of any responsibility for the violence committed in its name."[36]

In the wake of 9/11, charting a way between these two reference points is complicated by a third: the need to clarify the moral basis for a *self-regarding claim*, namely, indignation in response to a grievous injustice. Too often we are inclined to overlook duties (and injustices) to the self in our focus on rights and respect owed to others. That inclination, I want to argue, can be too charitable. In what follows I aim to provide moral grounds for self-regarding feelings of indignation while steering between the Scylla of apologetics and the Charybdis of chauvinistic criticism. Such self-regarding ideas, as should be obvious, encumber others, including strangers, with the duty to recognize and respect oneself. That is one implication of thinking in terms of basic human rights: all persons, including those who espouse human rights for others, are rights-bearers themselves.

I have organized the bulk of this book in seven chapters that concentrate on ethical theory and social criticism. The next chapter will examine efforts by scholars and public intellectuals to help us think about the relationship between Islam and terrorism in the wake of 9/11. After describing and assessing those views, in chapters 3 through 5 I will develop a normative understanding of the rights to life, security, and toleration that aim to deepen our understanding of what lies behind my assessments. There we will enter directly into a discussion of human dignity and its implications for thinking about basic rights and duties—especially respect, toleration, and recognition—within diverse, multicultural contexts. The idea of human dignity, I hasten to add, is not only a liberal or parochial Western creation. To make that point, in chapter 6 I will show how the grounds for thinking about human dignity and human rights provide a basis for dialogue with Muslim political theology. That discussion will open up more general reflections about the ethics of belief and the putative priority of religion to ethics, topics about which I will remark in chapter 7. That chapter will be followed by two appendices that focus on theoretical and practical moral questions surrounding the use of armed force in response to the attacks of 9/11.

Discussions of religious terrorism typically aim to render it intelligible. They speak to the enigma of killing conceived as a sacred duty. In the next chapter I want to examine various frameworks that help us wrestle with the relationship between the Islamic tradition and terrorism. Frameworks organize our perceptions and help make sense of our experience. They also help us refine some of our intuitions about how to assess others along with ourselves. Four such frameworks assumed center stage in the wake of 9/11, all of which reflect more general patterns in social criticism for thinking about political religion, normative inquiry, and multicultural politics. To their specifics it is now time to turn.

2

9/11 AND VARIETIES OF SOCIAL CRITICISM

Discussions of Islam and terrorism often aim to contextualize Muslim radicalism and render it intelligible. They speak to the incomprehension that follows upon religious violence. Here I want to examine four arguments—historical, economic, relativist, and internalist—that aim to help us grasp the relationship between the Islamic tradition and terrorism in the aftermath of 9/11. These arguments deploy one or another interpretive framework for "imagining religious terrorism," to paraphrase Jonathan Z. Smith. They try to make sense of what seems incomprehensible by invoking frameworks, contexts, or parallel examples in comparative ways. When confronted by what is unusual or incongruous, we typically think comparatively and analogically, drawing from more familiar areas of experience to help make sense of what seems new or radically different. We domesticate and sometimes try to humanize what is strange by looking for similarities in other domains of experience, recalling prior examples or precedents to help us understand what otherwise seems unimaginable.[1]

Yet the arguments I want to examine are not merely descriptive; they target more than our sense that religious violence seems inexplicable. They are forms of social criticism. They enable us to assess customs, practices, and policies that shape the direction of institutions and aspirations of public culture. Frameworks offer not only the promise that "in comparison a magic dwells," as Smith would have it.[2] Also, and equally important, they offer normative insights. They provide illumination in which the work of critical interpretation becomes possible.

In the wake of 9/11, social criticism that draws from historical arguments show how Muslim extremists draw on Quranic, legal, and other materials in Islamic tradition to justify committing terrorism in its name. They also show that moderate or more mainstream Muslims have normative resources within their tradition for condemning terrorism, thereby providing Muslims a basis for "connected criticism"—criticism that invokes rules and teachings that are indigenous to the terrorists' own background and beliefs.[3] The economic argument claims that religious belief is incidental to the causes of Islamic terrorism—that poverty, not religious conviction, fuels terrorist activity. On the strongest version of that view, Islam is epiphenomenal to the material factors that drive Muslim extremism. The relativist argument claims that we must stand in the shoes of Muslim terrorists before judging their conduct. On that account, appealing to what purports to be universal morality of human rights in order to judge Islamic extremism expresses a parochial, Western perspective. The internalist critique argues that the rise of Islamic terrorism raises questions that should be directed inwardly, toward an assessment of policies and practices of the United States both at home and abroad. One exponent of that argument assimilates a critique of terrorism into a more general critique of neoliberalism and global capitalism.

These lines of thinking capture intuitions that typically arise in response to an interpersonal or social trauma. We are often inclined to situate such events within a larger story, one with origins, authorities, and potentially analogous or telling incidents that provide reference points for us to consider as we try to make sense of what happened. We might seek out root causes and deeper motives to explain what happened and why people acted as they did. We might ask ourselves what might drive someone, the agent or agents of the action, to behave as they did—imagining how the world looks and feels when we place ourselves in another's shoes. And we might ask ourselves if we contributed to the events that transpired—whether we are implicated in the incidents that we lament. Such commonplace dispositions find voice in the historical, economic, relativist, and internalist accounts to which we'll soon turn our attention.

These four accounts also reflect a heightened level of sensitivity regarding Islam and its representations in the wake of 9/11, and each presses important insights about which I will comment in the pages that follow. They seek not to articulate bin Laden's particular grievances but to frame the rise of Muslim terrorism, or our judgments about such terrorism, within a wider narrative or explanatory account. But they all fail to face fundamental questions about human rights, the grounds (and limits) for respecting different beliefs, and the basis for expressing (and deserving) respect from others. Stated in the simplest terms, they fail to clarify whether citizens aggrieved by the attacks of 9/11 may justifiably feel morally indignant and expect their grievance to warrant respect (and potential action) from others. Putting ourselves in dialogue with these frameworks will enable us to grasp various challenges that arise when evaluating religiously authorized practices. Along the way, we will clarify some of the terms and aspirations of liberal social criticism as it bears on the ethics of religiously authorized violence, toleration, and the relationship between religion and ethics.

HISTORICAL ARGUMENTS

One way to address the Islamic extremism and terrorism of 9/11 is to say that there are legal precedents and doctrinal aspects within Islamic tradition that enable us to assess the use of violence for political or other purposes. Among the scholars who have embarked on a historical analysis of this sort, John Kelsay and James Turner Johnson stand out owing to their familiarity with the ethics of international affairs and, in particular, historical approaches to the morality of war in Western religion.[4] After reviewing bin Laden's many incendiary statements that killing Americans and Jews is a duty of all Muslims, Kelsay asks, "How, then, can one regard the judgment of Osama bin Laden as 'Islamic'? The short answer is, one cannot."[5] Drawing on traditional and contemporary Islamic teachings on war and peace,[6] Kelsay reports that there are places in Islamic doctrine that permit the use of force in defense and reprisal, but that nothing in Islamic tradition justifies indiscriminately killing Americans (or anyone else) as a "constant and considered policy."[7] Bin Laden's stand suggests an all-out war in an emergency situation to remove U.S. and allied forces from the Arabian Peninsula, the main lines of which run contrary to Islamic teaching. That teaching requires using limited means that prohibit treachery, cheating, and killing or mutilating children, women, and old men. Drawing on these and related materials, Kelsay concludes: "Extremely solid grounds exist . . . in Islamic tradition, for condemning the Sept. 11 attacks."[8]

In a similar vein, Johnson argues that bin Laden's fatwa, *Declaration on Armed Struggle against Jews and Crusaders*, makes several assumptions that are not found in traditional or mainstream Islamic approaches to war. The *Declaration* expresses a radicalized version of jihad that includes several distortions of juristic thinking about the legitimate use of force. First, bin Laden and his associates cannot presume the authority to promulgate a fatwa because they lack the necessary scholarly credentials.[9] Second, their fatwa distorts the original understanding of the "individual duty" to carry out a jihad. The juristic tradition authorized the idea of an individual duty in response to an emergency, understood as a military invasion. Johnson notes that "the statement from bin Laden and his associates, by contrast, postulates a broad and continuing state of emergency. . . . It is not a short-term response to the immediate emergency caused by a military invasion but rather a call to jihad that turns it into a conflict of cultures."[10] Further, bin Laden and his associates present the erroneous idea that territory that was formerly under Muslim rule properly belongs to the *dar al-Islam*, that such territory cannot be ruled by a non-Islamic government or its proxy, and that the only proper rule for such territory is Islamic law, the Shari'a.[11] All of these ideas depart from normative juristic tradition in Islam; indeed, they produce a permission for using force that traditional jurists sought to exclude. Bin Laden's fatwa likewise "leaves scant room for toleration of the 'people of the book,' as prescribed in the Qur'an, because under the extended definition of what constitutes an aggression against the dar al-islam, Jews and Christians present in dominantly Muslim societies become assimilated to this aggression."[12] The fatwa turns the idea of the defensive use of force into an offensive one. Johnson writes: "The traditional, normative conception of defensive jihad is still visible through bin Laden's reasoning, but its meaning has been distorted into a doctrine far removed from what the jurists who first formulated it had in mind and transformed into something they sought to make illegitimate: a justification for the waging of war nominally on behalf of the Islamic community but in fact by private individuals for their own goals."[13]

Kelsay and Johnson help to sort through traditional materials that Islamic social critics may use for internal critique, reform, and intellectual development. Identifying legal precedents or normative jurisprudence enables adherents within Islamic tradition to evaluate it from within and develop its intellectual and cultural resources for comparative ethics. Rather than expecting Muslims to adopt the language, ideology, and heritage of non-Muslim political morality, the work of Kelsay and Johnson invites Muslims to interpret and develop resources in their own tradition to evaluate acts of violence by fellow adherents.

Kelsay's book, *Arguing the Just War in Islam*, develops an extensive contribution to this line of thinking, providing an account of historical, cultural, and legal processes by which Islamic "men and women attempt to forge links between the wisdom of previous generations and the challenges posed by contemporary life, in hopes of acting in ways consistent with the guidance of God."[14] Kelsay calls "Shari'a reasoning" one of those modes. In Shari'a reasoning, "arguments are evaluated as better or worse, persuasive or not, in terms of the ways in which advocates of various positions make use of historical precedents."[15] Of special importance in Islamic tradition is a long-standing precedent against indiscriminate fighting, a precedent established as early as the ninth century ⬛⬛ by Muslim jurists who reasoned about the requirements of honorable conduct in war. About such reasoning and Islamic militancy, Kelsay writes:

> We should understand the arguments made by Osama bin Laden and other militants as genuine attempts to find guidance by engaging long-standing Muslim tradition. At the same time, it is clear that the framework of Shari'a reasoning is one in which disagreement is not only possible, but to be expected. Thus, even as we do well to analyze the texts produced by contemporary militants—advocates of the "new *jihad*," who style themselves inheritors of the mantle of Shari'a reasoning—we do well to raise questions about their arguments and, in particular, to note the kinds of criticisms made by other Muslims who are equally engaged by the notion of following divine guidance.[16]

Kelsay identifies contemporary Muslim writers who dispute bin Laden's arguments from within the framework of Shari'a reasoning, citing figures such as the Shaykh al-Azhar, Ysuf al-Qaradhawi, Shaykh Muhsin al-'Awaji, Safar al-Hawali, and Muhammad al-Khasif.[17] One way we might read bin Laden's *Declaration*, Kelsay observes, is as an appeal to the idea of acting under an "emergency" or acting in accord with the Islamic law of retaliation to justify the use of violence such as occurred on 9/11. At the end of the day, Kelsay notes, such a reading not only seems strained, it fails to enter fully into the tasks of Shari'a reasoning. He writes: "The *Declaration*'s call for indiscriminate fighting is problematic, because the authors fail to provide an adequate argument for the overriding of precedent [against indiscriminate fighting]."[18] In other words: If bin Laden and his associates believe that, on Islamic grounds, their actions may permissibly override restrictions on taking innocent life, they fail to establish that point.

For non-Muslims, however, this line of argument against bin Laden will likely not suffice. What is at stake for non-Muslims is a basis for *their* indignation, not someone else's. Strawson's more precise terminology regarding morally reactive attitudes, as I noted in chapter 1, would have us put the point this way: identifying Muslim bases for *indignation* fails to provide grounds for justifying the *resentment* of those who suffered the injustice. That is to say, providing grounds for Muslim social criticism—connected criticism—leaves questions about the moral grounds for non-Muslim grievance unanswered.

One way to address this difficulty is to say that historical arguments can identify conceptual parallels or overlapping ideas between traditions, thereby opening up one tradition to comparative and cross-cultural dialogue with another.[19] The idea is to identify analogies between Muslim and non-Muslim norms as a basis for cross-cultural reflection about (in this context) the morality of resort to armed force. Liberals, among others, should welcome such efforts insofar as they contribute to the prospect of tolerance, respect, and mutual understanding in the name of freedom and equality. And, as it bears on my argument, cross-cultural theorizing might open the door to expressing one's own grievances in ways that can gain a hearing more broadly.

Johnson points to several points of contact between Islamic approaches to war and the Western just-war doctrine:[20] "Both traditions link the right to use armed force to the exercise of legitimate governing authority for the protection and common good of the governed community. . . . Both traditions recognize that even the use of force justified in this way is not without limits when it comes to the question of who may be targeted and the means that may be used against aggressors."[21] In a similar way, Kelsay identifies several parallels between Islamic jurisprudence and the just-war doctrine's attention to proper authority, right intention, just cause, last resort, and the morality of war's means, including the principle of double effect.[22]

While it is true in a formal sense that Islamic teaching shares commonalities with just-war doctrine's basis for and limits to the use of force, I am not persuaded that Islam is as strict or that its limits are satisfactory. To be sure, Islam is not a religion of "total war" if by that one means "unlimited war"; there are limits to the use of force in Muslim tradition. But the important philosophical question goes beyond whether there are limits to the use of force in Islamic teaching to include whether they are drawn in the right places and in the right way.

Consider the historical material provided in *Arguing the Just War in Islam*, looking in particular at matters pertaining to the *jus in bello* in just-war doctrine—especially the principle of noncombatant immunity, which prohibits the intentional targeting of innocent persons in war. Kelsay observes that the writings of the Islamic jurist al-Shaybani (d. 804) and his colleagues suggest parallels between the principle of noncombatant immunity and Islamic tradition. Al-Shaybani and his colleagues specify persons who are morally immune from direct attack, establishing a precedent in Islamic law regarding honorable combat that follows a directive of the Prophet: "Do not mutilate anyone, nor should you kill women, children, or old men."[23] To this list al-Shaybani adds slaves, the lame, the blind, the helpless insane, and Muslims located in the midst of the enemy as immune from direct attack.[24] The problem with this list, of course, is that it excludes from the status of noncombatancy persons who may well be uninvolved in posing resistance, namely, young ablebodied men. Subsequently, al-Mawardi (d. 1058) moved Islamic thinking from listing persons who should not be directly attacked to an underlying principle that explains such a restriction: "as a general matter, they 'do not fight.'"[25] Three centuries later, Ibn Taymiyya (d. 1328) restricted the use of force in a way that combines a general principle with a list of examples. According to Ibn Taymiyya, war is not to be fought against those who "do not constitute a defensive or offensive power, like the women, the children, the monks, old people, the blind and the permanently disabled."[26] Kelsay summarizes Ibn Taymiyya's views: "The principle . . . seems to be that those who do not, or may be presumed not to, participate in the enemy's war effort are not to be the target of direct attack by Muslim forces."[27] This material by al-Shaybani, al-Mawardi, and Ibn Taymiyya underwrites the precedent against indiscriminate fighting in Shari'a reasoning that bin Laden's *Declaration* fails to override.

Al-Shaybani's, al-Mawardi's, and Ibn Taymiyya's lists and principles regarding the proper use of force appear to be the product of customary practices of premodern Muslim warfare. How they might contribute to the contemporary formulation of a deeper principle or value for restricting the use of force, and what that principle would be, remains unclear. Perhaps these Muslim writers had something like "proximity to conflict" in mind as a basis for denying persons immunity from direct harm.[28] That idea puts it within speaking distance of the just-war idea that one's role in war provides the basis for determining one's status as a combatant or noncombatant. On that view, one is a legitimate target because one poses a lethal threat or contributes in important ways to the marshalling of a lethal threat; against such threats, the use of force is justified. On those terms one could condemn the 9/11 attacks because they targeted persons who posed no serious danger to anyone.

But what we see in discussions by al-Shaybani, al-Mawardi, and Ibn Taymiyya remains too vague a basis for drawing a strong parallel with modern just-war doctrine's idea of noncombatant immunity. The Islamic idea that various persons or groups should not be fought when they are not posing a lethal threat could be explained in terms of a practical rather than moral motive: deploying force against them is an inefficient use of military resources. Using force in that way is to waste time and materiel.[29] Refraining from using force against nonlethal groups, in other words, can be justified entirely in prudential terms.

In my view, an account of immunity needs a more secure anchor, one that provides normative grounds for its observance along with support for feeling indignation when it is violated. When we avow a self-regarding grievance about another's wrongdoing, we have more than his or her wastefulness or inefficiency in mind. At the very least, when we do complain about another's inefficiency, our complaints gain moral traction when that inefficiency reflects a deeper problem, namely, another's disregard or disrespect.

One way to provide a more secure anchor to the norm of noncombatant immunity is to say that those who are not fighting or who pose no genuine threat possess immunity from direct attack because, as a matter of fairness, they have done nothing to warrant being attacked. The norm of reciprocity would support the idea that those who pose no harm should not be directly harmed. Perhaps the idea of reciprocity or fairness is implied by the idea that the Muslim authors in question are developing with regard to what it means to engage in "honorable conduct" in war. As it stands, however, the moral basis for assigning immunity remains vague.

Many modern Western exponents of just-war doctrine, in contrast, claim that identifying persons who are immune from direct attack "falls out" of a basic principle, namely, the idea that persons not directly or materially involved in assisting in a war do not forfeit their immunity from being directly attacked owing to a moral status or set of entitlements they may presume to possess. Walzer summarizes the point this way: "no one can be threatened with war or warred against, unless through some act of his own he has surrendered or lost his rights."[30] The idea of someone losing his or her rights is connected to the moral implications of that individual's conduct. Nonlethal persons are immune not because killing them would be a wasteful use of resources, but because such persons have done nothing to relinquish immunities that they possess by virtue of a basic value or entitlement that attaches to them. For that reason, directly imposing lethal threats on nonlethal persons is wrong. One major thrust of modern just-war theorizing has been to insist on a more precise determination of moral immunity (or liability) as a basis for distinguishing between combatants and noncombatants. On modern accounts of just-war doctrine, liability to direct attack turns on whether individuals lose their immunity because they violate (or possess the potential to violate) another's rights or endanger (or potentially endanger) others' lives.[31] The possession of rights is a theory-dependent concept that is attached to the notion that possessing moral status entails immunities from unprovoked harm or danger.

The concrete implications of this difference between a moral and prudential basis for assigning immunity to innocent persons is plain. A moral basis is free from contingencies that surround an army's potential success or failure in battle. It is absolute when set off against the demands of military interest or necessity. A moral basis thus generates a right that functions to trump utilitarian or other practical concerns. Understanding immunity from direct harm on prudential terms, in contrast, offers no such security. The right remains contingent on whether honoring it is in an army's overall military interest. If, for prudential or practical reasons, one can improve one's chances of success by directly killing or harming noncombatants, then their protections obviously erode. Such persons lack rights that function as trumps. Clarifying the difference between these two bases, then, would help settle whether, or to what extent, Islamic approaches to the ethics of war indeed cohere with the Western just-war ethics, especially the *jus in bello*.[32]

My difficulty with Islamic teachings about war congeals around this problem of vagueness or, more precisely, whether moral or prudential reasons serve as a basis for condemning indiscriminate uses of force. Perhaps Islamic scholars and intellectuals, informed by Kelsay's work and the commentary it generates, will develop an account of immunity that clarifies this matter, providing stronger moral bases for identifying common ground with modern just-war doctrine to express moral indignation in response to terrorism. As Kelsay notes in his earlier work, "a specifically Islamic contribution to the rules governing the conduct of modern war is still very much in process."[33]

A different historical argument, suggested in Rashid's comment in chapter 1, says that Muslims and non-Muslims should question those who reify Islamic traditions around some core ideas—in the case of terrorists, around the core idea of radical jihad. Recall Rashid: "The Taliban, like so many Islamic fundamentalist groups today, divest Islam of all its legacies except theology—Islamic philosophy, science, arts, aesthetics and mysticism are ignored. Thus the rich diversity of Islam and the essential message of the Koran—to build a civil society that is just and equitable in which rulers are responsible for their citizens—is forgotten."[34] On this view, Muslim extremists are guilty of overlooking the richness and plurality of Islamic history and culture. Rashid looks not to normative resources within Islamic juridical and moral reflection but to the plurality of sources that make up Islamic tradition. For Rashid, Islamic terrorists who justify their acts in light of some militant statements in the Qur'an or according to a radicalized version of jihad fail to recognize the Islamic tradition's many streams and sources, its richness, and its practices of peacemaking and reconciliation.

The apparent advantage of this approach, like other historical arguments, is that it avoids imposing some "external" account of Western morality onto Islam. That idea seems, on the face of it, entirely respectful of difference. For Rashid, the way to critique radical jihadists is to propose an alternative way of thinking about "tradition": traditions are typically plural and historical, not monolithic and frozen in time. On this view, Muslim terrorists are guilty of a kind of reductionism.

Yet such an alternative account is no less normative than one that directly raises normative questions about Muslim terrorism. Rashid's argument shifts the focus away from substantive matters regarding the content of Islamic tradition to formal matters regarding the meaning of the concept of tradition qua tradition. In that respect, it imposes a prescriptive view of a tradition as pluralistic and temporally distended. But that argument merely changes the subject, sidestepping whether radical jihadism is morally acceptable. In my view, whether Muslims experience tradition as historical and pluralistic or as reified, ahistorical, and monolithic is beside the point. The crux of the moral anxiety surrounding radical Islam turns not on such formal concerns but on substantive controversies surrounding the justification of, and respect for, grievances that arise in response to terrorism committed in the name of religion. I will turn to those matters in chapter 3.

ECONOMIC ARGUMENTS

A second line of criticism regarding Islam's nettlesome relationship with terrorism argues that the roots of terrorism have little if anything to do with Muslim faith. We must instead understand 9/11 and other recent terrorist attacks as the result of economic desperation. Indeed, the *Declaration* itself seems to invite an economic analysis. Bin Laden and his associates write:

> The Arabian Peninsula has never—since Allah made it flat, created its desert, and encircled it with seas—been stormed by any forces like the crusader armies spreading in it like locusts, eating its riches and wiping out its plantations. All this is happening at a time in which nations are attacking Muslims like people fighting over a plate of food. . . . We—with Allah's help—call on every Muslim who believes in Allah and wishes to be rewarded to comply with Allah's order to kill the Americans and plunder their money wherever and whenever they find it.[35]

Focusing on economic factors often proceeds on the notion that material interests rather than faith-commitments or ideals drive social movements and historical change such as those developing in the Middle East and Central Asia. We must not overlook the fact that terrorism is carried out by persons suffering from economic woes tied inexorably to the global effects of Western affluence, oil politics, and consumer culture. Echoing this line of thought, Anthony Lewis writes: "No one can doubt that the desperate conditions of life in Afghanistan provided nurturing ground for terrorism."[36] Similarly, Ellen Willis states in *The Nation*: "As with fascism, the rise of Islamic totalitarianism has partly to do with its populist appeal to the class resentments of an economically oppressed population and to anger at political subordination and humiliation."[37] Mashhood Rizvi is most explicit:

> The events of September 11 had little to do with Islam. . . . The world's most pressing problems do not result from either excessive or insufficient Islamic tolerance; nor are they the result of the caricatured portrait of Islam in the West and beyond—a portrait that has certainly tended to characterize Islam and all its followers as ignorant, brutal, confused, fundamentalist, and most recently "terrorists." Instead, and ultimately, the problem is the perpetuation of international systems of oppression and injustice.[38]

For these critics, focusing on the religious beliefs of Islamic terrorists may isolate the wrong explanation for their activity and end up blaming the victim.

Whether terrorism is in fact strongly correlated with poverty and, with that, a lack of education is not as obvious as it might appear.[39] That said, the economic argument has the merit of calling attention to the desperate economic conditions of Afghanistan and other parts of the world in which terrorism festers. Consider the fact that much of Afghanistan's economy over the past two decades has been connected to the international drug trade. Equally important is the fact of abject poverty and hopelessness in that country. Lewis rightly points to the need for humanitarian aid to those living in Afghanistan and fleeing to neighboring countries. Countless children in that region are continually at risk of dying from cold and starvation. Rashid writes: "Afghanistan has one of the lowest rated indices of the human condition in the world."[40] The infant mortality rate is 18 percent, the highest in the world, and a quarter of all children die before they reach their fifth birthday, compared to one-tenth of children in developing countries.[41] Small wonder, then, that American symbols of economic prosperity would be the target of anger and resentment. In 1998, the International Committee of the Red Cross reported that ninety-eight thousand Afghan families were headed by a widow, sixty-three thousand were headed by a disabled person, and forty-five thousand people were treated for war wounds in that year alone. The only productive factories are those that produce artificial limbs, crutches, and wheelchairs.[42] Madrassas, on the border of Pakistan and Afghanistan, succeed in recruiting young boys because those schools provide food and clothing, which are not provided in Pakistan's public schools.[43]

These facts are part of a wider pattern of poverty in the Arab world, the lamentable details of which are documented in a series of U.N. Arab Human Development Reports (2002–2005, 2009).[44] Those reports find, among other things, that about 50 percent of Arab women are illiterate, that the Arab region spends less than 0.5 percent of its GNP on scientific expenditures, that over the last millennium Arabs have translated as many books as Spain does in one year, and that the unemployment rate is 15 percent, the world's highest.

Yet focusing on economics and the lack of opportunity may distort our perceptions of bin Laden and al Qaeda. It is important not to overlook the bin Laden family's vast wealth and the class background of bin Laden's immediate lieutenants. As Jane Mayer makes clear in a *New Yorker* article that received virtually no attention in the wake of 9/11, the resources of Muslim terrorists are considerably more complex than an economic explanation for terrorism suggests.[45] The bin Laden family controls a five-billion-dollar-a-year global corporation that includes the largest construction firm in the Muslim world; Osama received between twenty-seven and thirty million dollars between the early 1970s and early 1990s.[46] Steve Coll writes: "Until Osama announced himself as an international terrorist, his family was much more heavily invested in the United States than has generally been understood—his brothers and sisters owned American shopping centers, apartment complexes, condominiums, luxury estates, privatized prisons in Massachusetts, corporate stocks, an airport, and much else."[47] The bin Laden siblings "financed Hollywood movies, traded thoroughbred horses with country singer Kenny Rogers, and negotiated real estate deals with Donald Trump."[48] Contrary to the idea that Osama is frustrated by the increased Westernization of Muslim culture and heritage, he and his family are deeply invested in American financial institutions. The bin Ladens have had a stake totaling two million dollars in the Washington-based Carlyle Group, a private firm that does a large amount of defense contracting. The family continues to have a stake, totaling about ten million dollars, in the Fremont Group, on whose governing board sits the former U.S. Secretary of State, George Schultz. Citigroup handles much of the bin Ladens' private financing and the family has equity investments in Merrill Lynch and Goldman Sachs.[49] Osama's wealth belies the idea that we can explain Muslim terrorism as a reaction to economic disenfranchisement wrought by global capitalism. With offices in London and Geneva and financial interests across the globe, the bin Ladens, including Osama, are corporate capitalists.

My point here is to complicate the economic picture of Muslim terrorism. It seems evident that terrorism finds its seedbed in economic desperation and political oppression. But it is equally true that those who orchestrated 9/11 are responsible for exploiting the Muslim poor. Moreover, an economic explanation poses the danger of shifting the blame for the economic woes of the Middle East and Arabian Peninsula entirely to the United States and Western economic actors. While many terrorists may very well be young people whose lives seem hopeless to them, we should remember that many Islamic countries have vast resources of wealth that are hoarded by a small group of families, including the bin Ladens, and that most women in Muslim countries are denied anything that remotely resembles equality of opportunity. The immediate answer to social injustice in many Muslim countries is for their political leaders to radically adjust patterns of economic distribution and opportunity within their own spheres of influence. Targeting the World Trade Center and the United States more generally obscures the massive economic problems facing Arab countries and shifts attention away from political and financial elites in the Middle East. An additional problem with the economic argument is that it ignores the explicit religious statements that bin Laden and his lieutenants made about carrying out the terrorist attacks. It seems counterintuitive, indeed condescending, not to take bin Laden and his associates at their word. As I indicated in chapter 1, bin Laden and members of al Qaeda have made repeated statements about the need to remove "infidels" from the Arabian Peninsula and other regions, and they describe those who sacrifice their lives on behalf of radical jihad as martyrs.[50] The terrorists self-consciously went through religious rituals in preparation for their fateful acts. Failure to grasp the religious motives and intolerance that fuels Muslim extremism is to impose a distorting, secularist mentality on international affairs. The frequent, explicit references to theological and normative Islamic ideas by leaders of al Qaeda cannot be ignored— as if we knew their motives better than they did.

THE RELATIVIST ARGUMENT

A third line of thinking, echoing the politics of recognition and postmodernism more broadly, states that Islam is too "other" to be subjected to social criticism by Western standards—that criticizing Islam is chauvinistic. The core idea is that non-Muslims, especially non-Muslim Americans, are arrogant to question Muslim belief and practice, as if non-Muslims had some privileged standpoint from which to evaluate Islamic tradition. Multicultural ethics and politics should be reluctant to pass judgment on those who claim the authority of another venerable tradition, especially if that judgment purports to rely on a point of view that claims to be ahistorical and impartial. Multiculturalists, among others, are suspicious of conceptual neutrality and typically claim that purportedly impartial perspectives mask ideological interests. This line of thinking develops aspects of the historical and economic frameworks, namely, that our thought forms and ideals are contingent, the product of social, economic, and political forces, not an outgrowth of reason operating in some pristine, contemplative sanctuary.

A version of this approach informs Stanley Fish's article "Condemnation without Absolutes," published soon after 9/11.[51] Arguing against the idea that 9/11 points to the inability of postmodernists to speak in moral universals,[52] Fish makes the following claim: "The only thing postmodern thought argues against is the hope of justifying our response to the attacks in universal terms that would be persuasive to everyone, including our enemies."[53] Fish suggests that social criticism cannot proceed unless critics first sympathetically understand the hatred that breeds terrorism against Western powers. He thus defends a qualified form of relativism in these terms: "If by relativism one means the practice of putting yourself in your adversary's shoes, not in order to wear them as your own but in order to have some understanding (far short of approval) of why someone else might want to wear them, then relativism will not and should not end, because it is simply another name for serious thought."[54] Criticism of Islamic terrorism is muted on this account because there are no universal canons of justice that apply to anything. Those who want to express their indignation without resorting to absolutes, according to Fish, "can and should invoke the particular lived values that unite us and inform the institutions we cherish and wish to defend."[55]

Fish's comments build on his skepticism about liberal political theory and Enlightenment philosophy more generally. In his mind, it is a mistake "to reify theory, to think that it has some independent existence (except in the precincts of philosophy seminars) and therefore to oppose it to something else. . . . There is no such thing as reason apart from its appearance in historical circumstances, an appearance that will always take the form of *reasons*, that is, of arguments already inflected and infected by some prechosen partisan vision or angle."[56] In places Fish speaks as if the entire project of rational discourse is post hoc—that efforts at rational justification are merely rationalizations, attempts to legitimize one's convictions under the guise of impartial argument. He writes: "Reasons, evidence, explanations, justifications—these inevitable constituents of thought do not guide or generate political decisions; they follow in their wake."[57] On those grounds, Fish polemicizes contemporary theory, especially "rational liberal theory with its abstract vocabulary of fairness, mutual respect, toleration, and so on," for its "penchant for thinking abstractly" and for holding to the false dream that such abstract thinking can make substantive differences in everyday life and practice.[58] The general problem with such thinking, he avers, is that answers derived from abstract reflection "are empty of substantive content—substantive content is what the abstracting process flees—and therefore they have no purchase whatsoever on the real-life issues to which you would apply them."[59]

Fish's polemics represent an obvious challenge to and rejection of the ideas I am developing in these pages. However distant his views seem from mine, I do grant some merit to what might be called, in his terms, his "prechosen partisan vision or angle." Among other things, Fish's comments after 9/11 have the merit of urging caution and self-reflexivity along with the need to expand our sympathies and imaginations, no small virtues in any society. Americans who are quick to criticize Muslim extremists may be naive regarding their own moral and political faults or about the extent to which the exportation of American cultural and economic values is offensive in many parts of the world. 9/11 dealt a stunning blow not only to American confidence, resurgent optimism, and sense of invulnerability, but also to the idea of American innocence. Bin Laden and his confederates singled out the United States as an exceptional evil in their ideological justification of the attacks and, with that, hit a deep nerve in American self-understanding. They made it plain that the globalization of Western values is neither culturally neutral nor obviously progressive, and that American policy, especially in Israel and the Middle East, is scarcely benign. Many Americans learned for the first time that they are deeply resented for their affluence, commercialism, isolationism, and support of Israel. One cultural outcome of 9/11 is that it produced a kind of exceptionalism in reverse, singling out the United States for its political, cultural, and economic arrogance. It is possible and necessary to listen to nonterrorists who don't endorse the racist and genocidal ideology of bin Laden, and yet feel suffocated by the United States' cultural, economic, and military ascendancy in the post–Cold War era.

That said, the demand to listen to the grievances of terrorists and their sympathizers differs from what Fish recommends. His defense of relativism is, as it were, simply overly simple. One problem is that his argument against moral universals fails to distinguish between the *range* and *weight* of moral claims. One can say, and Fish could say, that a judgment is justified according to a "local" set of beliefs and practices, but that it nonetheless applies without exception, absolutely. So Westerners might say that there is no exception to the fact that indiscriminate killing is always wrong. Fish equates *universals*, claims that are true for everyone, with *absolutes*, claims that cannot be overridden. Those who "invoke the particular lived values that unite us and inform the institutions that we cherish and wish to defend" can and should speak in unqualified terms. The challenge to social critics such as Fish is whether they have the temerity to utter an absolute condemnation without flinching.

In addition to confusing the distinction between universals and absolutes, Fish's understanding of universals makes no sense on its own. He conflates two claims: (1) there are no universals and (2) there are no universals "that would be persuasive to everyone, including our enemies." The second statement ties the nonexistence of universals to the fact of moral disagreement. But the fact of disagreement is no evidence against the existence of universals. Fish appears to conflate *de jure* with *de facto* universals. Earlier in his writings Fish makes the same mistake in a more general discussion of religion in the public square: "There are no reasons you can give to the devout," he writes, "not because they are the kind of people who don't listen to reason but because the reasons you might give can never be reasons for them unless either they convert to your faith or you convert to theirs."[60] But the fact that one's opponents are not persuaded by one's claims is hardly evidence that those claims are false or are only relatively true—true only to oneself. For Fish, it seems impossible to say that the person with whom one disagrees is thinking falsely or has adopted an unacceptable set of practices or beliefs. Small wonder, then, that it is difficult on Fish's terms to confidently articulate a moral grievance. The only basis for being confident that I am correct or am articulating an idea that might have general plausibility is when my "opposition" agrees with me or I agree with them. Surely that is absurd.

One of Fish's complaints about liberal theory—what he calls "strong liberalism"—is that it abstracts from substantive matters in everyday life, leaving such theory powerless to guide real politics and action. Fish writes as if liberal theorizing and practical ethics do or should operate in entirely separate domains, or that practical ethics does not exist at all. In his mind, "the theory project is coherent only within the terms of its elaboration as an academic enterprise, one populated by people who like to pose and present solutions to philosophical puzzles."[61] Such theory "is incapable of generating outcomes unless it is supplemented by the substantive considerations against which it defines itself."[62] Unfortunately, Fish fails to identify how substantive matters might, in a salutary way, "supplement" liberal theory or norms of liberal doctrine. On Fish's account, it would seem impossible to consider (for example) concrete feelings of indignation in any theoretical way.

Yet Fish's understanding of liberal theory's alleged powerlessness goes beyond that single oversight. He breezily overlooks the project of social criticism, whether liberal or otherwise. The entire thrust of social criticism, practical ethics, and comparative approaches to religious ethics, has, for decades now, been working to overcome the kind of complaints to which Fish directs his polemic. In other words, a more expansive and updated understanding of religion, philosophy, and public affairs would alert us to ongoing efforts to coordinate theory and practice in ways that avert Fish's complaints.[63]

Relativism as defended by Fish expresses the idea that thinking from another perspective is important and potentially instructive—that adopting the perspective of one's adversary "is another name for serious thought." Yet, as I will argue more fully in chapter 5, such openness to others should be provisional. I will call such openness "benefit-of-the-doubt-respect." To presume *a priori* that what I think *must* be self-justifying and parochial, however, begins by privileging the other in ways that is patronizing and uncritical. All too often, patronizing deference parades itself as "another name for serious thought." As I noted at the outset of this book, there are two dangers for non-Muslim social critics to avoid: ethnocentrism, on the one hand, and "favorable judgment on demand" (even when it is not demanded) on the other.[64] Serious thought requires us to think in terms that include but go beyond the first of these two dangers.

THE INTERNALIST CRITIQUE

The internalist critique picks up the self-reflexive caution at the heart of the relativist argument and presses it further into a bid for self-reflexive criticism. The core idea is that whatever criticism we are to practice in response to 9/11 should include policies and practices of the United States.

The internalist critique took on one theological expression in a conversation between the Moral Majority's Jerry Falwell and Pat Robertson on the Christian Broadcasting Network's *700 Club*. Two days after the 9/11 attacks, Falwell and Robertson exchanged these remarks:

JERRY FALWELL:
I agree totally with you that the Lord has protected us so wonderfully these 225 years. And since 1812, this is the first time that we've been attacked on our soil, and by far the worst results. And I fear, as Donald Rumsfeld, the Secretary of Defense, said yesterday, that this is only the beginning. And with biological warfare available to these monsters—the Husseins, the Bin Ladens, the Arafats—what we saw on Tuesday, as terrible as it is, could be miniscule if, in fact—if in fact—God continues to lift the curtain and allow the enemies of America to give us probably what we deserve.

PAT ROBERTSON:
Jerry, that's my feeling. I think we've just seen the antechamber to terror. We haven't even begun to see what they can do to the major population.

JERRY FALWELL:

The ACLU's [American Civil Liberties Union] got to take a lot of blame for this.

PAT ROBERTSON:

Well, yes.

JERRY FALWELL:

And, I know that I'll hear from them for this. But, throwing God out successfully with the help of the federal court system, throwing God out of the public square, out of the schools. The abortionists have got to bear some burden for this because God will not be mocked. And when we destroy 40 million little innocent babies, we make God mad. I really believe that the pagans, and the abortionists, and the feminists, and the gays and the lesbians who are actively trying to make that an alternative lifestyle, the ACLU, People For the American Way, all of them who have tried to secularize America—I point the finger in their face and say, "you helped this happen."

PAT ROBERTSON:

Well, I totally concur, and the problem is we have adopted that agenda at the highest levels of our government. And so we're responsible as a free society for what the top people do. And, the top people, of course, is the court system.

JERRY FALWELL:

Pat, did you notice yesterday the ACLU, and all the Christ-haters, the People For the American Way, NOW, etc. were totally disregarded by the Democrats and the Republicans in both houses of Congress as they went out on the steps and called out to God in prayer and sang "God Bless America" and said: "Let the ACLU be hanged"? In other words, when the nation is on its knees, the only normal and natural and spiritual thing to do is what we ought to be doing all the time—calling upon God.

PAT ROBERTSON:

Amen.[65]

Falwell defended his comments as making a theological rather than a legal statement, and clarified his theological claim to mean that God did not cause but permitted the tragedy by lifting "the curtain of protection" from the United States. Here, 9/11 is interpreted within a Christian theodicy that views the United States as generally enjoying divine selection and, with that, protection. But that selection is not unconditional; it includes certain moral expectations. On this account, the moral permissiveness of the United States has led to a loss of divine protection and exposure to the terrorists' attacks. The implication is clear: the best way to improve national security against future terrorism would be to advance the mission of the Moral Majority.[66]

But the internalist critique need not be Christian or theological. Two weeks after the attacks, Susan Sontag recorded this jeremiad in the *New Yorker*:

> Where is the acknowledgment that this was not a "cowardly" attack on "civilization" or "liberty" or "humanity" or "the free world" but an attack on the world's self-proclaimed super-power, undertaken as a consequence of specific American alliances and actions? How many citizens are aware of the ongoing bombing of Iraq? And if the word "cowardly" is to be used, it might be more aptly applied to those who kill from beyond the range of retaliation, high in the sky, than to those willing to die themselves in order to kill others. In the matter of courage (a morally neutral virtue): whatever may be said of the perpetrators of Tuesday's slaughter, they were not cowards.[67]

Sontag's critique is a hybrid of moral and political judgment. Like Falwell and Robertson, she views the attacks as a consequence of American practices and policies. And, also like Falwell and Robertson, she sees the atrocity as an occasion to comment on American public culture. Describing American leadership and journalistic commentary in the immediate aftermath of 9/11, Sontag writes: "Politics, the politics of a democracy—which entails disagreement, which promotes candor—has been replaced by psychotherapy. Let's by all means grieve together. But let's not be stupid together. A few shreds of historical awareness might help us understand what has just happened, and what may continue to happen."[68]

Yet Sontag's jeremiad does little to advance our comprehension or to clarify our indignation. She fails to indicate how the virtue of courage—a moral excellence of character—can be "neutral" unless one makes the false equation between courage and risk-taking. But courage involves risk-taking for good and noble reasons, not simply rashness or a willingness to take on danger.[69] Nor does she say how the attacks on 9/11 are a consequence of the bombing of Iraq or what "few shreds of historical awareness" might enlighten her readership. Bin Laden himself indicated well before 9/11 that his grievances were linked to American military activity over Iraq. We didn't need Sontag to tell us that.

Another version of the internalist critique claims not that 9/11 is an instance in which the United States "had it coming" but that terrorism is a function of what Benjamin Barber calls a "global democratic deficit": "the absence of democratic regulatory and legal institutions at the global level to contain and domesticate the anarchy of international markets, an anarchy that serves terrorism all too well."[70] Here terrorism is explicable as a function of cramped political options, repressive political regimes, and the forces of economic globalization that offer empty forms of freedom. As opposed to the theological-internalist critique of the right and the moral-internalist critique of the left, this is a political-internalist critique. It focuses not so much on the moral record of particular American policies and practices as on Americans' failure to reckon with the powers of globalization unleashed by a secular theology of neoliberalism.

Barber's argument is, among other things, a corrective to the economic argument's idea that exporting economic opportunity provides one sure way to remove incentives for terrorist action. For Barber, the exportation of free-market capitalism has let loose a materialist, consumerist anarchy that does little to satisfy deeper needs and yearnings for self-governance and self-command. Barber reminds us that exporting capitalism and exporting democracy do not necessarily go hand in hand. Democracy consists of institutions, norms, and traditions anchored to the idea that political sovereignty belongs in the hands of the people bound together as citizens under the rule of law. Understood appropriately, democracy can ensure that collective self-governance is not undermined by the pursuit of profit. As David Chase's brilliant depiction of violence and profiteering in *The Sopranos* makes plain, there is no reason to believe that unregulated capitalism and democratic practices go together. Quite the contrary: capitalism without political institutions to protect rights and enforce responsibilities too easily regresses into the feudal hierarchies of predation, patronage, and power from which modernity had hoped to escape. According to Barber, "The U.S. . . . has itself quite consciously conspired in the creation of an international 'order' that is actually an international disorder—a contrived war of all against all posturing as a free market but establishing conditions as favorable to the globalization of crime, weapons, prostitution, drugs, and terror as to the spread of unregulated markets."[71] And that fact, Barber contends, ought to remind us of globalization's deficit of democratic social and political institutions. Thus, he asks: In response to the 9/11 attacks, will the United States "grasp that interdependence means the anarchy of global markets and the anarchy of terrorism are linked, and that an appropriate response to them must be to find ways to globalize sovereignty and its defining democratic institutions?"[72] Americans have globalized the economy, trade, the free movement of human and natural resources, along with the many vices that accompany free market capitalism, but "they have not globalized the democratic, legal, and civic institutions that within nation-states contain and regulate capitalism and its free market institutions and prevent anarchy from prevailing."[73]

One plank of Barber's argument on behalf of the globalization of democratic institutions is to ensure a space for religious belief and practice, a space "in which both liberty and faith are secured."[74] He writes: "A just and inclusive world in which all citizens are stakeholders is the first objective of a rational strategy against terrorism, but a civil religion that imposes secularism or appears hostile to religion will not be adequate to the crisis of fundamentalism."[75] Allowing economics, materialism, and consumerism to dominate every sector of life has a leveling, one-dimensional effect that ignores deeper human longings and aspirations. Overcoming the global democratic deficit will have to create room for religious pluralism in a manner that follows the general contours of the American model. Barber suggests something along the lines of a global civic sphere: "Civil society at its best is that nonstate public realm where through free association we create the voluntary communities of education, culture, and faith that define our plural human character. Civil society is not coercive but it is public; it is free, but it is not private. It demands adequate space for all those activities that give meaning and dignity to life."[76]

Barber's prescription for the globalization of democratic institutions insists on protecting religious liberty and pluralism, not establishing a religious democracy or an antireligious secularism. That suggests that he has liberal democracy in mind, not merely electoral democracy. Electoral democracy alone, without liberal safeguards, has the potential to vote in a government dominated by a politically regressive religious majority, as we witnessed in Algeria in 1990. But Barber's prescription, duly amended, brings us full circle to the questions with which I began this book. Granting that democratic institutions here and abroad need to ensure greater protection for religious belief and practice, what sorts of beliefs and practices can be tolerated, and why? What expressions of belief and practice deserve respect and protection? Barber too quickly adverts to the idea that "the crisis of fundamentalism" is a symptom of religious repression brought on by secular politics. But seeing fundamentalism as a symptom of secularism fails to explain the presence of fundamentalism in countries such as the United States, where protections for religious freedom are secure.

The existence of fundamentalist groups that espouse intolerance along with other intolerant groups in the United States and elsewhere suggests that we do well to explore terms that set boundaries of toleration and provide a guide for tolerating the intolerant. More important, the presence of intolerant groups raises questions about how and on what terms various religious beliefs deserve tolerance and respect. To those subjects we will return in chapters 4 and 5, after we examine basic questions surrounding rights and values that undergird indignation in response to the attacks of 9/11.

Social criticism in the wake of 9/11 works to overcome our incomprehension insofar as it seeks to interpret the attacks within one or another narrative or explanatory framework. It captures and expresses intuitions that often guide our efforts to make sense of a social or personal trauma. Ethically speaking, however, the efforts I have examined in this chapter leave us without resources for expressing the (self-regarding) feeling of indignation—the moral outrage at the violent attacks and the religiously motivated antipathy that authorized them. To develop those resources, we must turn to ethical considerations regarding rights to life, security, and religious toleration. Social criticism with that more explicit normative agenda enables us to ponder the injustice done to the United States on 9/11. It takes up the challenge of articulating grounds for moral umbrage in a world of multicultural differences and religious diversity. To those subjects the next three chapters are devoted.

3

RIGHTS TO LIFE AND SECURITY

Readers of the last chapter might draw the following conclusion: social criticism launched from one or another historical line of inquiry—whether we are examining the social sources internal to a tradition or material interests that condition the conduct of its adherents—inevitably leads to a cul-de-sac in which we end up talking to (and about) ourselves.[1] Such seems to be the trajectory in the previous chapter insofar as it begins with social criticism of a historical sort and ends by examining forms of relativist and internalist commentary. On that inference, the effort to think about Islamic extremism in a historically conscious way sets us on a path that eventually curls back into various forms of self-analysis among Western intellectuals. Such self-analysis, moreover, ironically leaves behind the self-regarding considerations regarding the suffering of injustice that provided impetus for social criticism in the first place. The path of discussion down which we moved seems oddly unreflective—indeed, self-defeating: a tiger chasing its tail.

That is not a conclusion that I intend for us to make. I see no logic in the previous chapter that requires us to start from any one framework of social criticism and move to another. The connections I drew as we surveyed varieties of social criticism were meant to be illuminative and nothing more. Thinking from within the movements of history scarcely necessitates that we confine our conversation partners to those who are near and familiar.

More generally, as I will make plain in chapter 7, I see no need to bifurcate history and truth. Thinking from within a particular social location need not bar us from making nonrelative insights—discoveries that are true for ourselves as well as for others, differently situated. We measure the durability and potential generalizability of such discoveries by subjecting them to ongoing tests that draw from various insights, analyses, facts, and frameworks.[2] But the irony to which I just referred should warn us about difficulties that can accompany social criticism in the wake of a traumatic event, especially the challenge of keeping focused on self-regarding claims such as those bearing on suffering an injustice. In the aftermath of an atrocity, the risk of moving from grief to self-pity, from mourning to melancholia, is not to be underestimated.[3]

In this chapter I will self-consciously step off the path down which we moved in chapter 2. I want to indicate why, or on what grounds, we may say that Islamic terrorism is wrong—indeed, that all terrorism is wrong—in direct and unambiguous ways. The reasons on which I will focus our attention underlie the rule against killing and the rights to life and security. I want to examine such reasons as they are connected to the value of human dignity and the norm of respect for persons, a norm that produces basic human rights and the moral immunity from arbitrary harm or injury. Often we say that each person has a right to life and safety and that all persons are entitled to being secure from arbitrary violence and extreme danger. The "right" being named here should be understood as a justified claim cast in the form of an entitlement to the protection from certain harms or the provision of certain goods. The vernacular of rights is an abbreviation for a broader set of arguments about what persons are entitled to be free from or provided with. It serves as a kind of moral shorthand, and often shortcut, in moral argumentation to express our concerns about (among other things) the problem of personal injury. The aggression that occurred on

9/11 violated the right to life along with the right to security. What does this mean?

TRANSPARENT WRONGFULNESS

One approach to this question says that such aggression is so transparently wrong that any moral theory seeking to justify it disqualifies itself as implausible. On this view, we do not begin moral inquiry with a question about the possible justifiability of an act such as an atrocity. Rather, a decision about whether a particular action is justified "falls out" of a broader theory that must be designed in advance of any specific judgment. So we begin our inquiry at a second-order level regarding the general design of a moral theory and then refine it by testing it against strong, pretheoretical convictions.

Such an approach has three steps. First, we theorize about the normative terms for evaluating human behavior and institutions. One way to do that is to conceptualize about how to require, permit, or prohibit human conduct and then craft an account of appropriate directives in the form of moral absolutes and potential exceptions or anomalous cases. Second, we test that theory by seeing whether the exceptions or anomalous cases it seems to allow include obvious instances of wrongdoing. If it does, then we are to go back and refine that theory as a third step, tightening up its exceptional clauses to reduce its potential to permit intuitively wrongful actions.[4] Any moral theory that opens itself to the possibility of allowing for transparently wrong actions reveals itself as sorely deficient if not corrupt. Certain paradigmatic instances of wrongdoing, such as genocide, incest, or torture, require no sophisticated moral theorizing before we render a verdict about them. Rather, we use those secure judgments as reference points for determining how well a broader moral theory works. On this view, we don't need an elaborate moral theory of rights, such as a right to life or security, to express a grievance about 9/11 and events like it. The fact of injustice is obvious.

David Little develops a form of this line of thinking in his account of the nature and basis of human rights, focusing on atrocities such as the recreational or intimidational torture of defenseless innocents. Defending a version of rational intuitionism that draws from G. E. Moore, Little argues that we intuitively recognize the "transparent wrongness" of certain acts.[5] Such intuitionism, Little notes, differs from the "sensationalist intuitionism" of Hutcheson and Shaftesbury in that it holds that wrongness has certain irreducible cognizable features. Human beings may be expected to recognize certain acts "as deeply wrong, or taboo, and to begin to organize their lives accordingly, unless impeding or debilitating circumstances intervene to derail the prescribed recognition."[6] A taboo, Little adds, "is a sacred prohibition." It goes to the depths of human life and verges "upon a 'sacred' realm, a realm beyond daily experience that is at once powerfully mysterious and fascinating."[7] "To talk of taboos," Little adds, "is to talk, without embarrassment, of the inalterable and universal foundations of human life."[8] Little proposes that "paradigmatic Nazi atrocities provide a fixed reference point for interpreting and applying prohibitions against genocide, cruel and unusual punishment, torture, and the like, whatever variations and complications particular cases may generate."[9] One might say, following Albert R. Jonsen and Stephen Toulmin's account of casuistry, that a "locus of certitude" exists with reference to certain acts. Such acts serve as paradigm cases for moral judgment; ethical reasoning reflects on such cases in an *ex post* rather than an *ex ante* manner.[10]

In the previous chapter I gave one example of *ex post* reasoning in our discussion of Fish's understanding of rational argument. Little's understanding of *ex post* theorizing should be sharply distinguished from that of Fish, especially Fish's claim that "reasons, evidence, explanations, justifications—these inevitable constituents of thought do not guide or generate political decisions; they follow in their wake."[11] Fish's description fits the work of trial lawyers commissioned to prosecute or defend an accused criminal: they must produce the best possible argument given the claims and evidence put before them. Fish uses that kind of argument, which includes a "prechosen partisan vision or angle," as a model to make a case against the entire project of philosophical theorizing.[12] Little, in contrast, understands *ex post* reasoning not as a rationalization of a "prechosen partisan vision or angle" but as one step in designing a theory that possesses more than contingent or pragmatic foundations.[13]

That is not to say that history is irrelevant to Little's project. In his mind, the ban on torture is part of an emergent international consensus regarding human rights that materialized in the wake of the Second World War and its witness to the Holocaust and anticolonialist movements. The overall effects of fascism and colonialism, he avers, were to clarify our moral intuitions. Little elaborates:

> The record of atrocities committed in the name of fascism and colonialism served to shock people all over the globe into a new awareness of what we called the "modern potential for political pathology." It was not that in beholding fascist practices people came for the first time to believe that genocide or "geno-torture"—taking life or inflicting severe suffering on the basis of religious, ethnic, or racial criteria—was wrong and ought to be condemned and resisted. Rather, people came to see dramatized before their eyes the full pathological implications of certain discriminatory beliefs. Once the connections were demonstrated, all further arguments in support of those beliefs were silenced.[14]

Owing to an international human rights vocabulary, Little writes, "all sets of practical beliefs in all parts of the world are now standardly subjected to what one could call 'the antifascist test,' and its variant, 'the anticolonialist test.'"[15] Atrocities of one sort or another are subject to condemnation and resistance owing to a belief in human rights that "rests upon a few incontrovertible intuitions concerning some fundamental taboos."[16] Little's intuitionist line of argument is not irrationalist; it does not aim to disparage moral reflection. Rather, as I suggested earlier, it understands "such reflection to be after the fact, rather than before it."[17]

Little understands the growing consensus around human rights to pose a serious challenge to Alasdair MacIntyre, among others, who claims that the morality of the modern West has become fragmented and incoherent, disconnected from the human communities of tradition and social practice according to which Western morality once secured its authority. According to MacIntyre, the concepts that "inform our moral discourse were originally at home in larger totalities of theory and practice in which they enjoyed a role and function supplied by contexts of which they have now been deprived."[18] What we now possess, he avers, are "fragments of a conceptual scheme, parts of which lack those contexts from which their significance derived."[19] Lacking a common moral vocabulary, our current moral disputes are interminable, resting as they do on incommensurable moral foundations. "We possess indeed simulacra of morality," MacIntyre continues, "but we have—very largely, if not entirely—lost our comprehension, both theoretical and practical, of morality."[20]

On Little's account of the emerging global consensus about human rights, however, MacIntyre's obituary of moral coherence and consensus is premature if not entirely wrongheaded. As a factual matter, it does not square with current political developments and social movements. Little writes: "While it is true that under present international conditions by no means all human rights claims are satisfactorily accommodated, . . . it is hard to ignore the growing prevalence and significance of a common vocabulary in which claims from very different cultures are similarly articulated. . . . The fact these days that so much international attention is given to the petitions of human rights advocates all over the world—in the press, in diplomatic discussions, and in the reports of monitoring groups like Amnesty International, Human Rights Watch, and Helsinki Watch—attests to the remarkable momentum with which human rights are being internationalized."[21] Current global movements and political developments point to rather more than less agreement about some basic terms of common morality.

Little's understanding of the concept of rights is instructive. A right, he observes, "is an entitlement to demand a certain performance or forbearance on pain of sanction for noncompliance."[22] *Moral* rights are authoritative in that they take precedence over other actions; *legal* rights are warranted and enforced by a legal system. With those concepts in mind, Little identifies five characteristics of "the prevailing human rights vocabulary." A *human* right

1. is a "moral right advanced as a legal right," thereby constituting "a standard for the conduct of government and the administration of force";
2. protects "something of indispensable human importance";
3. is assigned as a natural right, irrespective of race, creed, ethnic origin, or gender;
4. may be suspended or forfeited under specific conditions, although some rights are indefeasible;
5. is "universally claimable by (or on behalf of) all people against all (appropriately situated) others, or by (or on behalf of) certain generic categories of people, such as 'women' or 'children.'"[23]

I agree with Little's fivefold summary. Human rights protect important human goods, are universal, and are prepolitical. They provide a basis for judging the conduct of governments and the administration of force by governmental and nongovernmental actors. They sort themselves out into claims that have different weights attached to them. They increasingly inform the moral claims (and indignation) that underwrite political changes in Eastern Europe, South Africa, and Southeast and Central Asia, to name only a few places. And they provide a basis for thinking about atrocities such as 9/11.

Little developed his general account of rights, rational intuitionism, and taboos prior to and apart from questions raised by 9/11, but those ideas directly inform how he assessed the attacks of that day. "The events of September 11," he writes, "bring us face-to-face with sacred matters. Acts of terrorism, particularly of the sort we witnessed in New York and Washington, D.C., are violations of something we all regard as a *taboo*—a taboo against the intentional targeting and destruction of defenseless civilians."[24] Echoing the idea that such acts are transparently wrong, Little observes that the events of 9/11 were literally "unspeakable" and "unthinkable."[25]

One problem facing this argument is the fact that certain groups do not have an obvious moral revulsion or settled intuitions about the wrongness that occurred. They do not find the events unspeakable. Despite the fact that Muslim leaders criticized the attacks, in many Muslim countries the event was followed by a conspicuous silence and, in some places, public celebration. Those facts suggest that less consensus exists about 9/11 as a human rights atrocity than many Westerners assume (or desire).

Aware of the problem that conflicting intuitions—or moral disagreement based on such conflicts—poses for an intuitionist theory, Little holds a clear position. Consider the case of torture as an example of wrongdoing. About persons who might doubt the taboo against arbitrary suffering as manifested in the practice of torture, he writes: "I would see no particular problem in describing as 'handicapped' or 'pathological' someone, or some group of people, who genuinely and systematically denied the universal and absolute wrongness of such a practice, particularly if such denials were acted upon."[26] There are times and places in which it is impossible to reason with persons who fail to recognize basic taboos.

In a subsequent exchange with Scott Davis in the *Journal of Religious Ethics,* Little found himself pressed to provide deeper reasons to justify the intuitions that animated (and continue to animate) the modern human rights movement.[27] Amplifying his line of argument, Little states: "The use of force, namely, the infliction of death, impairment, severe pain/injury, or confinement on other human beings, requires an extremely strong justification, wherever it occurs, for two principal reasons: the obvious adverse consequences that result from using force, and the strong temptation in human affairs to use force arbitrarily."[28] The first of these reasons appeals to immediate consequences, the second to the danger of a slippery slope, for thinking about the ethics of violence and coercion.

In offering this reply, however, Little seems to have departed from the method by which he sets out to think about cases of transparent wrongfulness. That method would have him prescind from identifying norms or reasons for condemning such wrongfulness *ex ante* and instead would ask him to turn the question of justification back to any questioner. If taboos (and their violations) are pretheoretical, then they don't need theoretical justification.

More worrisome in my mind are the reasons that Little cites for justifying the intuitions on which his judgments rely: immediate and long-term consequences of human rights infringements. These are obviously important moral concerns, but Little does not say enough about them. Surely we must ask what kinds of consequences have moral relevance to the presumptive ban on using force. I am presuming that by the phrase, "obvious adverse consequences," Little has in mind the morally adverse effects of rights violations on individual victims along with the body politic. That account would have us focus in principled terms on the inhumanity that such violence represents. But that is only a speculation on my part. Little might have in mind a more conventional utilitarian answer, namely, that such violence does more harm than good. On that view, we would ask if societies that carry out violence are better or worse off in the short or long run. Obviously that kind of analysis enters into the labyrinthine project of having to determine what is meant by "better" and "worse" and how to specify short- or long-term cost-estimations for determining the overall balance of utility and disutility. Given those uncertainties, we do well to inquire further into what is morally at stake in cases of unprovoked threats or acts of aggression. I will attempt to do so shortly.

Little notes that his list of primary taboos is small. That his list would include the wrongfulness of 9/11 seems plain. My view is that such an inclusion, however attractive at first blush, would not suffice to ground a moral grievance. I believe that it is too easy to dismiss the terrorists who attacked on 9/11 as suffering from a moral pathology or to state that they are morally handicapped. Moreover, I do not think it sufficient to say that the use of force is presumptively wrong because it has negative consequences without indicating what sorts of consequences are morally salient. Although I am sympathetic with the idea that paradigmatic instances of goodness or wrongdoing provide loci of certitude for practical moral reasoning, unfortunately we cannot say, paraphrasing Little, that practical beliefs in all parts of the world are now standardly subjected to what one could call "the antiterrorist test."[29] The culture of apology and excuse surrounding terrorism to which I referred in chapter 1 suggests that matters are more complicated—or at least that our practical beliefs require more extensive moral theorizing. For these reasons, more needs to be said about the moral stakes involved in the attacks of 9/11 and events like it. What can be said?

I began this chapter by talking about the rule against killing and the rights of life and security on the assumption that those concepts need philosophical vindication. Operating behind the rule against killing is the idea that individuals have an interest in being left alone, an interest in being secure against arbitrary threats of death, injury, or serious danger. That is because each person's life is *his* or *her* life. The possessive pronoun is meant to express a personal interest, a key concept that grounds rights-talk. Also, and more importantly, it points to an existential fact that has important moral implications. Each of us can say, "My life is intimately mine, uniquely and specially so." As Nancy Davis observes, we are understandably partial about attaching value to the security of our own individual lives.[30] Such partiality, Davis writes, calls "for other peoples' recognition . . . that (by my lights) my life has the greater value to me."[31] Davis calls this an "agent-relative" perspective to underscore its first-person character.[32] The core notion is that "a person's life is of special value to the person whose life it is" as opposed to a value more generally.[33]

The idea that "my life is intimately mine, uniquely and specially so," is often understood on analogy with a property right, a possession that other persons are not entitled to seize or jeopardize. Viewed more accurately, the idea grounds the commonsense understanding of responsibility, the idea that we are to deliberate about and order our lives over their duration. In carrying out that responsibility we put a distinctive stamp on our existence, marking ourselves off from other persons. There is a truth to metaphysical individualism (although only a partial truth). Without having a right to a secure life, we would be unable to exercise the capacity to deliberate about and order our lives as our own.[34] We are individually responsible for assuming ownership of our lives, of sorting out what is right and good by our own lights. For that reason we say that each person has inherent dignity by virtue of the capacity for moral subjectivity, "the capacity to lead and take responsibility for one's own life," as Stephen L. Darwall puts it.[35] Accordingly, the agent-relative perspective that we take toward the value of our own lives points to a deeper, more general value at stake when considering rights to life and security: the importance of freedom as the condition for envisioning and acting on our respective visions of the good. Our dignity attaches to our existence as moral subjects, with capacities for defining and acting on fundamental, self-defining commitments.

I began this book by describing its moral outlook as generally connected to the liberal tradition, and now we can see how that is so. The basic idea is to affirm the value of autonomy as a basis for living a good life. Recall my reference to Will Kymlicka in chapter 1: "We lead our life from the inside, in accordance with our beliefs about what gives value to life," and we are free to question those beliefs in light of whatever information we acquire.[36] Liberalism is premised in part on our need for the freedom to choose and critically to revise our commitments against a background of meaningful frameworks and options. For liberals, autonomy is valuable as a necessary ingredient in one's pursuit of the good. It enables us to place our first-order, more immediate desires in critical frameworks that provide terms according to which we determine whether such desires are indeed desirable.[37] Seen in that way, autonomy is, in the words of David A. J. Richards, the "capacity for rationally self-critical evaluations of wants and plans."[38] You can hardly call such a pursuit "yours" if you have not been given, or have not assumed, the freedom to define and, if necessary, revise your account of the good. Freedom is a condition of assuming personal responsibility for defining the goods that shape one's *telos*. In this way, we can see how the rights to life and security are meant to protect individuals so that they may carry out their obligations: to Allah, Torah, Jesus, human flourishing, dharma, the pursuit of pleasure, or the maximization of utility, to name several of the most prominent options. The rights to life and security are presumed in any framework that understands human beings as having self-defining obligations.

Rights to life and security can thus be conceived in these foundational terms. I wish to add that they are to be understood as universal but not absolute.[39] Although each person is entitled to assume such rights-claims are by no means indefeasible. They may yield to the defense of other rights in situations of moral conflict.

As I noted above in our discussion of Fish, there is a distinction between a universal claim and an incorrigible one, recalling the difference between the range and weight of a moral concept.[40] On my view, a right may have a universal range but it may give way to more demanding rights or goods in situations of moral complexity, when rights conflict. That is to say, there are universal grounds for embracing rights, rights that are "only" *prima facie* or presumptive. On my view, we say that there is a universal presumption against killing and injury that must be overridden by other, weightier goods in order to justify the use of force. Put simply: there is a *prima facie* duty not to kill, injure, or endanger others, the violation of which shoulders a considerable burden of proof.

Yet the ideas that I am developing here go beyond standard accounts of liberal doctrine by probing more basic dimensions of autonomy and self-determination. To usurp someone's personal sovereignty (and responsibility) over his or her life is radically to determine another's fortune—to make an ultimate decision about another's fate. The intimacy of one's existence, the fact that it is one's *own* life, suggests specialness akin to a sacred trust. Although life is a personal possession in a unique sense, we do not come to possess it through will or ingenuity. Phenomenologically speaking, we experience it as bestowed. Admittedly there is a certain paradox to these notions: we are responsible for our own lives, but we also know that we are not entirely sovereign over our existence, for we are not self-originating. That *I am* is not a personal achievement, a matter of works. Hence metaphorical language about the "giftedness" of life. That language points to radical dependence, to an emptiness or nullity when it comes to being in command over one's own origination. That I am something rather than nothing is a fact for me to possess and cherish; it is not something that I can claim as an accomplishment. The phrase, "It's *my* life," distills a perception about the possessive dimension and the dependent, gifted quality of our lives as individuals. When that gift is at risk of being arbitrarily jeopardized or seized, we rightly respond by acting self-protectively.

These claims say as much about the values of autonomy and personal responsibility as they do about our dependence and contingency—features of our existence that liberal doctrine sometimes overlooks. It is impossible to disregard conditions of human finitude, the "thrownness" of existence into a particular time, habitat, and culture. Our existence is conditioned by basic necessities, uncontrollable forces, and the experience of lack and luck.

Typically, we view these aspects of the human condition as opposed to one another, believing that our freedom and our finitude pull us in opposite directions or identify features of existence that are contradictory. Reinhold Niebuhr famously exploited the implications of this dualism.[41] One aspect of the duality points to our unboundedness and individuality, the other to our encumbrances, vulnerability, and social ties. But in fact the relationship between these two dimensions of our lives is reflexive insofar as our freedom is such to reveal our finitude. It enables us to assume a perspective on ourselves according to which we can see that we are dependent and therefore bounded by needs, longings, and vulnerabilities. That is to say, our power of self-reflexivity enables us to discover conditions that are essential to freedom's own expression—externalities without which we could not exercise our choices and potentialities, the material from which we must evaluatively choose as we develop our character. Our freedom is embedded in bodily, social, and cultural exigencies, and that fact underscores our basic finitude.

Taking these strands together, we can say the following: existence is "given" in that we are not self-originating; it is metaphorically understood as a gift that has been received, a trust to be protected. Further, existence as *human* existence presumes conditions for experiencing life "from the inside"—for defining and ordering one's self-defining commitments. Hence the interest that we have in moral subjectivity: it provides the condition for pursuing all of our other interests. Having a right to life and the related right of security is derivative upon the interests in being a moral subject, in being creatures with the capacity to lead and take responsibility for our own lives and dependent on conditions that enable us to exercise that capacity. When someone seeks arbitrarily to endanger that capacity and its supporting conditions, we are justified in forming a moral grievance against that encroachment. Such an infringement is a violation of what it means to assign respect to persons as moral subjects with inherent dignity—with capacities to define and, if necessary, revise our respective visions of the good. To be sure, our freedom is bounded, as I have noted. It also marks the boundary of others' freedom and functions to set restrictions on their pursuits. Honoring that boundary is one expression of respect for persons. It provides the basis for a moral immunity from arbitrary, direct harm and potential injury.

On this line of argument, we say that persons as moral subjects deserve respect as ends in themselves, as objects of unquantifiable worth. That fact generates rights or entitlements to which all persons are bound. Rights do not generate a basis for respect; rather, the demands of respect generate rights such as the immunity from arbitrary harm or aggression. Such rights encumber others regardless of whether they endorse the visions of the good that such rights are designed to protect.

This immunity provides the moral grounding for the conviction that unprovoked or arbitrary acts of danger or violence are unjust, that they violate the norm of respect for persons. It also grounds the conviction that arbitrary acts of aggression are unjust insofar as they compromise a community's capacity to produce the conditions of a common and secure life and violate the general terms of peace on which communities and states rely. Each of us depends on social, political, and cultural conditions that others put at risk when they initiate war, criminal violence, or other forms of unjust coercion. Therein lies the general basis for a community's right to use force: a community provides the intersubjective conditions in which we exercise our capacities as moral subjects. Here we see metaphysical individualism's incompleteness: we do not develop our lives in isolation but in dialogue with others, an intergenerational dialogue that both creates and presupposes social customs, political institutions, and cultural traditions. These goods have value in that they provide the ambient structures within which persons' lives are constituted over time, the horizon of meaning according to which we gain sense and direction in our pursuits of the good. Our respective pursuits of the good are not solipsistic or monological; they involve social sources, a "common life."

The right to defend a common life is but an extension of the right to be secure from another's unprovoked threats of arbitrary, injurious action. Insofar as our identity is bound up with the intersubjective and intergenerational experience of community and culture, collective security is a basic moral value, for it provides a shield behind which individuals, as moral subjects, can interact and develop their respective visions of the good life.[42] To be sure, the formation of civil society—of mutuality and association—is complex. It develops less as a result of explicit transfers and exchanges among citizens than from shared experiences, customs, and cooperative activity that grow and change over time.[43] This fact does not mean that civil society is reducible to ethnic or cultural solidarity, only that societies develop historically and contingently. Like personal friendship, civil society materializes from the alchemy wrought by finite freedom—emerging from a mix of reason, affection, collective memory, and pure accident. Societies and the political institutions that protect them are less a product of rational, deliberate transfers of power than of the gritty, organic facts of history, opportunity, creativity, and struggle. Viewed in these terms, communities have the right to be left alone on the premise that they provide a sphere of freedom along with material and cultural conditions on which we depend in our pursuits of the good. The right to be secure from external threats thus generates the more general duty to protect the institutional structures with which persons-in-communities form themselves over time.

In the modern age, the state coordinates the political institutions that aim to protect individuals and their associations in civil society, the natural and social sources of a common life. States have security rights and international laws to protect them. Without the guarantee of noninterference, states and the groups that inhabit them would be unable to develop the political arrangements and institutions that condition and reflect the aspirations and beliefs of their people.

This fact should remind us of the important distinction between state and society in political ethics. Individuals and social groups have legitimate expectations that the state will organize the mechanisms of power to provide for a society's collective security.[44] A state's right to use force generates the duty to protect its citizens from those who unjustly seek to seize life, liberty, and the conditions of security on which the exercise of those goods relies. For that reason, the ethics of international relations considers the sovereign state to be the key unit for thinking about a community's formal structure. The state has the responsibility for protecting the nation, or nations, that reside within it.

We can thus say that states have the right not to be interfered with, all else being equal—that arbitrary aggression violates states' rights of security and the good of international peace and order more generally. Owing to that violation, unprovoked aggression is an occasion for moral grievance and may warrant an armed response. The moral wrong of aggression and the need to protect citizens and their common life provides one reason for overriding the presumption against war and killing. Those who volunteer or are enlisted in the service of that responsibility may be justified in using force—lethal force if necessary—against persons who have coordinated their efforts to threaten others' lives and liberty.

On this line of thinking, 9/11 was a moral atrocity because it consisted of deliberate acts of massive destruction and killing of persons who did nothing to forfeit their entitlement to respect and safety. The attacks violated as basic a set of human rights as one can imagine, and they did so on a vast scale. Terrorist attacks such as occurred on 9/11 seek to inflict injury on everyday people in a way that is both random and indiscriminate. They single out people on the basis of who they are rather than for having done something that might pose a lethal or serious threat to others. One reason we say that acts of terrorism are wrong is that they target innocent people along with the social and political institutions in which they carry out meaningful activities. Bin Laden made no case for the attacks of 9/11 to explain why the *prima facie* rights to life and security of those targeted may be justifiably overridden. Nor is it clear, as Johnson notes, that bin Laden and his associates possess the authority to authorize any such use of force.[45] The attacks of 9/11 violated rights to life and security, rights so basic that any religion or worldview failing to honor them appears unworthy of allegiance; one can scarcely imagine a humane social life without them. Whatever else a group, culture, or tradition might pursue, these rights (and the dispositions to act on them) are axiomatic. As I will make plain in chapter 7, they provide terms central to an ethics of belief.

MORAL AGENCY AND THE
LOGICAL ENTAILMENT OF RIGHTS

The idea that respect for persons as free and finite moral subjects grounds basic rights bears strong resemblance to moral theories that defend human rights in light of invariant features of moral agency. Appeals to moral *subjectivity* resemble appeals to the demands of moral *agency* insofar as both arguments attend to entitlements that can be derived from what might be called the interior features of human action. But there are important differences between claims that derive from respect for the capacity of moral subjectivity, on the one hand, and claims that derive from an analysis of invariant aspects of human agency, on the other. With that in mind, I want to distinguish my argument from the defense of human rights that has been developed by the philosopher Alan Gewirth. Gewirth constructs an account of universal human rights that turns on an analysis of moral agency, focusing on the necessary conditions of human action—conditions that imply claims to which all persons, on pain of contradiction, must affirm. Such claims, Gewirth argues, generate rights that aim to protect and, under certain circumstances, enhance human capacities to act purposively.[46]

Gewirth's argument proceeds in two steps. The first step examines necessary features of human action on the premise that human action provides the context for the general subject matter of morality. We think of morality, in other words, in terms of human action and not something else—the movement of the stars, the behavior of animals, and the like. Analysis of human action reveals that it possesses two proximate necessary conditions that all agents must at least implicitly claim for themselves. Those two conditions are well-being and freedom, "where freedom consists in controlling one's behavior by one's unforced choice while having knowledge of relevant circumstances, and well-being consists in having the other general abilities and conditions required for agency."[47] All rational agents, Gewirth adds, regard their freedom and well-being as necessary goods insofar as these conditions must, of logical necessity, be presupposed in all purposive human activity. "Since agents act for purposes they regard as worth pursuing . . . they must, insofar as they are rational, also regard the necessary conditions of such pursuit as necessary goods."[48] All rational agents necessarily rely on the goods of freedom and well-being as invariant conditions of action, whatever those agents' ends might be.

From this claim Gewirth develops an account of human rights, building on the putative logical connection between necessary goods and rights. From the statement, "My freedom and well-being are necessary goods," it logically follows, according to Gewirth, that one should say, "I have rights to freedom and well-being." The affirmation of freedom and well-being is not merely a factual statement about rational agency; it also carries one's advocacy or endorsement. It is a prescriptive claim insofar as one is saying that he or she *must* have freedom and well-being as necessary features of any and all purposive activity. Moreover, it is a prudential claim: the entitlement is grounded in the rational agent's needs as someone who wants to pursue his or her own purposes.[49] This prescriptive-prudential claim implies correlative duties for other persons. The goods of freedom and well-being establish, at a minimum, the claim to the noninterference of others along with their help in certain circumstances.

The second step in Gewirth's argument universalizes the insight garnered from the first. It requires that we assign to others the same rights to freedom and well-being that we claim for ourselves. Called "the Principle of Generic Consistency" (PGC), this principle combines the formal consideration of consistency with the material consideration of the generic features of the rights of agency.[50] The PGC entails the "*equality of generic rights*, since it requires of every agent that he accord to his recipients the same rights to freedom and well-being that he necessarily claims for himself."[51] Each rational agent must admit that others have as much right to the goods of freedom and well-being that she or he does, since the reason for which she or he claims them also applies to others.[52]

In this way, Gewirth seeks to proceed from the invariant conditions of moral agency to argue on behalf of objective claims that protect or promote those conditions, claims that are then universalized according to the PGC. His argument seeks to have as few incontrovertible claims as possible and relies on logical terms that we all clearly understand and accept. Yet Gewirth's argument involves a philosophical sleight of hand. The fact that a rational agent necessarily affirms goods of freedom and well-being as conditions of action scarcely grounds a direct right to these goods. The argument lacks directness because it by no means follows, as Gewirth would wish, that one's endorsement of a necessary good establishes an objective claim on others. By this I do not mean to rehearse the is-ought problem, the difficulty of moving from factual statements to moral ones. I rather mean that I see no logical connection between identifying the necessary conditions to purposive action, on the one hand, and an entitlement to claims that aim to protect those conditions, on the other. Someone who frustrates another's purposive activity may undermine a need. But that frustration does not obviously infringe on a basic right. More must be said for us to proceed from values ingredient in an agential need to the existence of a basic right. Gewirth fails to close the gap between needs and rights.

Anticipating this challenge, Gewirth wishes to strengthen the importance of the prescriptive-prudential need for freedom and well-being by distinguishing those goods from other kinds of needs. He thus differentiates between the endorsement of freedom and well-being and other forms of endorsements, such as the claim, "I must have a Florida vacation." A necessary good, in contrast to a recreational wish, is "confined to the truly grounded requirements of agency; hence, it correctly characterizes the indispensable conditions that all agents must accept as needed for their actions."[53] One might say that freedom and well-being are deep, invariant needs whereas other needs or desires are not. For that reason they are qualitatively different and thus make a justifiable bid as entitlements.

However true it is that certain needs are more fundamental than others, that fact fails to close the logical gap between needs and rights. All that Gewirth can show is that some needs have less potential to make a bid for becoming rights, not that some needs secure their bid to being rights. Gewirth needs to add a substantive claim about the value of proximate necessary conditions for purposive agency, and that claim is lacking. That is to say, Gewirth needs to develop a more robust account of value regarding those conditions, one that renders intelligible the importance he wishes to assign to constitutive agential needs. Such an account would bridge the gap between needs and rights. It would do so by introducing a concept that mediates between needs and rights, namely, the idea of respect. As that idea bears on Gewirth's analysis, respect would pertain to, or would be demanded by, the deep goods of freedom and well-being. Rights would make sense, then, as an expression of respect for proximate necessary goods of moral agency. But Gewirth is silent about substantive values of this sort.

In my mind, it makes greater sense for human rights theory to focus on the dignity of the agent as a moral subject rather than on the invariant conditions of moral agency. Focusing on the invariant conditions of freedom and well-being, whether or not that includes the idea of respect, abstracts too austerely from our capacities and needs as embodied subjects. We do better to attend first to the entitlement of respect due to persons valued as having dignity before asking if their freedom and dependence give rise to claims of one or another sort. Attention to the conditions of moral agency and the claims that they might generate arises after we assign a substantive value—and the requirement of respect—to agents as persons viewed with embodied desires, deliberative capacities, and aspirations for a good life.

What Gewirth *can* do is to develop an account of human rights that proceeds in an indirect manner. The argument would proceed as follows. Assuming that freedom and well-being are necessary conditions of purposive agency, I act on the "pain of contradiction" when I arbitrarily undermine the basic conditions necessary for other persons' actions. The argument would recognize that all persons act on such conditions, and then would assign to me the duty to respect the same conditions for agency according to which I wish my agency to be respected. In effect, the argument would combine the Golden Rule with the Principle of Generic Consistency, and it would rely on the correlation between rights and duties. The argument would begin with the duty to respect the conditions of others' agency on pain of contradiction. When that duty is universalized, it then creates obligations for others to respect the conditions of my agency. Those obligations then imply self-regarding entitlements, or rights that I may claim for myself. What Gewirth succeeds in establishing is the idea that consistency requires others to respect my prudential interests in well-being and freedom along with the idea that I am required by consistency to respect theirs. On this account, rights fall out of a prior set of duties. For that reason I call it an indirect method of establishing human rights.

My argument, in contrast, relies on moral subjectivity as a substantive value that requires respect and proceeds to establish some basic rights in a direct manner. Like Gewirth's argument, it acknowledges the fact that "we lead our life from the inside, in accordance with our beliefs about what gives value to life,"[54] or, in Gewirth's terms, that a rational agent "is a prospective agent who has purposes he wants to fulfill."[55] But unlike Gewirth, I want to say that moral subjectivity is intrinsically valuable, that it has inherent dignity. Moral subjectivity is that endowment according to which we order our lives. It is the *sine qua non* of the moral life. We thus begin by establishing not the "equality of generic rights," as Gewirth does, but the equality of persons as bearers of dignity that requires respect.

"Respect for persons" demands that we are to respect *that* persons have moral subjectivity, not that we respect *how* persons exercise their subjectivity. That is to say, we respect others' authority to make their own decisions even when we decline to esteem the judgments they make. Of course, we may indeed endorse how others exercise their moral subjectivity, but such esteem differs from respect that we assign to them "as persons." We can respect another's point of view without having to share or endorse it; indeed, we can respect others even if we judge their choices as being less than admirable. But there are limits to our deference: we typically deny others our esteem when they fail to assign respect to other persons.

These ideas trade on important distinctions between respect and esteem, distinctions that have become considerably more charged in multicultural settings within which persons or groups demand recognition for the particular practices and traditions according to which they find meaning. Such expectations raise difficult questions about the importance, grounds, and limits of toleration in a world of multicultural differences. Those who were aggrieved by the attacks of 9/11 understand their indignation in normative terms, as grounded in a moral condemnation of Islamic terrorism. Indignation sounds intolerant, and intolerance seems to chafe against liberal sentiments. How to sort out these points regarding tolerance, respect (including self-respect), and recognition in a public culture characterized by grave differences is less than straightforward. To those concerns, along with their connections to liberal doctrine, we must therefore turn.

4

TOLERATION, EQUALITY, AND THE BURDENS OF JUDGMENT

Earlier, I stated that Muslim (and other) extremists should respect basic rights of life and security even if they don't endorse the visions or ways of life that those rights function to protect. That claim invites us to consider connections between acts of religious violence and religious intolerance. Violence that targets victims on the basis of their creed or religious heritage obviously disregards the lives of the individuals so targeted; it also expresses intolerance of those victims' tradition, community, or worldview. As I noted earlier, we object to terrorism because it targets persons on the basis of *who* they are rather than for *what* they have done. That simple statement contains a deep philosophical point about the level of disregard expressed by agents of religious violence. A religious zealot's putative grievance surrounding a discrete act or policy might be masking a deeper intolerance of his or her victim's very existence based on that victim's beliefs. In such cases religion functions both as a warrant for using violence and as an explanation for why certain persons or groups are targeted. In the wake of 9/11 and other similar acts, we do well to explore issues of tolerance—or its absence—along with its connection to violence carried out as a sacred duty.

By "toleration," I mean the practice of deliberately refraining from interfering with an opposed other when one believes that such interference is within one's power.[1] We tolerate another's belief or behavior when we intentionally subordinate our disapproval of another's belief or behavior to another value. For liberals, that latter value is respect—respect for the other's attachment to her belief or the goods she assigns to her behavior. Toleration consists in respect for the other's authority to determine and revise his or her understanding of the good life.[2] When we tolerate, we shift our perspective from another's particular beliefs to the person who holds them. Toleration is shaped by a tension between one's self-respecting adherence to one's own beliefs and normative standards, on the one hand, and respect for another's humanity and authority to determine his or her beliefs or practices, on the other.

Describing toleration in terms of this tension sheds light on its demands on our moral psychology. We tolerate not when we decline to share or endorse someone else's beliefs, attitudes, or practices, but when we disapprove of them. Toleration is not a matter of being neutral about another's views; it presumes a negative judgment. Our judgment is bracketed, however, by the assignment of respect to the bearer of those beliefs, attitudes, or practices as someone of inherent dignity.[3] We leave it to others—those whom we tolerate—to sort out their visions and pursuits of the good despite the fact that we find something about those visions that we dislike. One question is how far toleration can be endured given the fact that it includes the background condition of dislike or disapproval. Typically, we draw limits around toleration at that point where the agent of our (bracketed) disapproval acts to harm innocent persons or undermines socially important goods. In those cases, our respect for one person is overridden by rival concerns—others' personal welfare, for example. Our perspective then shifts from the humanity of the person we tolerate to other values—values that generate concern about real or potential victims of injustice. Our respect for the humanity of those whom we tolerate should not come at the expense of others' humanity and well-being.

With these thoughts in mind, I want to discuss matters of toleration with an eye to assessing the intolerance of Islamic extremists as revealed in their incendiary remarks regarding Israelis, Americans, and American supporters or sympathizers. The comments I cited at the outset of chapter 1 reveal connections between religious intolerance and religious violence in the ideology of al Qaeda. Bin Laden's intolerance aims to animate violence that is sanctified by religious commitment. "As for the fighting to repulse [an enemy]," he and his colleagues write, "it is aimed at defending sanctity and religion, and it is a duty as agreed [by the ulema]. Nothing is more sacred than belief except repulsing an enemy who is attacking religion and life."[4] The hijackers who died on 9/11 were praised as martyrs, and the event was described as one in which "America [was] struck by Allah the Almighty in one of her vital organs."[5] Obviously we cannot downplay the role of religious conviction in the plans and actions of Muslim radicals. Three years before 9/11, bin Laden stated: "Every Muslim, from the moment they realize the distinction in their hearts, hates Americans, hates Jews, and hates Christians. This is a part of our belief and our religion."[6]

On the argument I want to develop, we should find these and related comments morally offensive for reasons that go beyond the lethal threats that they are meant to authorize. Moreover, we should find these comments offensive apart from their hatefulness. We should find them offensive because they are fundamentally and unashamedly intolerant.[7] They fail to honor the value of human dignity and the respect for persons that it entails.

REASONS FOR TOLERATION

One way to get a handle on extremist sentiments is to invoke the distinction between *tolerating* and *endorsing* another's beliefs, building on John Rawls's argument regarding the "burdens of judgment" in his understanding of moral disagreement, toleration, and political liberalism. For liberals, intractable moral differences occur for understandable reasons, and such differences need not prevent parties from respecting each other—or expecting respect *from* each other—according to the constraints of basic rights and claims of justice. This Rawlsian explanation of disagreement is an alternative to "Tower of Babel" accounts of religious and moral difference, where factors other than overweening pride, culpable ignorance, or what some religious believers call "sin" or "fallenness" explain why people hold differing beliefs. Rawls's account has important implications for thinking about what opposing persons or groups owe each other. I will return to it shortly.

First, however, we might ask whether it is fair to expect religious extremists (or others) to tolerate persons whose practices they do not endorse. That question is complicated by the fact that toleration appears to be a Western and parochial norm. To assume that what Westerners find normative applies to others seems insensitive to cultural and religious differences and appears to involve the affirmation of particularity masquerading as universality.

Richard Rorty raises this problem in his discussion of political and social justice and defense of what he calls "postmodernist bourgeois liberalism," providing a platform for the sort of argument we found Fish avowing in chapter 2.[8] Rorty frames his argument by distinguishing between two sets of philosophers that have emerged from the Enlightenment: absolutists and pragmatists. The former rely on an Enlightenment rationalism according to which "there is a relation between the ahistorical essence of the human soul and moral truth, a relation which ensures that free and open discussion will produce 'one right answer' to moral as well as to scientific questions."[9] To this Rorty contrasts a pragmatist theory with roots in the Hegelian idea that "there are no ahistorical criteria for deciding when it is or is not a responsible act to desert a community, any more than for deciding when to change lovers or professions."[10] Absolutists, Rorty avows, "talk about inalienable 'human rights' and about 'one right answer' to moral and political dilemmas without trying to back up such talk with a theory of human nature." Pragmatists, in contrast, "consider talk of 'rights' an attempt to enjoy the benefits of metaphysics without assuming the appropriate responsibilities."[11] They thus "still need something to distinguish the sort of individual conscience we respect from the sort we condemn as 'fanatical.' This can only be something relatively local and ethnocentric—the tradition of a particular community, the consensus of a particular culture. According to this view, what counts as rational or as fanatical is relative to the group to which we think it necessary to justify ourselves—to the body of shared belief that determines the reference of the word 'we.' "[12] Rorty in effect replaces the search for universal foundations for human rights with the affirmation that local traditions provide.

But Rorty overlooks the real work that human rights can perform, namely, regulating how people from different traditions and cultures deal with each other in cross-cultural situations. These contacts occur not at some abstract level of philosophical theorizing but in the real-life encounters and political disputes, whether we are thinking about desires for political autonomy in Kosovo and Palestine, genocide in the Sudan, or economic development and environmental degradation in Central and South America. Human rights perform their practical work in contexts outside bourgeois insularity and isolation from cross-cultural encounters. They provide voice to the complaints and expectations that arise in those encounters, mediating social criticism among those who find themselves in that liminal, interstitial space between their own traditions and others'.

Moreover, Rorty concentrates narrowly on our responsibilities toward persons beyond our culture while ignoring the task of establishing mutually recognized guarantees for the protection of all persons, including ourselves. If 9/11 teaches anything, it teaches the importance of self-regarding claims involved in feeling indignation along with the challenge of establishing the basis for a moral grievance that is more than a complaint articulated narcisstically to ourselves. Rorty's postmodern bourgeois liberalism risks sacrificing one's entitlement to (receiving) respect from others. The challenges of coexistence in a globalized, pluralistic public culture scarcely entail sacrificing the good of self-respect, a good that is often inseparable from relationships shaped by expectations of mutual respect.

With these thoughts in mind, let us return to matters of religious toleration. Liberals hold the idea that toleration is a basic right for reasons that are much more elementary and practical than the metatheoretical discussion of rights that we find in Rortyean thinking.

One plank of liberal argument—contrary to Rorty's claim that certain liberals adopt a line of reasoning in pursuit of "one right answer"—is that we tolerate different worldviews and practices on the premise that there are reasonable grounds for disagreement and that, barring socially damaging consequences within the constraints of fairness, everyone has an equal right to believe as they do. One morally offensive aspect of radical Muslim politics—indeed, of religious extremism and intolerance more generally—is that it seems unable to respect or tolerate persons holding views that it does not endorse. It only respects persons and values that can be endorsed on a certain Muslim interpretation of the good, of what is Islamically "endorseable" (on a particular, normative account of Islam). Non-Muslims and moderate Muslims should be critical of radical Islamists because their beliefs prevent them from recognizing this distinction between respecting or tolerating, on the one hand, and endorsing, on the other. That failure has enormous moral and practical implications in a world of multicultural differences.

There are two claims, then, to develop here: whether there are reasonable grounds for disagreement, and how to understand the moral grounds of freedom of conscience and the demands of toleration and respect. Let us take each in order.

The first claim identifies factors that help explain why conscientious and reasonable people disagree about some fundamental convictions. Rawls calls these factors the "burdens of judgment."[13] They point to aspects of our reasoning other than self-interest and ignorance that indicate why people arrive at quite different views of and orientations toward the world and our lives with one another. Although Rawls does not attempt to provide a comprehensive list of such burdens, his account is instructive insofar as it disabuses those who view all disagreement as a matter of power, egoism, or intractable religious conviction. The main point is that there are understandable reasons for disagreement and that it is unfair to assume peremptorily that those with whom one disagrees are beyond the pale of reason or that others are not entitled to respect.[14] Consider the following six reasons why we should expect disagreements to arise about matters of moral and religious conviction:

1. Empirical and scientific evidence bearing on a case or world-view is conflicting and complex. Facts in support of one or another viewpoint do not always line up on only one side, and identifying which facts are relevant to any side of a dispute involves the exercise of judgment.

2. How much weight to assign relevant facts is also a matter of judgment, even when we agree about which facts are relevant and which are not. That is to say, the importance that we assign to specific facts in moral argument is not self-evident, and the importance that we do assign can nonetheless vary in degree.

3. The rules or guidelines that bear upon a problem are open-ended and indeterminate, requiring interpretation and practical understanding about which reasonable people can differ.[15] Not infrequently we disagree about how to interpret the meaning of a rule, especially when we seek to apply it to marginal cases or to circumstances that the rule was not originally designed to address. The moral rule or rules pertinent to a case are not self-interpreting, and interpretations of them, along with their supporting grounds, invite different points of view.

4. Our assessments of facts and concepts are shaped by our course of life, which modifies our outlook as we grow in experience, and which differs from person to person. This fact is made more complex by the different kinds of roles and communities out of which our experience grows. Rawls notes, "In a modern society with its numerous offices and positions, its various divisions of labor, its many social groups and their ethnic variety, citizens' total experiences are disparate enough for their judgments to diverge, at least to some degree, on many if not most cases of any significant complexity."[16] Personal background and experience—in all of their diversity—inform our practical understanding of the meaning and implications of moral convictions.

5. Different kinds of normative concepts may bear on a case or controversy, and these may enjoy different degrees of importance or weight on each side of an issue. For example, adjudicating between concerns for equality and freedom—assuming clarity about the meaning of these concepts—requires us to judge their meaning and relative weight.

6. The practical requirements of institutionalizing a set of values allows for limited possibilities.[17] It is thus necessary to make some selection of values and to understand how they may restrict each other in the design of social and political institutions. Setting priorities and coordinating values with each other involves difficult decisions and practical reasoning. Again, we are met with the challenges of interpretation and judgment.[18]

Owing to these factors, we cannot expect conscientious persons always or easily to arrive at the same conclusion about matters of dispute, even after a free and open discussion. The burdens of judgment set limits on what we can expect when attempting to persuade others of our own point of view. Those burdens thus help to endorse "liberty of conscience and freedom of thought."[19] They point to epistemic limits on reaching consensus. Hence one reason for religious liberty: answers to life's basic questions are not obvious or self-evident, and people of good will face obstacles to arriving at the same point of view.

That fact points to the second crucial issue, the idea of religious freedom and equal liberty. Rawls rightly notes that the burdens of judgment "are of first significance for a democratic idea of toleration."[20] Terrorists trained by al Qaeda, as I noted earlier, are virulently intolerant of Israelis, Americans, and their sympathizers. For liberals and other democrats, one of the great challenges of 9/11 has involved reckoning with the limits of toleration, accustomed as liberals are to tolerating others, including at times the intractably intolerant.

Here the critical question is: What *value* is at stake in religious freedom and toleration? Often we answer that question by citing the value of civic peace or the prevention of social conflict. On that account, toleration is viewed as a matter of achieving a *modus vivendi*, a compromise for handling disputes based on the prudential estimation that everyone is better off by tolerating different practices and beliefs. But a *modus vivendi* is contingent on achieving a balance of power among rival factions; should an imbalance occur, those in the minority are vulnerable to discriminatory treatment. That fact along with the experience of radical intolerance prompts us to plumb toleration's moral depths. We must therefore reconsider the moral values or principles that are at risk in contexts where individuals may be harmed owing to their religious or other comprehensive doctrines. Morally speaking, what do intolerant groups such as al Qaeda deny to others?

The answer is simple: equal liberty. Rawls puts this point indirectly in his discussion of toleration when he writes: "It seems that an intolerant sect has no title to complain when it is denied an equal liberty. At least this follows if it is assumed that one has no title to object to the conduct of others that is in accordance with principles one would use in similar circumstances to justify one's actions toward them. A person's right to complain is limited to violations of principles he acknowledges himself."[21] That is to say, those who deny freedom to others, including religious freedom, act inconsistently when they claim such freedom for themselves. They fail to respect others as equals and instead assume a position of superiority, drawing on religious confession and authority to support their stance. Intolerant persons ask for themselves what they deny to others, thereby assuming or acquiring a greater share of freedom in matters of religious or moral conviction.

On this view, toleration is not a utilitarian doctrine whereby we agree to disagree on the estimation that we are better off in the long run under a regime of toleration rather than in a regime ruled by, say, conformist religious authority. Rather, toleration is a rule-governed activity, grounded in principle and involving norms of justice that are connected to the value of equality.

SUBMISSION AND RESPECT

To be sure, the ideas of equal liberty and equal respect are relative newcomers to the history of political philosophy. They have their own history and, with that, their own conceptual firmament. Stephen L. Darwall briefly traces the genealogy of the idea of equal respect as it developed in early modern Western thought and, in the process, identifies one possible obstacle to its widespread acceptance. Central to our understanding of equal respect, Darwall reminds us, is the distinction between two forms of subjection, each of which presumes a different relationship to authority. One relationship is that of *submission* to authority; the other is *respect* for it.[22] Submission is the acknowledgment of *de facto* authority, the status of being ruled. It expresses no view about that authority; one can submit to a rule that one considers unjust. Respect, in contrast, expresses a normative attitude toward authority; it involves the subject's internal acceptance of a sovereign's rule. Therein lies the difference between submission and respect. With respect, "although the subject is governed by the sovereign *de facto*, there is a sense in which she also governs herself, since she is not submitting to something she does not herself accept."[23] One can respect authority out of awe because it has superior dignity, as in hierarchical relationships, or one can respect an authority because it has equal dignity, thereby entailing mutual or equal respect. In either forms of respect—hierarchical or mutual—the core idea is that there is something about authority that satisfies an independent norm. Respect for authority, unlike submission, is contingent upon meeting criteria that stand apart from the authority's control of power. The authority merits respect by virtue of possessing certain admirable qualities. Those who respect authority on such terms are ruling and being ruled at the same time.

Ideas about authority and religious belief, as they first developed in early modern Europe, were complicated by the fact that individual and institutional authority were seen as divinely willed and dependent upon obedience to God. Central to this picture of authority was the idea of theological voluntarism and divine command morality, defended by Duns Scotus and William of Ockham in the late medieval period and subsequently developed in the political theologies of the mainline Reformers. Luther and Calvin both believed that moral and political authority derives from God's will as expressed in divine commands. Luther held that "God is He for Whose will no cause or ground may be laid down as its rule and standard; for nothing is on a level with it or above it, but it is itself the rule for all things. . . . What God wills is not right because He ought, or was bound, so to will; on the contrary, what takes place must be right, because He so wills it."[24] Luther continued this line of reasoning in "Secular Authority," in which he sought to "establish secular law and the sword, that no one may doubt that it is in the world by God's will and ordinance."[25] Drawing exclusively on biblical passages (especially Romans 13), Luther claimed that it is "sufficiently clear and certain that it is God's will that the sword and secular law be used for the punishment of the wicked and the protection of the upright."[26] Luther developed these ideas in part to confine the reach of secular authority to the realm of external behavior, arguing that faith was the Christian's individual responsibility and thus not subject to coercion. "Where temporal power presumes to prescribe laws for the soul," Luther writes, "it encroaches upon God's government and only misleads and destroys the souls."[27] Yet Luther had no compunction about enjoining public authorities to punish those who practice the Catholic Mass. "If cursing and swearing are forbidden in a country," Luther reasoned, "it is still more right here that the lay lords should prohibit and punish, because such blasphemy and such insults to God are as evident and public in the Mass as when a rascal blasphemes in the street."[28]

Similarly, Calvin sought to assert a theological basis for government, relying exclusively on biblical materials to justify the existence and duties of civil authority. Like Luther, Calvin argued on behalf of limited government by distinguishing between the inner and outer "governments" of the Christian, the former of which is ruled by God alone. Yet Calvin quickly qualified that distinction by asserting that the two governments are not antithetical. According to Calvin, "civil government has as its appointed end, so long as we live among men, to cherish and protect the outward worship of God, to defend sound doctrine of piety and the position of the church, to adjust our life to the society of men, to form our social behavior to civil righteousness, to reconcile us with one another, and to promote general peace and tranquility."[29]

When political authority is grounded in theological terms in this way, Darwall notes, "there will be an obvious sense in which religious difference will seem to contest political authority, at least potentially."[30] Those who worship God differently, or who worship a different deity, will have reason to question the *de jure* authority of a sovereign. At a minimum, they will see a potential conflict between obedience to divine and political authorities. Central to the problem of religious toleration in early Europe, "was the idea that the authority of human beings and human political institutions derives from God's superior right of command, that to be a human moral subject is to be *subject to* God's authority."[31] The opportunities for violations and umbrage are clear. Darwall observes: "In a world in which dignity and moral identity are gauged by *subjection*, by the relation human individuals and institutions have to superior divine authority, an attack on God must be understood as an attack on the source of one's own dignity and, hence, as a personal insult which, if not avenged, risks dishonor and devaluation to oneself, as it does to anything whose dignity derives from God's."[32]

This is not to say that a regime of toleration is impossible in a politics premised on theological voluntarism. Early modern Europe eventually produced a regime based on a *modus vivendi*, a civic peace seen as serving the interests of all. Yet, as I noted earlier, such an arrangement is unstable insofar as it is based on enlightened self-interest instead of normative principles that stand apart from contingencies surrounding the distribution of power; should the balance of power shift so that one religious group assumes dominance, the freedoms assigned to other groups may decrease or disappear. For such citizens, subjection becomes a matter of submission to authority rather than respect for it.

In contrast to a regime of toleration premised on submission and mutual advantage, there is the idea of mutual respect. Central to this idea is a feature of human beings to which I referred in chapter 3, namely, moral subjectivity, "the capacity to lead and take responsibility for one's own life."[33] We need freedom to choose and critically to revise our commitments against a background of meaningful options. On that view, autonomy is valuable as a necessary ingredient in one's personal pursuit of the good. We thus assign to each person the authority to lead his or her own life as an expression of respect for her intrinsic dignity as a free and equal person, respect that is constrained by fairness and mutual respect. Religious toleration on this view expresses respect for this intrinsic dignity.[34] What is salient about religious toleration understood along these liberal lines, Darwall notes, is "its centrality to political institutions that express *respect* for the dignity any individual has in herself, independently of her religious belief and practice—respect for citizens as equals."[35]

Such are some basic differences between submission and respect, along with their respective understandings of authority and their implications for thinking about religious toleration. More recent discussions of toleration in political philosophy would have us understand it along social contractarian lines, and it is about those ideas that I wish to comment here. My view does not defend religious toleration within the framework of Rawls's contractarian contribution to liberal doctrine, however much my references to Rawls might otherwise suggest. For contractarians, principles that regulate social life are fair if they would be agreed upon by contracting parties who are deprived of information about their particular life circumstances as they deliberate about the moral design of social and political institutions. Rawls's contribution to social contract doctrine is a thought-experiment famously known as the veil of ignorance, which he deploys for conceiving the terms on which religious toleration would be impartially accepted by contracting parties. Situated behind the veil of ignorance, contracting parties do not know in advance their own personal characteristics, including whether they will be religious, or what religion they would espouse if they are religious. In designing fair principles of social cooperation, they must reckon with the possibility that, once the veil is lifted and they see society's arrangements and their individual characteristics in some detail, they might be persons who hold religious beliefs that are not prevalent in society. Rawls argues that contracting parties who lack information about their particularities behind the veil of ignorance would nonetheless grasp that believers of all different sorts attach great importance to the freedom to practice their religion as they please. With this fact in mind, they would agree that a fair framework for religious pluralism would be one that assigns all persons the equal right to freedom of conscience. Forced to legislate in an impartial way, contracting parties would agree to principles that protect religious liberty.[36]

Rawls develops this account with an eye toward protecting religious minorities from various forms of majoritarianism including the confessional state. That is to say, his argument presumes basic institutions of the modern nation-state. The problem with Rawls's contractarianism is that it does not obviously extend globally, beyond the institutional boundaries of the state. Indeed, when discussing matters of international justice, Rawls does not include equal liberty of conscience as a principle in his account of the law of peoples.[37] This omission allows him to say that some nonliberal societies—what he calls "decent societies"—should be tolerated and accepted in the foreign policies of liberal regimes. My argument, focusing not on contractarian premises but on the idea of moral subjectivity, avows that equal liberty of conscience is a fundamental human right. That right puts principled limits on the actions and intolerance of others that would be difficult to build from Rawls's account.

It might be thought that I am espousing the idea of autonomy as a "comprehensive ideal," understood as intrinsically valuable because it reflects our rational nature. Often liberal thinking takes up this line of argument (often ascribed to Kant) and is targeted by critics who insist that we might (or should) have higher ideals than the good of freedom. But that is not the line of liberal thought that I am advocating here. I am rather defending a conception of autonomy as that which enables us to learn and assess what is good in life. This idea presumes that we have an essential interest in developing beliefs about value and revising those of our beliefs that we judge to be mistaken.[38] On this view, autonomy refers, in the words of David A. J. Richards, to "capacities of persons to entertain and act on second-order desires and plans self-critically to have and revise a form of life."[39] Accordingly, autonomy is not arbitrary willfulness, raw egoism, or some notion of independence according to which a person is abstracted from context and relationships. Autonomy is rather "a capacity for rationally self-critical evaluations of wants and plans."[40] Mill writes in the same vein: "It is the privilege and proper condition of a human being, arrived at the maturity of his faculties, to use and interpret experience in his own way. It is for him to find out what part of recorded experience is properly applicable to his own circumstances and character."[41] This appeal to moral subjectivity is only one of Mill's arguments in defense of toleration; other arguments on which he relies impute to autonomy an intrinsic value or an instrumental value on behalf of socially important goods. But the idea of moral subjectivity is central to Mill's defense of individual rights along with other liberal theories.[42] Echoing this notion, Rawls himself writes of the capacity "to form, to revise, and rationally to pursue a conception of the good."[43] The capacity to review and evaluate our ends is one of two "moral powers" (along with the capacity for a sense of justice) that Rawls identifies in his account of the "conception of the person."[44] We assign authority to individuals owing to respect for their dignity as moral subjects with the capacity to form and revise their views of the good life. For that reason we must establish (or protect) institutional mechanisms to ensure a principled defense of religious toleration.

IMPLICATIONS OF TOLERATION FOR OTHERS

The right of religious liberty has second-person implications, constraining others with moral obligations. That is to say, the right of religious liberty entails the *self-regarding* fact that others, including strangers, have a duty to respect oneself. In human rights doctrine, all persons are rights-bearers, including those who espouse human rights for others. Although that obvious fact underlies anxieties about others' intolerance, it is often ignored given the tendency in discussions of religious toleration to focus on other-regarding duties—on responsibilities owed to others as subjects of one's respect. I want to emphasize that the right to equal liberty imposes duties on everyone, generating the duty of toleration premised on the norm of respect for persons. On this view, we have grounds to expect others, including violent religious extremists, to tolerate persons whose ends they do not endorse within constraints implied by equal liberty.

Again, there are two related reasons to justify that expectation. One is epistemological, premised on the burdens of judgment; the other is ontological, premised on the "distinctive dignity of moral personality."[45] The first reason helps to explain why persons see the world differently, the second reason indicates why we should respect persons who see the world differently and why we are justified in expecting others to reciprocate that respect. Different persons and worldviews lay claim to toleration at a *prima facie* level owing to the humility implied by the burdens of judgment as well as the norms of respect for human dignity and equal liberty.

How does this account bear on the question of whether to expect others, including non-Westerners, to tolerate religious differences? The duty of toleration makes a bid for acceptance without asking skeptics or others to submit to it from a position of inferiority or domination. It operates within a set of expectations shaped by the norms of reciprocity, human dignity, and equal respect.[46] The point is not to avow parochial attitudes that blithely champion Western values. It is rather to identify facts about persons and human knowledge that asks for others' respect and offers them as moral terms for others to consider as free and equal persons.

Social criticism that proceeds along these lines thus urges a kind of moral steadiness. The disposition to assess others can insist on respect for basic rights in ways that can also acknowledge cultural and other differences. Those who are intolerant for religious, gender-based, racial, class, or ethnic reasons deny an entitlement owed to everyone given our capacities as moral subjects whose freedom is necessary to pursue and, when necessary, revise our final ends. Such an entitlement is a condition for any person to be a moral agent; to deny such a claim is not only to deny a right but to disregard a basic dimension of another's humanity. Such disregard deserves to be named and judged. Engaging in social criticism along such lines, I hasten to add, presumes (or should presume) confidence in one's own dignity as entitled to equal respect. Hence the need for moral steadiness: social criticism attentive to respect for persons must include considerations of one's own (equal) dignity as a moral subject. Whether a relation of equality is only a narrow or parochial ideal is handled by a question that Rawls puts to this kind of discussion: "In what other relation can a people and its regime reasonably expect to stand?"[47]

Rawls's way of asking this question reflects his tendency to think in terms of rights in institutional contexts, even when he is thinking about matters of human rights and global justice. Hence his reference to "a people and its regime." But the question he asks clearly has ramifications beyond relationships among individuals in their role as citizens or between regimes in international relations. Persons—whether fellow citizens or fellow humans—deny others equal respect and equal liberty when they fail at a *prima facie* level to tolerate others' authority to make and revise their own basic commitments. The intolerant treat others as second-class persons, inferior and subordinate to their own way of being. Intolerant persons who expect others to accept such a second-class status ask them to submit to the authority of their views without also asking if such a relationship can be self-respecting for those on whom such authority is imposed. Obviously it is not. Liberal social critics, when pressed to clarify the expectations surrounding the idea of equal respect, should amend Rawls's question: In what other relationship can fellow human beings reasonably expect to stand?

5

RESPECT AND RECOGNITION

One of my aims in this book is to make sense of the idea that moral indignation felt in response to an atrocity can be connected to the idea of respect for persons and their inherent dignity. Advancing that aim was the main goal of chapter 3. I have also said that persons who grossly violate basic rights such as respect for persons do not deserve the kind of sentiments or attitudes that recognition typically requires.[1] That statement is more complicated than it might first appear. It trades on two assumptions along with an ambiguity that we do well to clarify. One assumption is that being recognized by others is desirable, that it contributes to our sense of who we are and how we relate to the world. As I am using it here, to *recognize* is to acknowledge someone or something as valid, important, or perhaps even good. "Recognition" means more than perception or awareness; it also means acknowledgement in a strong sense. It involves some measure of deference if not support or affirmation. And it involves important psychological elements. Increasingly we believe that our identity and self-image are bound up with how others see us—that who we are is intersubjectively conditioned.

The second assumption is that recognizing someone involves, in part at least, respecting him or her. Therein lies an ambiguity. It concerns the *type* of respect that would provide a basis for recognizing someone in the strong sense I just mentioned. Typically, such respect proceeds on terms that assign positive value to indigenous or "local" features of another's self-understanding. But recognition that is tied to *that* account of respect seems to ask for more than the idea of "respect for persons" typically suggests.

Ambiguity about the meaning of respect can be clarified by distinguishing between what Darwall calls *recognition respect* and *appraisal respect*. Simply put, recognition respect is "the disposition to weigh appropriately in one's deliberations some feature of the thing in question and to act accordingly."[2] As it bears on interpersonal relations, recognition respect means that persons "are entitled to have other persons take seriously and weigh appropriately the fact that they are persons in deliberating about what to do."[3] Recognition respect assigns appropriate regard to an other as moral subject, as an end in him- or herself. That is how we normally speak of "respect for persons." Appraisal respect, on the other hand, is the disposition to esteem a person based on certain excellences of character or action understood in relation to appropriate standards.[4] This latter form of respect involves a specific or context-bound evaluation.

Darwall's distinction enables us to get a handle on a deeper anxiety to which some of my opening comments alluded, namely, the grounds for desiring and assigning recognition. If, as we tend to believe, one's identity is bound up with recognition from others, and if such recognition depends on securing respect from others, then denying respect to others has high stakes. It not only passes a negative moral judgment, it threatens to remove an important basis for others' self-esteem. It has the potential to deliver a damaging blow to another's self-image.

But that anxiety trades on another ambiguity, one that requires us to distinguish between Darwall's notion of *recognition respect*, on the one hand, and the notion of *group recognition as a social source for identity*, on the other. The former concept, as I have noted, consists in the disposition to assign respect on the basis of another's dignity as a moral subject. That idea lies behind my liberal account of toleration in the previous chapter. But the latter concept, group recognition, asks for more.[5] Such recognition asks for a kind of disposition to esteem particular expressions of tradition, custom, or ongoing social practice as having dignity. Often such demands are linked to "being true to oneself," of establishing identity and difference in the face of homogenizing social and cultural forces. What is nettlesome is whether "being true to oneself" deserves the recognition that it sometimes demands.

This challenge is acute in cases regarding groups, such as al Qaeda, that espouse a distinct, reformist brand of Islamic tradition in their justification of terroristic violence. But that challenge isn't peculiar to al Qaeda; it is a challenge that accompanies any form of religiously authorized violence that violates human rights. Religious terrorism—or critiques of religious terrorism—implicate deep beliefs according to which individuals form relationships and identity. To condemn violent acts that are carried out as a sacred duty appears to intrude on matters of conviction and faith, matters that typically link up with claims for recognition in a multicultural world. Moral condemnation and the indignation it expresses make claims that are potentially sacrilegious to those who are so judged. That is to say, indignation appears to move social criticism into the realm of *disrespect*.

To these ideas—considerations of respect and their implications for recognition and identity—this chapter is devoted. With those concepts and distinctions in view, we can then see more clearly what I mean by saying that the atrocity of 9/11 consists of a violation of respect for human rights, and that persons who fail to respect rights do not deserve the kind of attitudes or sentiments that recognition typically requires.

RECOGNITION RESPECT AND APPRAISAL RESPECT

Respect, Darwall observes, consists in "a disposition to weigh appropriately in one's deliberations some feature of the thing in question and to act accordingly."[6] Distinguishing between recognition respect and appraisal respect clarifies two ways in which we deliberate in light of features of other things or persons. Darwall calls recognition respect "giving appropriate consideration or recognition to some feature of its object in deliberating about what to do."[7] For example, we assign such respect to others' feelings, the law, social institutions, or roles. We say that we respect the institution of law to explain why we act in a law-abiding way. That respect does not rely on esteeming any particular law; it is generic. More important for our purposes is the fact that all persons are said to deserve this form of respect. We are entitled to have others take seriously and weigh appropriately the fact that we are persons when they deliberate about what to do. Obviously others are entitled to the same form of treatment, the same "respect for persons." Recognition respect, then, is identical with "moral requirements that are placed on one by the existence of other persons."[8] Recognition respect views others as ends in themselves, as having a basic dignity that deserves appropriate weighing when we deliberate about how to act.

Appraisal respect, in contrast, is merited. Such respect turns on characteristics that make someone deserving of positive appraisal. "Its exclusive objects," Darwall observes, "are persons or features which are held to manifest their excellence as persons or as engaged in some specific pursuit."[9] Appraisal respect is tied to particular facts about a person's exercise of agency. We may admire or envy someone with special gifts, but we assign appraisal respect based on how they try to use them. And we carry out that appraisal in light of judgments that are categorical, not in light of how they benefit oneself or advance one's own interests alone. Appraisal respect is principled.

We might sharpen the distinction between these two forms of respect with an eye to another's feelings. With recognition respect, I respect the fact *that you have feelings* in my deliberations about how to act. I should be courteous and mindful of you as an equal. In that way my conduct is constrained. With appraisal respect, I would be required to respect the *feelings that you have* in my deliberations about how to act. I would exercise such appraisal respect based on a principled judgment about the merits of those feelings and whether they indeed justify responding to you as you might value.

One reason that I might judge your feelings as unworthy of appraisal respect is that they are disrespectful of others. That fact indicates one way in which recognition respect and appraisal respect are connected. Typically we assign appraisal respect to someone based on his or her recognition respect for standards of a pursuit or of behavior more generally. We might esteem a tennis player for her prowess in competition, but we would deny her appraisal respect if she laughs at her opponent's errors, contests every close call to throw off her opponent's concentration, or heckles her opponent in the course of the match.[10] Our appraisal respect of such a player would turn on whether she can act according to basic expectations within the standards of her pursuit. Because she fails to respect the standards associated with being a good sport, we deny her positive appraisal respect regarding her performance as a tennis player.

Appraisal respect, then, depends in part on whether a person being appraised restricts his or her conduct in light of the requirements of recognition respect. This is not to say that abiding by recognition respect is sufficient to secure appraisal respect, only that it is necessary in appropriate contexts.[11] To grant appraisal respect on more permissive terms would seem to assign "respect on demand," contrary to the grounds on which appraisal respect is granted. Darwall clarifies: "There will be connections between the grounds of one's appraisal respect . . . and the considerations which one takes as appropriate objects of recognition respect. For example, if one judges that someone is not worthy of (appraisal) respect because he is dishonest, one is committed to recognition respect for considerations of honesty. Our appraisal of persons depends on whether they show the appropriate recognition respect for considerations which merit it."[12]

Darwall's account of respect helps us understand why the indignation felt in response to 9/11 is tied to a respect for persons and basic human rights. The grievance is connected to values that we understand as inherent in the idea of "respect for persons." Those who were victims of attack were denied recognition respect in the deliberations among the Muslim extremists who planned and carried out the atrocity. Moreover, those who denied such recognition respect do not deserve appraisal respect. They do not deserve our esteem. Quite the contrary: owing to their disregard for recognition respect in their deliberations and actions, we can say that they committed a gross and flagrant injustice.

HERMENEUTICAL CRITICISM AND THE POLITICS OF DIFFERENCE

Denying appraisal respect to those who fail to exhibit recognition respect, I suggested earlier, goes beyond passing a negative moral judgment about another's actions or character. It threatens to remove an important basis of another's self-esteem. If one's identity is bound up with recognition from others, and if such recognition depends on securing respect from others, then withholding or denying respect can deliver a damaging blow to another's self-image.

On this premise, a moral judgment has high stakes, psychologically speaking. And that fact invites us to reflect about the challenge of social criticism and disagreement in a world that has become increasingly aware of multicultural differences. In his discussion of multiculturalism, Charles Taylor has done as much as anyone to clarify these stakes, and I want to consider his views here. I will identify his account as one of hermeneutical criticism because it draws its core ideas from the science of interpretation and the norms of understanding that shape intellectual work with cultural, legal, and theological materials. Hermeneutics is mindful of the social processes of representation and understanding, especially the fact that our knowledge-production is historically and linguistically mediated. These are crucial discoveries that lie at the heart of the linguistic and cultural turn in the humanities today. In many ways this form of criticism shadows the varieties of social criticism I discussed in chapter 2 given their sensitivities about representations of Islam. Those sensitivities reflect wider concerns about the politics of difference and the danger of passing ethnocentric judgments about others' conduct or character simply because they are different—likewise a preoccupation with hermeneutical criticism given the latter's awareness of the contingency and particularity of culturally mediated thought and judgment. Efforts to address ur incomprehension in response to Islamic extremism that prevent critics from making quick, chauvinistic judgments are to be welcomed. Such judgments, we should now see, are not only unfair to moderate Muslims, they can have damaging effects on those who are prejudicially judged. For that reason, they are doubly wrong.

Taylor developed a way of getting a handle on anxieties surrounding multiculturalism in an intellectual and political context focusing not on 9/11 but on minority and nonmainstream groups' claims for cultural survival and about how to consider the worth of another culture. Yet his ideas have broader implications that invite discussion. One of Taylor's core insights is that we are liable to commit an injustice against individuals or groups by failing to recognize their distinctive ways of producing meaning and culture. Denying recognition has the potential to demean and degrade those to whom that denial is directed simply because they are different. That problem is exacerbated by the worry that criteria for assigning (or denying) respect seem tied to a specifically Eurocentric way of thinking about persons and obligations. Judgments based on that point of view seem to be not universal or impartial, but prejudicial and question-begging. Taylor summarizes the general premise behind this anxiety:

> The thesis is that our identity is partly shaped by recognition or its absence, often by the *mis*recognition of others, and so a person or group of people can suffer real damage, real distortion, if the people or society around them mirror back to them a confining or demeaning or contemptible picture of themselves. Nonrecognition or misrecognition can inflict harm, can be a form of oppression, imprisoning someone in a false, distorted, and reduced mode of being.[13]

The stakes turn on persons' self-interpretations. Justice in multicultural contexts seeks, among other things, to protect members of minority or nonmainstream groups from internalizing self-deprecating images, which often result from ethnocentric attitudes and practices by members of the dominant culture. As a corrective, multicultural justice often invites persons to "fuse horizons" with the cultural legacies of nonmainstream groups so that members of such groups avoid internalizing condescending or imperialistic attitudes imposed from without.

Taylor moves toward this proposal by developing a philosophical genealogy that describes how modern societies have come to value group-related recognition as a claim of justice, and how that value has developed out of Enlightenment concerns for human dignity, equality, and authenticity. Two political movements have emerged from this legacy: the politics of dignity and the politics of difference. The politics of dignity has generated a set of universal human rights, applicable to individuals regardless of their group membership. It is the sort of argument that I have been defending in these pages. In the political sphere, this legacy has helped secure democratic protections for civil equality and personal liberty, assigning entitlements and immunities to individuals regardless of race, background, or creed. By contrast, the politics of difference asks that we esteem the unique identity of an individual or group. A chief characteristic of this legacy is individuals' or groups' desires to be recognized for their distinctness and authenticity, not their universal dignity. Kant and Mill are (for different reasons) the standard-bearers for the politics of dignity; Rousseau, Herder, and Fanon are (in different ways) spokespersons for the politics of difference. The politics of dignity applies moral or political principles impartially; the politics of difference calls for special considerations that seem partial to a particular way of life.

For those concerned about protecting cultural distinctiveness, assimilating difference into a uniform understanding of human dignity constitutes a dangerous leveling process, for it homogenizes difference into a single mold. It thereby compromises authenticity, the value of being true to one's own measure, one's own originality.[14] As it has come to develop in the late twentieth and early twenty-first centuries, the politics of difference has grown critical of how the politics of dignity has institutionalized a standard schedule of equal rights and expectations. Those advocating the politics of difference argue, among other things, that some individual rights need to be subordinated to collective aims, especially when the survival of a minority group is at stake.

Concrete tensions between these two legacies have appeared in Canada's effort to accommodate Quebeckers' demands for linguistic and educational restrictions in the name of preserving a Francophone society. They have likewise appeared in efforts by various groups to secure exemptions from legal prohibitions or requirements in order to protect traditional customs,[15] to fund special programs that call attention to the legacies and merits of minority cultures, to acquire special representation rights,[16] or to acquire some measure of sovereignty within a state's territory.[17]

Taylor argues that the need to modify individual rights in light of the collective end of cultural survival can be met straightforwardly. Group-specific claims made on behalf of Quebec, for example, can be accommodated by distinguishing between essential and nonessential rights. Taylor remarks: "One has to distinguish the fundamental liberties, those that should never be infringed and therefore ought to be unassailably entrenched, on one hand, from privileges and immunities that are important, but that can be revoked or restricted for reasons of public policy—although one would need a strong reason to do this—on the other."[18] For Taylor, fundamental rights include rights to life, liberty, due process, free speech, and freedom of religion. So long as a society adequately safeguards these rights, it may restrict other liberties for some collective goals, for example, by legislating language restrictions in education and commercial signage.

Taylor's endorsement of essential rights would thus produce a resounding condemnation of the attacks of 9/11 as clear violations of the rights of life and liberty. The importance of essential rights lies behind the feeling of moral indignation and the confident expression of a moral grievance. But Taylor's attention to the politics of difference invites us to take up a broader question, namely, some groups' claim about the equal *value* of their cultural practices. This demand has something other than cultural survival at stake; it requires nonmembers to appreciate another's standards and customs, moving cultural politics toward what Darwall calls appraisal respect. Herein lies one challenge of multiculturalism. It asks, how is one to interpret and evaluate groups' claims to moral worth? When multicultural differences arise, on what basis is appraisal respect to be assigned? These sorts of questions bid us to consider the moral worth of cultures with notably different values and practices. Such considerations along with diffuse cultural pressures to assign esteem might weaken the moral confidence that a commitment to essential rights endeavors to underwrite.[19] For that reason we do well to consider them at some length.

Taylor's reply to the challenge of considering the moral value of other cultures attempts to provide an alternative to the "demand for recognition of equal worth, on the one hand, and the self-immurement within ethnocentric standards, on the other."[20] Ethnocentrism consists in the reflex assumption that one's standards are morally superior to those one is judging. Recognition on demand, in contrast, asks that we view another culture favorably simply because it is different, premised on the idea that any judgment of another culture is inescapably ethnocentric.

In his attempt to go beyond these approaches, Taylor recommends two distinct claims. The first, weaker claim is that we should not discount *a priori* the value of other cultures. We should be open to the equal worth of another culture, adopting a presumption that should shape our stance when setting out to study the other.[21] Not unlike an act of faith, this presumption claims that "all human cultures that have animated whole societies over some considerable stretch of time have something important to say to all human beings."[22] Cultures that have "articulated their sense of the good, the holy, the admirable" for large numbers of people over a long time "are almost certain to have something that deserves our admiration and respect, even if it is accompanied by much that we have to abhor and reject."[23] Presuming the worth of another culture, Taylor adds, is a "starting hypothesis" for cross-cultural inquiry, but its validity "has to be demonstrated concretely in the actual study of the culture."[24] Failure to hold such a presumption is clear evidence of cultural prejudice.

Taylor combines this claim—that we should not discount *a priori* the value of other cultures—with a stronger one. Drawing on the hermeneutical theory of Hans-Georg Gadamer, he argues that we achieve a true understanding of others as the result of a "fusion of horizons," which "suppose that we have been transformed by the study of the other, so that we are not simply judging by our original familiar standards."[25] In such a fusion, we develop "new vocabularies of comparison," leading to judgments that presuppose revised norms, a *tertium quid*.[26] Here one's standards of judgment are vulnerable to revision upon encountering other cultural practices or beliefs. Such a fusion does not require that we change our judgments about another's customs or practices, only that our judgments derive from standards that have been revised in the process of studying the other. Taylor writes: "We learn to move in a broader horizon, within which what we have formerly taken for granted as the background to valuation can be situated as one possibility alongside the different background of the formerly unfamiliar culture."[27] In this way we are to test our initial presumption of equal worth: if we find support for that presumption, "it is on the basis of an understanding of what constitutes worth that we couldn't possibly have had at the beginning. We have reached the judgment partly through transforming our standards."[28]

Combining these two claims appears to enable hermeneutical criticism to avoid ethnocentrism and recognition on demand. Taylor avoids the former by saying that any judgment of another culture results not from imposing one's putatively superior standards, but from applying standards that, in part at least, have accommodated themselves to the other culture's norms and way of life. He avoids the latter by saying that *respecting* another culture does not necessarily mean *admiring* it. Putting matters more precisely using Darwall's terms, Taylor could say that assigning recognition respect does not mean assigning appraisal respect. But hermeneutical criticism does not quite embrace these terms. Taylor is saying that something more than recognition respect and something less than appraisal respect is needed in cross-cultural comparisons and criticism. I will call this *benefit-of-the-doubt respect*. It is granted through an act of faith, a presumption of equal value, which is then subject to further study and validation.

Benefit-of-the-doubt respect mediates between Darwall's notions of recognition respect and appraisal respect and captures, I believe, the intuitions that lie behind Taylor's weaker proposal regarding appropriate dispositions in multicultural contexts. Benefit-of-the-doubt respect consists of a presumptive openness to listen to and learn from others, and thereby to broaden the horizon within which one holds normative standards. It does not require one to relinquish one's standards, only to grasp and considerately reckon with a wider range of arguments and interlocutors according to whom one's ideas seem arguable or contested. Such presumptive openness is what is typically expected of students as they learn about other cultures: they must come to understand viewpoints and ways of thinking that are not their own along with the challenge of articulating their ideas to a wider, more diverse public. In that way they can learn about beliefs and commitments that shape others' perspectives and develop the capacity for imagining and articulating their own constitutive beliefs in ways that can become deeper and more sophisticated. Such (dialogical) openness recognizes that others deserve to be respectfully accounted for while also recognizing that the fact of intellectual, cultural, ethnic, class, or religious difference does not justify a patronizing deference to others' mores and practices. On those terms the good of equal respect can be realized.

I believe that Taylor's weak claim is all that we need to navigate the world of cross-cultural social criticism and multicultural politics, and that his strong claim regarding the need to fuse horizons asks too much. Indeed, it is not obvious that Taylor's strong claim is needed to support his weak claim, or that the two claims are necessarily connected.[29] Herein lies the first of three difficulties in Taylor's position and some of the temptations of hermeneutical criticism more generally: one can be presumptively open to another culture's merits without fusing horizons as a basis for nonethnocentric evaluation. Nonethnocentrists can assign benefit-of-the-doubt respect without also having to transform their standards when evaluating others. Taylor's weak claim urges humility when evaluating other practices, and humility is surely a virtue in matters of multicultural justice. But asking for a transformation of standards demands too much, for it implies at an *a priori* level that one's norms need to be substantively revised to be adequate to their task. We've seen a version of this problem in Fish's argument and we encounter it here in a more thoroughgoing discussion of pluralism and cultural differences.

The problem, stated differently, is that Taylor exaggerates the extent to which multicultural differences challenge ethical reasoning and moral judgment.[30] As a result, he exaggerates what is required to overcome those differences. It is not clear why the problem of resolving differences is any more severe in a multicultural situation than in a situation of diversity that characterizes most single cultures. Why is multicultural disagreement any different from disagreement in our own culture? Why not handle multicultural disagreements the same way that we handle disagreements within our own culture, for example, through a kind of rich and complex practical rationality that takes into account various claims, utilities, principles, commitments, and/or goods that are (often but not always) attached to customary practices?

Attention to multiculturalism might *explain* how some cultural differences have materialized and why they produce acute tensions. Moral judgment in a multicultural situation implicates identity and thus implies expressing potentially unflattering images of others when negative evaluations occur. Given the role of linguistic differences in multicultural disputes, moreover, disagreements may rely on misunderstandings that produce deeper offenses of one or another sort. Further, in multicultural disputes whole cultures might be implicated; to disagree with a representative member may suggest disagreement with the majority in another culture or subculture, and the risk of offense is obviously high if one's judgments are wrong. But these dangers can be easily overdetermined or rendered excessively exotic, especially when compared with disagreements within a single culture. Debates in multiculturalism too easily presuppose a vast chasm between "us" and "them," as if clashes within a culture were somehow less offensive and more easily resolvable than clashes between cultures.

Put in other terms: there are no formal differences between reproachful judgments about Muslims who authorize terrorism, Native Americans who hunt and kill whales, and parents who are members of the Church of the Firstborn and who refuse lifesaving antibiotics for their child with pneumonia.[31] If no formal difference exists among such judgments of reproach, then methods for handling more proximate differences should be considered as a way of handling more remote cultural differences as well. That is to say, if we surrender the notion that intercultural disagreements are somehow more exotic or more intractable than intracultural disagreements, we can overcome some of the concerns about ethnocentrism and get on with the challenge of finding terms for deliberation without requiring participants to transform their values in the process. *In short, multicultural disagreements are typically a species of moral disagreement.*

The effect of seeing pronounced differences within, as well as between, cultures should be to relax some anxieties about ethnocentrism. We can thus demystify difference, or see difference as more pervasive than discussions of multiculturalism tend to suggest. If worries about ethnocentrism help fuel apologetical tendencies, moreover, then relaxing anxieties about the former may go a long way toward removing incentives for the latter. In cases of internal or external disputes, disagreements require individuals or groups to adjudicate their conflicting visions of the good life, but those disputes should not necessarily require members of both groups to revise their standards as a deliberative virtue.

Yet it remains unclear whether hermeneutical criticism's "fusion of horizons" can avoid some problems associated with ethnocentrism, and herein lies a second problem with Taylor's argument. Note that a fusion of horizons involves a mutual transformation of norms. Fusing horizons avoids either culture's imposition of its values onto the other by transforming each set of standards into a *tertium quid*. In other words, a fusion of horizons is a reciprocal venture, moving toward a common point or horizon from "both sides." Judgments that would derive from the perspective of a nonmainstream culture must be revised for the fusion to be symmetrical with its mainstream alternative. That is to say, preventing ethnocentrism by means of a fusion of horizons ought to affect another's cultural standards no less than one's own. Otherwise the language of *fusion* is misplaced. But if that is true then the fusion is syncretistic, thereby spoiling the integrity of the other's cultural standards. Seeking to avoid ethnocentrism through a fusion of horizons compromises the integrity of the other's norms. While this solution is less imperialistic than conventional forms of ethnocentric judgments, it hardly ensures respect for unadulterated versions of another's beliefs.

A final problem with the idea of a fusion of horizons concerns its desirability. When confronted by patriarchy, racial supremacism, religious discrimination or zealotry, ecologically doubtful customs, or other illiberal sentiments, it is not clear why we would want to "have been transformed by the study of the other, so that we are not simply judging by our original familiar standards."[32] Many illiberal sentiments can be found within a variety of cultures, even those that have "articulated their sense of the good, the holy, the admirable" for large numbers of people over a long period of time.[33] Moving toward what Taylor calls a "broader horizon" may paradoxically require feminists, antiracists, religious liberals, or environmental advocates to narrow the range of goods they seek to protect.[34]

It seems more reasonable to adhere to Taylor's weak claim independently of its connection to a fusion of horizons: Multicultural justice requires humility as a virtue in which cross-cultural inquiry demands presumptive openness to the moral value of another culture. I call this presumptive openness benefit-of-the-doubt respect. Benefit-of-the-doubt respect can provide a "starting hypothesis" that must be "demonstrated concretely in the actual study of the culture," as Taylor says.[35] But such demonstrations need not require cultural and social critics to compromise their standards or to fuse their beliefs with those of others, for do to so may be to capitulate to unacceptable customs or norms.

ON BENEFIT-OF-THE-DOUBT RESPECT

Concerning benefit-of-the-doubt respect, Darwall would doubtless have us ask about the restrictions it places on our conduct or dispositions, and what those restrictions have as their basis. To those questions we can say that, like all respect, benefit-of-the-doubt respect consists in "a disposition to weigh appropriately in one's deliberations some feature of the thing in question and to act accordingly."[36] Benefit-of-the-doubt respect thus serves as a basic principle for an ethics of heterology, our normative stance toward interacting with and evaluating others. Benefit-of-the-doubt respect imposes restrictions on attitudes or judgments that are negatively prejudicial in our deliberations about a thing or person. That is to say, it requires an openness to listen and learn from cross-cultural inquiry and engagement, a refusal to presume that another's customs are inferior simply because they are different. In this way, the restrictions it imposes on our deliberations are self-reflexive. They ask us to reflect on our own manner of responding to difference, to be conscious of our fallibility and the limitations of our particular perspectives. In addition, benefit-of-the-doubt respect imposes restrictions on attitudes or judgments that are positively prejudicial in deliberations about and with others. It requires an openness to be critical of others in cross-cultural inquiry and engagement, a refusal to presume that another's customs are superior or less fallible simply because they are different.

On this latter point we see a connection between benefit-of-the-doubt respect, recognition respect, and appraisal respect. Upon assigning the benefit of the doubt to other customs, beliefs, or practices, we inquire into their respective visions of the good and their manner of treating their own adherents as well as others. Customs, beliefs, or practices that assign recognition respect move one step toward earning appraisal respect. Such customs or beliefs honor human dignity, a baseline value that I defended in chapter 3. By the same token, customs or beliefs that deny recognition respect to others undermine the grounds for securing appraisal respect. They violate the basis for treating others as possessing human dignity, the idea that all of us are free and equal. On those terms we can say, as I stated earlier, that persons who fail to respect rights do not deserve the kind of attitudes and sentiments that group recognition typically requires. To assign appraisal respect to such customs or beliefs is to offer recognition on demand and to contradict the very grounds for being respectful at all. Recognition respect thus puts limits on how we assign appraisal respect. Customs or beliefs that deny recognition respect to others undermine the basis for treating persons as free and equal and forfeit any presumptive claim to our esteem.

6

RELIGION, DIALOGUE, AND HUMAN RIGHTS

My argument on behalf of rights to life and security is tied to the value of human dignity and the norm of respect for persons. That norm lies behind the idea that all persons have a *prima facie* right to be left alone, to be free from acts that arbitrarily threaten to seriously compromise personal freedom and the infrastructural conditions that enable us to deliberate about and pursue our visions of the good. In liberal thought, the value of human dignity is attached to our capacities as moral subjects, as persons with the ability to order our actions toward ends that we embrace and may revise in light of information made available to us through social and cultural processes. Without protections to carry out such deliberations, we would lack the space necessary to exercise our capacities as moral subjects.

The value of human dignity, grounded in moral subjectivity, and the corresponding norm of respect for persons likewise lie behind a principled defense of religious toleration. The *prima facie* entitlement to lead one's own life is a corollary of the norm of respect for one's intrinsic dignity as a free and equal person with the authority to envision and act on an account of the good. One way that well-ordered and just societies institutionalize respect for this intrinsic dignity and the corresponding idea of equal liberty is by protecting religious freedom.[1]

By now it should be clear that the rights of life and security and the right of religious liberty share an inner logic. Each person has a *prima facie* entitlement to lead his or her own life without arbitrary harm or injury owing to the demands of respect for his or her intrinsic dignity as a person. That idea of intrinsic dignity likewise assigns individuals the *prima facie* authority to pursue and, if they wish, revise their comprehensive beliefs. Respecting other persons means, among other things, leaving them alone in body and soul to pursue their lives without arbitrary interference.

Notions of dignity, respect, and rights focus our attention on matters of philosophical anthropology—the idea of the human person and basic human capacities in relation to broader values or goods. I gestured in this direction of philosophical anthropology when discussing toleration in chapter 4. Recall that when describing submission, respect, and grounds for religious toleration, I drew on Darwall's distinction between dignity that is imputed to persons by God as understood in a picture provided by theological voluntarism, on the one hand, and dignity that is inherent to persons in the picture provided by a philosophical understanding of moral subjectivity, on the other. One way to understand basic norms in liberal social criticism is to see them anchored to a philosophical anthropology of a specific sort.

Yet viewing dignity in light of those two options appears to undermine any *religious* understanding of inherent human dignity, mutual respect, and the equality of persons. It suggests that respect for the inherent worth of persons and the idea of equal liberty must take their bearings from secular moral philosophy, leaving the notion of human dignity sacrificed at the altar of divine command morality. Echoing this idea, Michael Ignatieff writes: "The dispute comes down to this: the religious side believes that only if humans get down on their knees can they save themselves from their own destructiveness; a humanist believes that they will do so only if they stand up on their own two feet."[2]

Readers familiar with religious thought and ethics know that Ignatieff's comment oversimplifies. The idea that dignity is imputed by God is a legacy of theological voluntarism, not theology tout court. More specifically, and as I'll make clear at the conclusion of this chapter, the idea of dignity as imputed by God is a feature of divine command morality tied to an account of *special revelation* as distinct from *general revelation*. The latter account blurs the distinction between divinity and humanity by pointing to features that the latter shares with the former. A not inconsiderable swath of contemporary theology—including some Muslim thought—has moved in this direction, developing an understanding of human dignity premised on a version of natural theology and ethics, one that identifies the transcendent ground of dignity as an inexorable feature of the human personality.

Such ideas complicate the distinction between thinking philosophically and theologically about human dignity and human rights and open up some promising territory for conversations between secular liberals and theologians, religious intellectuals, and political thinkers of a theistic bent, including Muslim intellectuals. Indeed, thinking along such lines can expand representations of Islam to include a wider array of moderate and moderating voices than my references to Islamic thinkers has provided thus far. Facilitating such conversations about shared bases for rights, moreover, can help legitimate the human rights project by establishing various avenues of consent to the demands generated by such rights.[3] The point of such dialogue, in other words, is to explore prospects for an overlapping consensus according to which basic rights might find support from different, nonsecular visions of human nature and the good.[4] Establishing this support is part of what I will call the *desideratum of cosmopolitan legitimacy*. That desideratum aims to strengthen connections between the human rights regime and different religious (and other traditions) on the premise that human rights can be tied to more than one set of thick or comprehensive doctrines about the good. Pursuing that desideratum in the context of 9/11 and its aftermath invites us to embark on a cross-cultural discussion of Muslim theories of human dignity and religious toleration.

Such a dialogue might also help us understand toleration in richer ways. Toleration is often thought of as a "negative virtue," a disposition to avoid interfering with others based on their beliefs and practices. On that view, toleration is a form of restraint and noninterference, a specification of others' negative liberty. One downside of that account is that it permits toleration to settle into incuriousness so that toleration becomes what Barbara Herman has called a "laissez-faire virtue."[5] It need not be open or engaged. But toleration that is wedded to respect for another's dignity suggests more than noninterference and negative virtue; respect for persons suggests the responsibility to understand the humanity of others, including their constitutive beliefs. Others are due respect by virtue of their having the capacity to work out a vision of the good life, however different it is from one's own.[6] Viewed in light of offering benefit-of-the-doubt respect (chapter 5), toleration opens one to conversation and cross-cultural engagement. Benefit-of-the-doubt respect entails greater engagement with others than does toleration understood as noninterference alone.

Over the past thirty years there has been a vigorous and wide-ranging discussion of Islam, human rights, and democracy. Scholars and activists such as Abdul Aziz Said, Mohamed Allal Sinaceur, Abdullahi an-Naim, Mohamed Talbi, Sohail Hashmi, Akbar Ganji, Khaled Abou El Fadl, Abdolkarim Soroush, Leila Ahmet, Anina Wadud, and Abdurrahman Wahid, among others, have wrestled with the teachings of Islamic tradition in light of Muslims' experience of Western colonialism, the vastly different contexts of Muslim political life today, and various political ideologies and philosophical arguments. These writers draw on previous efforts to think about human rights and Islam by, for example, Sayyid Qutb and Abul A'la Maududi, as well as Marxist theory, theories of secularization, theories of literary interpretation, and historical criticism.

In this chapter I want to explore accounts of Islamic human rights in dialogue with liberal ideas on the premise that benefit-of-the-doubt-respect, along with the desideratum of cosmopolitan legitimacy, urges cross-cultural dialogue. I will not presume to summarize or comment upon the vigorous and extensive debate among modern Muslims.[7] I rather want to limit my discussion to two contributions to Muslim thought, by Abul A'la Maududi and Abdulaziz A. Sachedina, respectively, focusing on points of convergence and divergence between their religiously-informed account of human rights and political ethics, on the one hand, and liberal norms and ideas, on the other. Their views help to identify both the limits and the promise of thinking about human rights within the framework of religious tradition, along with the challenges that accompany seeking the desideratum of cosmopolitan legitimacy for human rights doctrine and its commitment to human dignity.[8]

ISLAMIZING HUMAN RIGHTS

To some religious thinkers, Muslim and non-Muslim alike, the problem with secular philosophy is that it appears to connect moral norms to contingent foundations. On that view, moral norms seem unreliable when compared to those revealed by the absolute and unchangeable will of God; political authority vested in the human will alone leaves rights subject to the vagaries of ambition and desire. Given that concern, religious political ethics sometimes describes the difference between theological and secular philosophy as the difference between eternal, impartial, and stable foundations of authority, on the one hand, and temporal, partial, and contingent foundations of authority, on the other.

Such a framework informs how Abul A'la Maududi (1903–1979) develops his account of the relationship between Islamic and Western human rights doctrine. Maududi was an influential source of thought and inspiration for Pakistani and broader Islamic revivalist and fundamentalist movements and the founder of Jamatt-i-Islami in 1941, a religious party with strict, militant, anti-Western beliefs that produced the hundreds of madrassas where many members of the Taliban were taught the Qur'an and Islamic doctrine.[9] Maududi's widely disseminated and influential treatise on human rights describes them not only as compatible with Islamic tradition but made better when conceived in Islamic terms.[10] Central to his work, especially *Human Rights in Islam*,[11] is the aim of redefining human rights within an exclusively Islamic framework and, in the process, polemicizing Western political philosophy and practice.[12]

On Maududi's account of Islamic political theology, all authority derives from God, who appoints human beings as his vicegerents to carry out his will on earth in accord with rules revealed to the Prophet. In his mind, because authority is bestowed on all of humanity and not one person or group, the norms of equality and democracy are compatible with Islamic teaching. Sovereignty is vested first in God who then bestows on all of humanity the task of representing his will in earthly affairs. For that reason, Maududi writes, "every person in Islamic society enjoys the rights and powers of the caliphate of God, and in this respect all individuals are equal."[13] In this way, Maududi seeks to wed theological ideas with democratic norms. Sovereignty does not lie first in the popular will as it does in Western democratic theory, but in the divine will, which authorizes humans to develop political life in order "to fulfill the purpose and Will of God."[14]

From within this theological framework Maududi proceeds to describe the complementarity and difference between what he calls "fundamental rights" and the rights owed only to citizens living in an Islamic state. One thrust of his argument is that all Muslims and non-Muslims have basic human rights:

> Human blood is sacred . . . and cannot be spilled without justification. It is not permissible to oppress women, children, old people, the sick or the wounded. Woman's honour and chastity are to be respected under all circumstances. The hungry person must be fed, the naked clothed, and the wounded or diseased treated medically irrespective of whether they belong to the Islamic community or are from amongst its enemies.[15]

Maududi adds to this list a fairly standard schedule of human rights, including the right to life and safety; equal protection before the law; equal freedom; basic material necessities, and the right to cooperate.[16] But these rights are inferior in quality and quantity to the rights enjoyed by citizens of an Islamic state. That is to say, they are supplemented by specific rights that are owed only to citizens (including non-Muslims) in an Islamic state, rights that guarantee the following: security of life and property; honor; sanctity and security of private life; personal freedom; dissent and protest; freedom of expression, association, and conscience; protection from arbitrary arrest; the right to "avoid sin"; and the right to participate in the affairs of government.[17]

Basic human rights and the specific guarantees found in an Islamic state are grounded in the fact that all persons derive from the same parents, created by God. All persons are therefore equal in the eyes of God, regardless of "colour, race, language or nationality."[18] In this same spirit, Maududi identifies basic laws of war, including restrictions on the right to resort to war as well as on the conduct of war. Those latter restrictions include honoring rights of noncombatants and combatants, and they prohibit killing certain groups of people (monks, women, children, the old, the infirm), along with torture, theft, dishonoring the dead, or attacking wounded soldiers. All of these restrictions are derived from the Qur'an or the hadith of the Prophet.[19]

What is crucial in Maududi's mind is that all such rights and norms have an irrevocable quality. Human rights are granted by God, Maududi says, not by "any king or by any legislative assembly." Rights on the latter description "can . . . be withdrawn in the same manner in which they are conferred"; rights conferred by God, in contrast, cannot be abrogated or withdrawn.[20]

For Maududi, then, Islamic tradition—not philosophical reason—is both necessary and sufficient for securing the authority of human rights. His view of reason is that of revealed epistemology, according to which reason cannot make claims to truth apart from information provided by divine revelation. About the "fallacy of rationalism," Maududi writes: If one "speaks as a Muslim, may he be orthodox, a liberal thinker, or a reformer, whatever be the case, he is expected to talk within the orbit of Islam with the Qur'an as the final authority and within the fundamentals of religion and the laws of Shari'ah as enunciated in the holy Qur'an."[21] Maududi thus appears to exemplify the sort of theological voluntarism about which I previously spoke. Political authority and wisdom derive from God's will, which sets the rules for proper conduct and legislation. Non-Muslim citizens in a Muslim state—those who hold a different account of God, or who have a different understanding of the relationship between divine and human authority, or who are atheists—would seem vulnerable to discrimination of one or another sort. They would be citizens without equal rights to practice their beliefs openly or to express political dissent.

But Maududi does not see these matters as posing a problem for Islamic teaching. On his account, the proper understanding of equality in Islam guarantees religious liberty. Non-Muslims in a Muslim state will have "full freedom of conscience and belief and will be at liberty to perform their religious rites and ceremonies in their own way."[22] That is because, according to the Qur'an, "there should be no coercion in the matter of faith (Q 2:256)." That liberty, moreover, extends to the right to "propagate their religion" and "to criticize Islam within the limits laid down by law and decency."[23]

Maududi first presented his thoughts on Islam and human rights in January 1948, less than a year before the United Nations promulgated the Universal Declaration of Human Rights.[24] In his mind, Islam in both theory and practice anticipated the U.N. rights initiative, rendering that initiative redundant or inferior for its lack of stable foundations and consistent enforcement. Despite the fact that Westerners have professed a commitment to human rights, Maududi remarks, rights "have been violated and trampled upon at different places, and the United Nations has been a helpless spectator."[25] He thus warns against Muslims looking for guidance from the West.[26]

What is missing from Maududi's account, however, is explicit affirmation of human dignity and the entitlement to respect that such dignity confers. Maududi prefers the language of equality and the implied notion of equal respect, but his views fall short of securing the value of the human person as a baseline for understanding the grounds of respect. We do not find him affirming the idea that, as the Declaration puts it, "all human beings are born free and equal in dignity and rights." Nor do we find the idea that we are to recognize "the inherent dignity and the equal and inalienable rights of all members of the human family."[27] In short, there is no philosophical or theological anthropology of the sort that enables us to understand the *humanity* behind human rights doctrine.

We are left with human rights that are relative to the history of Islamic doctrine and law. Missing in Maududi's account is explicit and unambiguous defense of the liberty to renounce one's religion, including Islam. Silence on that matter is troublesome given the criminalization of apostasy in many Muslim countries. Maududi also pays scant attention to gender equity; what he does say about women focuses on the duty to honor their chastity. His account of equality in the eyes of God, regardless of "color, race, language or nationality," omits gender as a crucial marker of identity and a potential cause of discrimination. That omission is a problem given the fact that (during Maududi's time as well as today) women possess second-class status in many Muslim countries and that family law in Islam does not assign the same rights to women as to men in matters of divorce or inheritance.[28]

These oversights are part of a larger problem with Maududi's views, namely, his misconception of the universality of human rights. Universality, properly understood, would hold not only that Muslims have grounds for respecting the rights of all, but that all persons are under the same obligations to each other, Muslim and non-Muslim alike. Maududi fails to grasp that the truly liberatory potential of human rights doctrine lies in the fact that it entitles all persons to equal treatment on the same grounds. It does not assign equal rights to one group, in this case non-Muslims, on terms that are the sole prerogative of another group. Assigning human rights in that way would put non-Muslims in a subservient position to Muslims, contrary to the aim of human rights doctrine to establish a common basis for assigning basic entitlements to all.

As I noted above, Maududi first presented his views on Islam and human rights the same year in which the United Nations released its Universal Declaration of Human Rights. Foremost in his mind is the fact that Islam boasts stronger grounds and a better historical record for honoring human rights. He cites the legacy of Western colonialism, racism, and inhumanity in war as evidence of the unreliability of secular human rights doctrine. Islam, Maududi avers, has no comparable legacy of slavery, embraces members of all races, and has elaborate restrictions regarding conduct of war and the humane treatment of captives that establishes a high bar of justice and compassion. He concludes his treatise on an apologetic note: "It refreshes and strengthens our faith in Islam when we realise that even in this modern age which makes such loud claims of progress and enlightenment, the world has not been able to produce more just and equitable laws than those given 1,400 years ago."[29]

Maududi's apologetic agenda is flawed, however, by his religious chauvinism. He both defends the superiority of Islamic doctrine while omitting critical attention to some of its blind spots. What he offers by way of contributing to an overlapping consensus on human rights is thus extremely limited. Certainly his account of religious toleration and the proper conduct of war provide clear moral resources for condemning radical Muslims who advocate religious violence and intolerance. Likewise, his claims in support of economic rights and equality before the law fall into the plus column for persons interested in social justice. But his failure to grasp the underlying foundations of equality in human rights doctrine leaves him without resources to think about social problems such as discrimination against women or those who convert from Islam to another tradition or who reject theistic beliefs. Nor is he able to provide a normative basis for humane treatment of noncombatants and combatants in war apart from the ad hoc reasoning found in the Islamic sources on which he relies. These are serious deficiencies.

I have suggested that part of Maududi's problem lies in the failure to produce a philosophy of the human person, the humanity behind human rights doctrine. Maududi understands rights for all persons as one piece of a larger account that includes the idea that specific guarantees accorded to non-Muslims within Muslim regimes are superior to basic human rights, however much those specific guarantees omit reference to gender equality and place non-Muslims in a subservient position in Muslim regimes. A theological account that entitles persons in an egalitarian way must say more about how and why all human beings are entitled to basic claims. For such an account we must press further into more recent work in Islamic political theology. With those thoughts in mind I would have us turn to the ideas of Abdulaziz Sachedina and his defense of democratic pluralism on Islamic grounds.

Sachedina is a modern scholar of religion and Islamic jurisprudence whose work, *The Islamic Roots of Democratic Pluralism*,[30] sets out to establish Quranic grounds for religious toleration premised on the idea of universal human dignity and the equality of all persons under God. In his mind, Muslim teaching about the superiority of Islamic tradition is the product of a particular period in Islamic history that provides no basis for doctrine regarding intrareligious or interreligious relations today. Sachedina urges Muslims to revisit the Qur'an and Islamic tradition with an eye to their meaning and their contexts of production. That task must be carried out, he adds, in light of contemporary exigencies, including the fact of religious pluralism and the existence of the global nation-state system. Sachedina speaks in no uncertain terms, focusing on those who rely predominantly on Islamic jurisprudence for thinking about matters of religious diversity and toleration today: "Most of the past juridical decisions treating non-Muslim minorities have become irrelevant in the context of contemporary religious pluralism, a cornerstone of interhuman relations."[31]

Central to Sachedina's constructive interpretation of Islamic scripture and tradition are two claims: first, that all persons have inherent, God-given dignity in virtue of their innate potential to know universal human values and, second, that no inherent tension exists between reason and Islamic revelation. According to Sachedina, the Qur'an provides guidance that illumines humanity's innate disposition to know the good and to avoid evil, but it does not offer radically new information for humanity's benefit.

Sachedina's argument recalls the medieval synthesis of faith and reason in the West, the effort to wed Greek and Christian theological ideals. Echoing the Mu'tazilite approach to Quranic interpretation and view of human nature, he holds that "human beings, as free agents, are responsible before a just God," and that "good and evil are rational categories that can be known through reason, independent of revelation."[32] That fact blurs the domains of philosophy and theology, reason and faith, moral insight and divine command. Sachedina thus challenges the assumption of Islamic fundamentalists that non-Muslims are to be treated with less than equal dignity and respect, or that sources of moral knowledge are the exclusive possession of persons who profess Islamic belief.

For Sachedina, the Qur'an is an authority that points beyond itself to the authority of innate reason as a stable and reliable guide for human relationships and political life. Muslims believe that God implanted in humanity "a natural predisposition to acknowledge the lordship of the Creator."[33] There are Islamic grounds, in short, for the idea of "natural religion," the idea that we can know that God exists by reason, unaided by revelation.[34] Muslims also affirm, according to Sachedina, the natural human endowment to intuit universal values based on a belief in the God-given capacity to know and do the good. We are all capable of grasping "universal, objective criteria that intuitively inform some essential principle of just and equitable interpersonal relationships."[35] Sachedina writes that "no human being . . . can claim ignorance of the ingrained sense of wrong and right."[36] Accordingly, all are encumbered with social responsibility: "The natural knowledge of good and evil makes injustice in any form inexcusable."[37]   *FITNA*

The Arabic term for this natural capacity is _fitra_. _Fitra_ provides intimations of the knowledge of God and the fact of divine judgment, and it provides basic moral knowledge. Stated in terms of religious scholasticism, _fitra_ is that innate capacity of the human intellect presupposed by the natural law.[38] "The function of the _fitra_," Sachedina writes, "is to provide moral direction to individual and social activity by interrelating this and the next world in such a way that human religiosity finds expression in the perfection of public order and institutions."[39]

This feature of human nature and knowledge ought to help Muslims address what Sachedina views as an epistemological crisis in Islam.[40] That crisis turns on whether Muslims are to rely solely on the Qur'an and Islamic juridical thinking for their moral guidance and political governance, or whether non-Muslim sources also provide moral authority. Sachedina claims that the impulse in Islam toward emphasizing exclusivism and divine command theology is a reaction to Islam's cultural and political decline in modernity, and it contradicts the Qur'an's message of the unity of humanity.[41] Muslim fundamentalism "stems from the acute awareness of a disparity between the divine promise of success for the believers of Islam and the historical development of the world controlled by nonbelievers."[42] Sunni writers in particular have been prone to address this crisis by turning exclusively to revealed sources and Islamic jurisprudence.[43] But the epistemological crisis wrought by that disparity should not obscure resources in Islamic thought for affirming an inclusive, pluralist vision. Islam affirms the existence of general moral principles " 'inspired by God' that do not require any justification independent of the naturally given process of reasoning."[44] The purpose of revelation is to "clarify and elucidate matters that are known through the human intellect."[45]

The concept of *fitra* thus provides the background for considering freedom of conscience and religion, based on the Qur'an.[46] Owing to the idea of *fitra*, Sachedina avers, the Qur'an "treats all human beings as equal and as potential believers in God before they are sorted into membership in various religious communities."[47] That is to say, the idea of *fitra* for Sachedina parallels the idea of moral subjectivity in liberal doctrine. Each idea—*fitra* and moral subjectivity—identifies the locus of human dignity and provides the basis for assigning (and expecting) respect. [48] In Sachedina's view, the value of dignity derives from capacities of human cognition, focusing as he does on the powers of reason. For him, each person is owed respect owing to the "special honoring of humanity as the carrier of the 'noble nature.' " That fact, in turn, "is connected with universal ethical cognition."[49]

Human dignity is thereby grounded on a rationalist rather than a voluntarist basis. That is not to say that Sachedina pays no heed to the idea of autonomy. Autonomy for Sachedina is connected to the idea of individual conscience, what Sachedina calls "the autonomous individual conscience."[50] The key point in his account is that each person is endowed with the "divinely ordained right . . . to determine his or her own spiritual destiny without coercion."[51] There are indubitable grounds for freedom of conscience in Islamic tradition that parallel those provided by Locke in liberal thought. In Islam, on Sachedina's reading, each individual is personally responsible for his or her salvation.[52] Accordingly, a person's ability to reject or accept faith "presupposes the existence of an innate capacity that can guide a person to a desired goal. This innate capacity is part of the human nature—the *fitra*—with which God shapes humanity (K. 91:7–10)."[53]

Sachedina notes that the concept of *fitra* lies at the heart of early Muslim thinking regarding religious difference and toleration. Important in that regard is how Muhammad transformed the Arabian Peninsula from a cluster of diverse, polytheistic tribes to a region committed to monotheism and social responsibility. *Fitra* helps make sense of "the strong impetus that the Koran provided to the social and institutional transformation from a tribal, kinship-based-society to a cosmopolitan community in which the nature of social and individual identity and meaning were determined by shared commitments (*al-ma'ruf*)."[54] Sachedina observes that the first decades of Islam provide numerous examples of religious toleration under the first caliphs because non-Muslims outnumbered Muslims in conquered territories.[55] Although religious toleration in those years falls short of the ideal today, it involved a core concept from which modern Islamic thinking can take its bearings. Key to those early years was the idea of "competing with one another in good works." That is to say, public morality, not individual belief, became the cornerstone of social relations. According to Sachedina, in matters of coexistence among several faith communities, "it was personal morality founded upon the dictum of 'competing with one another in good works' that defined the ultimate human community."[56]

That idea had *fitra* and religious freedom as its basic premise. Sachedina writes: "Without first recognizing the Koranic notion of freedom of conscience as part of the noble nature (the *fitra*) with which God has endowed each human being, it is fruitless to speak about an Islamic paradigm for human organization in which 'competing with one another in good works' serves as an ethical principle of pluralistic coexistence."[57] Muslims should be reminded of the importance of good deeds and character when assessing others. True Islam, Sachedina remarks, "is seen by the Koran in the moral quality of a person's life rather than in external appurtenances."[58]

The notion that Islam is the sole basis of moral and political wisdom and the belief that the revelation to Muhammad supersedes all previous revelations arose after the Prophet's rule. According to Sachedina, the idea of Islamic supersession finds no support in the Qur'an.[59] As he describes matters, Islam first embraced a universalist message, the idea that all persons—Muslims and non-Muslims alike—were heirs to the same parents and shared a common destiny. But when "Muslims began to expand the mission of Islam to create a world-wide society under their political domination, Islam was conceived as a political ideology that would first rule over and then supersede all other communities."[60] With Islamic expansion came Islamic triumphalism. Islam's "universal narrative that emphasized the common destiny of humanity was severed from its universal roots by the restrictive Islamic conception of a political order based on the membership of only those who accepted the divine revelation to Muhammad."[61] Juridical rulings that developed a triumphalistic ideology, important to Islamic fundamentalists and extremists today, were conditioned by "the beliefs, desires, hopes, and fears of that classical age."[62]

Sachedina's views should remind us that some theological arguments are not necessarily at odds with philosophical arguments—at least when both affirm the norm of respect for persons on the basis of moral subjectivity. Indeed, what we see in Sachedina's account is a critique of a certain version of divine command morality and, by implication, theological voluntarism. Sachedina provides a basis for the norm of respect not by affirming an alien dignity to human beings, imputed by God, but by affirming the idea that "all persons are created in the divine nature."[63]

Yet we should note an important distinction here, a nuance that distinguishes Sachedina's views from my own and liberal social criticism more generally. The difference between Islam (on Sachedina's description) and liberal thought lies in the fact that *fitra* names a morally positive disposition, one that justifies us in assigning dignity to persons. *Fitra* refers not only to a capacity to know moral universals, but to "the natural inclination toward obedience and doing good, the straight path."[64] Sachedina's theological anthropology thus appears to posit innate moral goodness and a relatively optimistic view of human nature. We assign dignity, on his view, on terms that fall somewhere between what we have been calling recognition respect and appraisal respect. Like recognition respect, respect for human dignity on Sachedina's terms is universal. But for Sachedina, respect is assigned on the basis of an appraisal: a judgment about the moral quality of human dispositions that relies on an account of "the straight path." Liberal social criticism, in contrast, makes no such evaluation as a basis for recognition respect. When it comes to assigning recognition respect, it is morally neutral about the dispositions of humans as subjects. By "morally neutral" I mean that liberal social critics assign recognition respect in ways that prescind from making judgments about the good or goods that an individual seeks. Liberal social criticism assigns authority to the human person not on the basis of her specific goods but by virtue of being a subject with the capacity to envision and act upon an account of the good.

Herein lies a liability in Sachedina's argument from a liberal viewpoint: if dignity is assigned on the basis of possessing good dispositions, it may be too easily forfeited by persons who are judged to be less than good. That fact opens the door to states or nonstates that might seek to justify their actions for paternalistic reasons, setting policies and practices that purport to do good for their constituencies. That is to say, respect that is secured on the basis of an appraisal may be denied when certain conditions are not met, thereby undermining individual protections from abuses of power. Assigning respect on that score renders it vulnerable to others' endorsement. For liberals, reference to dispositions that abide by what Sachedina calls "the straight path" suggests a relatively narrow range of options for envisioning and acting on an account of the good. More to the point, in liberal social criticism, dignity is assigned on a noncontingent basis. Recognition respect—respect owed to individuals by virtue of their moral subjectivity—places strong limits on what others can claim to do on their behalf. Most importantly, one's own claim to recognition respect cannot be denied or forfeited on the basis of others' appraisals of how one's subjectivity is exercised.

So much, then, for possible lines of convergence and divergence between Sachedina and liberal social criticism regarding religious toleration. What of the question of respect for persons, especially rights to life and security, in the ethics of war? It would seem that *fitra*, the basis for respecting religious differences, ought to provide grounds for respecting other rights as well. That is to say, reference to *fitra* would seem to provide one way to address questions I put to Kelsay in chapter 2 regarding reasons for limiting the violence of jihad: innocent persons are to be treated as possessing inherent dignity. That fact puts a limit on what others may do in situations of conflict.

On this matter, Sachedina is less extensive in his analysis than he is in his discussion of religious difference. He suggests some concrete implications of *fitra* for the conduct of war, saying that the use of violence in Islamic tradition should aim toward restorative justice, a process that "can restore to the people their God-given dignity through the *fitra*."[65] That claim would suggest that violence is both justified and limited by respect for human dignity.

But Sachedina says less on the question of war's limits in jihad than one might expect from his argument. To be sure, attention to limits is not absent from his account. In his mind, one basis for putting limits on violence, especially retributive violence, is the virtue of forgiveness as understood in Islam. What lies behind this virtue, and the critique of human arrogance that it entails, is the idea of human unity under God the Creator.[66] Moreover, like Western just-war doctrine, Islam developed "proscriptions on the use of unnecessary force to procure the peace." But, as we saw in my discussion of Kelsay's argument, the ban on unnecessary force can be justified in prudential rather than moral terms. What we need from Sachedina is a more explicit moral grounding for thinking about questions of the *jus in bello* in jihad, one that coheres with the theological anthropology that underwrites his account of respect for human dignity.

SPECIAL AND GENERAL DIVINE COMMAND MORALITY

Maududi's and Sachedina's contributions to Islamic political thought open up a number of possible comparisons for thinking about religion, toleration, and human rights along with the challenges involved in pursuing the desideratum of cosmopolitan legitimacy. Before concluding this chapter I want to focus on three.

First, and perhaps most obviously, the differences between Maududi and Sachedina should remind social critics never to homogenize religious traditions or assume that they offer a clear consensus about philosophical, social, or political ideas. Social criticism that pays attention to religion must be informed and discriminating. It must heed not only differences between religious belief and secular thought where such differences exist, but also conceptual, historical, and theological differences among religious traditions and subtraditions, denominations, and sects. Truly informed cultural and social criticism cannot continue to proceed in the dark when it comes to the kaleidoscopic array of religious belief, commitment, and practice on the global stage today. Distinctions need to be grasped not only between religious traditions but within them.

One way to distinguish what Maududi and Sachedina say about Islam and human rights is to note how their views fall out of two different accounts of revelation and divine command morality. Herein lies my second point. Accounts of revelation work in different ways to generate or connect with metaethical grounds that authorize moral commands. One way to mark those different ways is to distinguish between *general revelation* and *special revelation*. General revelation, as summarized by Robert Merrihew Adams, "takes place through facts about life and the world that are generally accessible to human beings, and through tendencies of belief and feeling that are natural to human beings or at least widely and commonly present in people in different places, times, and cultures."[67] In theories of general revelation, a divine command is mediated through reason and common human experience and thus is universally accessible, at least in principle. "The cross-cultural tendency of people to regard lying as generally wrong, for example, can be regarded as a general revelation of a divine prohibition."[68] Special revelation, on the other hand, requires specific epistemic sources and "takes place through more particular phenomena that have a more or less precise location in history."[69] Examples of special revelation include "divine commands made known through sacred texts, authoritative traditions, or unique personal inspirations."[70]

Maududi's and Sachedina's political theologies respectively fall into theories of special and general revelation. Maududi seeks to authorize human rights entirely in terms of the Qur'an and the hadith of the Prophet. Such is the method of a theory of special revelation: it authorizes duties and virtues exclusively in terms of historically revealed teaching. For Sachedina, avowing this form of exclusivism is a reaction to the wider cultural and political forces in which modern Islam finds itself. In his view, Muslim political theology must take its bearings from the natural human endowment to intuit universal values based on a belief in the capacity, given by God, to know and do the good.

This difference between Maududi and Sachedina complicates the impression, espoused by Ignatieff, that theological accounts of human dignity and moral norms all stand at considerable remove from secular accounts. Such an impression would surely be true if we were only thinking of the kind of Islamic political thought represented by Maududi. But Sachedina's understanding of *fitra,* along with his views of natural theology and moral reason, assign human dignity on much different terms: as intrinsic rather than as imputed, owing to capacities that we all naturally share and that entitle us to respect on equal terms. For Sachedina, it is wrong to assume that human dignity is sacrificed on the altar of divine command morality. Quite the contrary: Sachedina defends an account of rights that is Islamic and rational, theological and philosophical. That fact reminds us that a theory of general revelation poses few if any problems for a common morality. As Adams notes about general revelation, "principles that have wide enough acceptance to be genuinely a part of common morality can plausibly be regarded (by divine command theorists) as commands of God generally revealed."[71]

My discussion of Maududi and Sachedina opens up a third point, namely, that theories of special revelation and its version of divine command morality do not necessarily generate "critical distance" from secular practices or institutions—distance that might be the basis for assigning religious ideas special wisdom or esteem. Not infrequently, apologists of religion—or those who bemoan the decline of religion in the public square—assign a privileged place to religious discourse and morality because it answers to an authority that stands apart from the state and everyday politics. Apologists of religion who think along those lines might find a lot to commend about Maududi's appeals to religious belief and tradition as a way of resisting secular Western ideas. For some intellectuals who worry about the decline of confidence and trust in religion's role in political matters, religion offers the potential to disrupt centers of power, especially state power, and offers an alternative story by which adherents can forge identity and community.[72]

But Maududi's example shows that a mode of reasoning shaped by a theory of special revelation and revealed epistemology is hardly free of cooptation or cultural accommodation. Indeed, Maududi's views do nothing to disrupt entrenched gender hierarchies or the criminalization of religious apostasy. Whatever resistance or disruptive potential his claims might pose to Western ideas should be assessed on terms that allow us to ask whether such resistance is progressive or regressive. Religion might offer what appear to be countercultural claims only to sanctify cultural practices and prejudices that have little to recommend.

That is to say, how one views religion as a source of resistance raises normative questions about the ethics of belief. Claiming that special revelation is culturally enlightened can simply be a form of thinly disguised religious apologetics, providing cover for various forms of political and economic special interests in tandem with historical nostalgia. At the very least such claims beg questions about how political religions and their relations to power are to be evaluated. That fact requires us to think more generally about the relationship between religion and ethics—about the putative priority of religion to ethics. To those more abstract issues we are now in a position to turn.

7

LIBERAL SOCIAL CRITICISM AND
THE ETHICS OF BELIEF

ON THE PRIORITY OF RELIGION TO ETHICS

The norms of respect for human dignity and equal liberty enable liberal social critics to assess radical Islam and its connection to the events of 9/11 along with other political religions and similar movements that seek to disrupt peaceable formations of public life. At a minimum, those norms provide a basis for determining whether religious and cultural traditions are regressive or progressive when they claim to resist power structures and social practices. More generally, an ethics of belief that builds on liberal commitments invites us to reconsider what I have called the priority of religion to ethics.[1] That priority would have us hold that moral norms acquire their meaning against a backdrop of deeper convictions. Accordingly, moral norms draw not from some putatively neutral source of impartial reason but from particular webs of belief on which they rely for their sustenance and authority. Religious adherents are thus expected to adjust their judgments or perceptions of experience to the world picture or constitutive beliefs to which they subscribe when those judgments or perceptions call into question their wider convictions. On the view that religion is prior to ethics, radical challenges to one's world picture or constitutive beliefs derive from judgments that are relative to altogether different frameworks.

The metaphor "webs of belief" suggests the idea that different religions along with their respective moral norms are clearly marked off from each other. The image is revealing: webs not only have elaborate interconnections and internally reinforcing strands but also clear external boundaries. We can thus understand why the priority of religion to ethics creates strong barriers to criticizing anything beyond the borders of one's own tradition. On the assumption that norms are relative to discrete and bounded background beliefs, applying norms to practices that are authorized by other traditions or worldviews cannot but seem imperialistic to those who are judged. By the same token, if moral norms depend on webs of belief for their intelligibility, it is difficult for a stranger to grasp another's indignation that might arise in cross-cultural encounters when such indignation is not stated in terms that are indigenous to that stranger's own convictions. Instead, another's indignation becomes reducible to an expression of his or her group psychology.

One point of this book is that the priority of religion to ethics and the barriers it imposes on social criticism must be reconsidered insofar as the values of respect for persons and equal liberty are at stake in controversies regarding religious belief and practice.[2] That reconsideration has disquieting implications for those whose philosophy or theology inoculates piety from others' social criticism. Adherents of religions who deny respect for basic human rights might ask their fellow practitioners to revise their expectations and beliefs about the putative merits of such rights in light of broader background claims. That request should be vigorously denied.

ON THICK AND THIN MORALITY

For liberal social critics, the idea of reconsidering religion's priority to ethics can be refined by way of a spatial metaphor: thick and thin morality. But those terms might court confusion. Frequently they track the division between the private and public spheres of social life, distinguishing our private lives as persons with beliefs and heritages, local solidarities, and personal tastes from our public roles as citizens with political rights and obligations. Or they track the difference between two kinds of loves: preferential love—love of the "near neighbor"—on the one hand, and nonpreferential love—love of the neighbor "qua human existent"—on the other.[3]

Those differences do not capture how I am invoking the image here. We should instead think of the concepts of thick and thin morality as designating, respectively, the inner and outer layers of the moral life. Thick morality consists of our denser moral understandings and names those goods that we endorse or that we believe make a claim for our endorsement. It uses the language, as Walzer puts it, of "moral maximalism."[4] Thick morality identifies the deep, inner reasons and self-defining commitments according to which we find purpose and direction in life. Thin morality, in contrast, places limits on how we carry out those thicker commitments and purposes. It consists of norms and ideas that, compared to our denser moral understandings, are general and abstract. Thin morality speaks in the language of rights, freedom, and the claims of decency. It speaks in the language of "moral minimalism."[5]

The distinction between moral minimalism and maximalism invites us to ask whether the former is embedded in the latter and, if so, whether it retains any real traction when it is detached from denser commitments. Call this the challenge of intellectual holism. Intellectual holists question the possibility of detaching thin from thick morality. They doubt the idea that morality comes in anything less than whole cloth. Walzer, for example, argues that thin morality cannot but arise from deeper moral understandings and commitments. Thin and thick morality alike are products of social history, thick being prior to thin. Walzer writes: "Minimalist meanings are embedded in the maximal morality, expressed in the same idiom, sharing the same (historical/cultural/religious/political) orientation. Minimalism is liberated from its embeddedness and appears independently, in varying degrees of thinness, only in the course of a personal or social crisis or a political confrontation."[6]

On that view, thin morality provides terms or values according to which we sympathize with the suffering of others elsewhere, but our sympathy only makes sense to us when it is attached to our denser understandings. It may overlap with others' sympathies and moral claims but it is not an expression of morality conceived outside of history and context. Walzer states: "The morality in which the moral minimum is embedded, and from which it can only temporarily be abstracted, is the only full-blooded morality we can ever have."[7]

What may be overlooked in that account, and what I want to focus on here, is the work that thin morality performs in relation to thick morality. Thin morality requires us to pursue our ends within a set of boundaries. It imposes "side-constraints," defining the outer contours within which we seek and embrace the good by our lights.[8] More to the point, minimal morality blocks religious believers from elevating their religiously based moral norms above basic moral principles. And it does so by virtue of a value that attaches to the very idea of being a moral agent and having human dignity. That value, and the entitlement that it confers, must be heeded as a constraint on whatever other values or goods we wish to pursue.

The norms of respect for persons and equal liberty are part of thin morality. They present neither the whole of morality nor all of its utopian aspirations. They do not spell out the full range of entitlements owed to all persons, although the views on which they depend provide a basis for affirming not only civic and political but also basic social and economic rights—rights that entitle persons to the concrete conditions necessary to exercise genuine human agency.[9] As I have developed the idea of human dignity and its implications in this book, the norms of respect for persons and equal liberty provide the normative contours for our more engaged and committed pursuits. They mold and constrain how we are to interact with others. Whatever else we may seek according to our denser moral understandings, our pursuit of those ends must be bounded by respect for persons as having inherent dignity and equal liberty. Any morality, religious or otherwise, that fails to heed the value attached to moral subjectivity denies others their entitlement to exercise their moral responsibilities as free and equal persons.

We might simplify this idea by thinking about these two moralities in a first-order way. Thin morality defines a set of obligations that I must heed in my various commitments and pursuits. But how we are to understand the basis of those obligations is a matter of dispute. According to the argument in this book, we should recognize thin obligations as deriving not from one's deeper convictions but from what it means to be a subject with convictions in the first place. We can grasp thin obligations not by virtue *of the goods* to which we are committed but in response to others *with goods* to which they are committed. Thin obligations arise in response to the fact that others are moral subjects, each of whom lives life "from the inside" and possesses the authority to envision and (within limits) pursue his or her own vision of the good. Thin morality has as its basis each individual's dignity as a moral subject, a dignity that we are all obligated to recognize and respect.

It may seem that my account assimilates itself to Walzer's understanding of minimal morality's relationship to maximal morality. Concepts of "self," "authority," "entitlement," "freedom and finitude," "human dignity"—crucial to my argument throughout these pages—all smack of liberal notions that have their own history, politics, and institutional formations. Avowing rights to life and security along with the duties of toleration seems to repose, finally, against the background of thicker understandings that are parochial and particular. As a descriptive matter, the priority of thickness to thinness—and the priority of belief to ethics—seems undeniable.

But that account can't be right. Imagine a world picture that assigns to its adherents the notion that they are the sorts of beings who do not, cannot, or should not deliberate about and revise their understandings of the good. That is to say, suppose a world picture that denies its adherents the idea that they are moral subjects. Their thoughts and feelings are to be are conditioned entirely by the claims of the world picture to which they are heir and to which they are to abide. They understand "responsibility" to mean functioning as instruments to carry out a certain set of policies or directives, but not in ways that allow those adherents to reflect on the meaning of what they are doing or to change their attitudes toward it. Would we assign to that world picture the name "thick morality"? Surely we would not be satisfied by saying only that such a world picture is clearly illiberal. We would ask, "In what meaningful sense does it deserve to be called a 'morality'? In what meaningful sense are its adherents moral subjects rather than automatons?" Trading on the concept of "the moral" requires us to accept a basic assumption, namely, the fact of moral subjectivity. (Putative) moralities that deny their practitioners moral subjectivity—the freedom to adopt and revise their commitments against a background of cultural and other beliefs and ideals—trade on counterfeit currency. They deny the terms according to which we can have any expectation of genuine moral responsibility.

All of this is to say that when we ask about whether or on what terms relatively different moralities can be compared and criticized, we are presupposing some underlying invariants—especially the idea that moral responsibility assumes the existence of human subjects rather than instruments of another's will. Given the conceptual invariant of human subjectivity and the idea of dignity that it confers, we can speak in terms of thin morality, and apply its norms, without having its presumptions assimilated into any one particular maximalist account. Rather, it is a precondition for the existence of any maximalist account.

All of this is to say that liberal social criticism, with its particular history, politics, and institutional formations, opens up a nonrelative insight about morality itself. Put more abstractly, we need not bifurcate history and moral truth—as if the historicity of one point of view disables it from discovering a nonrelative idea.[10] The fact that a point of view derives from a contingent social location—one that could have assumed a different historical formation, were it not for this or that seemingly arbitrary cause—does not undermine its potential for generating a universal insight. Stated in other terms, we do well to distinguish between the *accessibility* of an idea and its *status* as true or false. The fact that an idea has not been timelessly accessible does not render it untrue. What liberal social critics call attention to from within their historic location and vantage point is an insight about what we intuitively and invariantly presume when we invoke the term "morality." No notion of "the moral" coherently denies the notion that human beings are moral subjects.

If I am correct about this view of human subjectivity and its bearing on morality in general and thin morality in particular, then we must reverse the priority with which I began this chapter. Given that minimal morality exists not by virtue *of the goods* to which I am committed but as someone in response to others *with goods* to which they are committed, we must presume the priority of thin to thick morality. Minimal morality names and develops the basis on which we can speak of moral responsibility at all. That is to say, whatever particular features describe any one maximalist morality, it must presume the existence of moral subjects, each with the capacity to reflect on and revise their respective pictures of the good life. Particular features of a maximalist morality enable us to distinguish it from another such morality, but *any* account of morality must repose against a universal assumption: the idea that adherents have moral subjectivity. A world picture or web of belief that denies that assumption forfeits its claim to espousing a morality of any sort. For that reason we must affirm the priority of thin morality to any thick version.

Another challenge posed to my account would introduce metatheoretical considerations about intellectual holism from a different starting point. It would launch itself by posing a substantive challenge to the moral anthropology presupposed by liberal social criticism, arguing that the account of moral subjectivity to which I subscribe is overly optimistic about human nature—that human beings, lacking supernatural healing and guidance, lack the capacity to reflect on and revise their picture of the good life. On that account, my differences with Sachedina in the previous chapter pale in comparison to a darker or more "realistic" account of human volition as weak and prone to self-aggrandizement at the expense of another's good. Call this the Augustinian challenge to the liberal account of minimal morality I have been defending. On the Augustinian view, the will is fallen and stands in need of divine grace to direct it toward ends beyond heedless self-love and the will-to-power—what Augustine knew as *libido dominandi*. God's healing and redirection, moreover, reorder the will for a life of desire of and affection for the Supreme Good. God's work transforms the power to choose, what Augustine understood as the *liberum arbi-*

trium, to a will that loves the Good for its own sake and all things as they participate in the Good. Such a will thereby experiences true freedom, liberated from the vices of self-aggrandizement and anxious self-absorption. The practical effect of such divine reordering is to direct the will toward the ends of the common good, neighbor-love, and proper self-love. Accordingly, for Augustinians the idea of human subjectivity must repose against a thicker account of humanity's place in the cosmos along with the will's fallibilities and frailties.

But that challenge to liberal social criticism is more complicated, and potentially weaker, than it first appears. The key question is whether one views human beings as endowed with dignity owing to our capacity to envision our ends and revise our purposes against a backdrop of meaningful options. As I noted in chapter 6, for liberals, dignity does not reside in the capacity to make the *right* choice, only in the capacity to make choices that are meaningful to the subject on his or her account of the good, choices for which she or he is morally accountable. Not infrequently religious adherents speak of human dignity in such terms—as endowing human beings with grounds for respect owing to our capacities to freely will the good and exercise our capacities as morally responsible. Theological versions of that idea describe humans as endowed with inherent dignity as creatures of God, understanding dignity in terms of moral subjectivity as I have been describing it. For example, in the *Declaration on Religious Freedom,* Roman Catholic social teaching avows that

> it is in accordance with their dignity as persons—that is, beings endowed with reason and free will and therefore privileged to bear personal responsibility—that all men should be at once impelled by nature and also bound by a moral obligation to seek the truth, especially religious truth. . . .
>
> However, men cannot discharge these obligations in a manner in keeping with their own nature unless they enjoy immunity from external coercion as well as psychological freedom. Therefore, the right to religious freedom has its foundation, not in the subjective disposition of the person, but in his very nature. In

consequence, the right to this immunity continues to exist even in those who do not live up to their obligation of seeking the truth and adhering to it.[11]

Note that Catholic teaching, like liberal doctrine, does not claim that individuals forfeit their dignity by virtue of failing to seek or adhere to the truth (understood in Catholic teaching as "true religion" which "subsists in the Catholic and apostolic Church").[12] On the Catholic view, "God has regard for the human person whom He Himself created; man is to be guided by his own judgment and he is to enjoy freedom."[13] If Augustinians view the will as providing the capacity to (accountably) envision and revise the pursuit of the good, then they too can enjoy shared ground with liberal social critics regarding the norms of respect and equal liberty.

What is crucial is whether Augustinian morality (or any religious morality) elevates its religiously authorized norms above minimal moral principles, leaving the former immune from criticism by the latter. Insofar as Augustinians (or, again, other religious adherents) understand respect for human dignity and equal liberty as setting the contours for their commitment to the common good, neighbor-love, and proper self-love, then they can join cause with liberal social critics.[14] On the other hand, if Augustinians deny dignity to human beings on the view that, without grace, humans are not entitled to basic respect, then liberals and Augustinians part company. For liberals, requiring us to make "right choices" as the basis for assigning respect would be to conflate recognition respect with appraisal respect. Liberal social criticism rejects that conflation.

ON PROXIMITY AND DISTANCE

Describing the relationship of thin to thick morality as I have—as constraining and constrained—is meant to distinguish this level of liberal social criticism from another level, which might be best captured by the spatial metaphors of distance and proximity. Again, some clarification is in order. Frequently that distinction is meant to track the difference between objectivism and relativism, or be-

tween general and local knowledge, or between ethics characterized as a "view from nowhere" and ethics characterized by appeals
to tradition or moral particularism. But that is not how I am invoking the distinction here. Instead, we should think of the distinction
as marking a pair of extremes that a liberal social critic's attitude
toward difference should avoid. At this level there is an ethics that
shapes one's stance toward topics of analysis, topics that include
religious belief and practice. That is to say, there is an ethics to
the practice of social criticism itself. Liberal social criticism of the
sort I've practiced here mediates between dismissing otherness and
romanticizing it. And it does so guided by a basic liberal value,
namely, respect for persons.

As a way of reflecting on the ethics of social criticism, this level
has us think in a second-order way. We should see it as marking
the outer boundaries for anyone practicing the craft. As with thin
and thick morality, here too we are thinking in terms of moral contours—this time with an eye to the practice of social criticism itself.
Social criticism that operates from excessive distance risks becoming formalistic and impersonal—criticism "of witchcraft as written
by a geometer," in Clifford Geertz's memorable phrase.[15] I hope to
have made it clear that excessive distance can generate a disposition that too easily fuels chauvinistic judgment. It encourages habits that fail to assign the benefit of the doubt to others and, instead,
dismisses them with a reflex-generated sense of superiority. Social
criticism that suffers from proximity, in contrast, risks speaking
in the vernacular, producing criticism—again echoing Geertz—"of
witchcraft as written by a witch."[16] I hope to have made it clear
that proximity can generate a disposition that too easily yields recognition on demand. It encourages habits that go beyond assigning
benefit of the doubt to others and instead embraces them with reflex-generated esteem.

One challenge of liberal social criticism turns on thinking with
these two levels—thick and thin, far and near—in relation to each
other. In this book, I have sought to draw on moral minimalism's
norm of equal human dignity and respect for persons to navigate
a path that is neither too distant from nor too close to its subject
matter. The ideas of equal liberty and respect for persons should

be seen as mediating principles, enabling us to step back, self-re-flexively, from behaviors and traditions that invite critical inter-pretation. The "self-reflexive" rider is crucial here. It captures our distanciation along with our mindfulness of that fact in the exercise of respectful social criticism. For liberals, intellectual practices are themselves ruled-governed activities, guided by basic values. If liberal social critics are going to apply their principles to others, we must do so in ways that are consistent with our own convictions. Expecting others to grasp the meaning of respect should be articulated and defended in a manner consistent with that expectation.

One of my aims in these pages has been to develop the meaning of basic moral claims in relation to religious violence and intolerance in a way that is mindful of liberal ideals. As I noted in chapter 1, one task has been to mediate between apologetics and ethnocentrism by including the value of respect as a central criterion. We are now in a position to bring that mediating aim into clearer focus. A liberal ethics of belief, guided by the value of respect, clearly distinguishes between apology and respect. It refuses to conflate respect with reflex-affirmation and instead views such affirmation as a form of patronizing deference—a form of condescension. Respect must be granted on terms other than the fact of "difference" alone. Moreover, a liberal ethics of belief clearly distinguishes between respect and chauvinistic judgment, which is but another form of condescension and disregard. A liberal ethics of belief begins from a disposition of benefit of the doubt given the dignity of all persons along with an understanding of our own epistemic limitations. That disposition honors the value of respect in the very act of comparing and evaluating different cultural traditions and practices.

We can bring these two levels (first-order and second-order reflections) into focus by noting how they share an inner connection with the idea of respect for persons. But they do so in different ways. At a first-order level, when thinking about the moral quality of our interactions with others, respect serves as a norm that ought to guide our attitudes and conduct. Thinking in those terms understands respect for persons as a fundamental obligation—a *norm* that we are to obey. At a second-order level, when thinking about the ethics of social criticism, respect serves as a criterion that ought to guide how we carry out the practice of criticism itself. Thinking in those terms understands respect for persons as a *virtue*, a disposition that inclines us to exercise our critical capacities in a certain way. As both norm and virtue, respect for persons, and the value of human dignity to which it is conceptually attached, guides the manner in which we should think about social controversies in a pluralistic, multicultural world.

Considerations of respect, of course, include expectations about how one ought to be treated by others—about the concrete implications of *mutual* respect. Throughout these pages I have sought to coordinate normative considerations of respect with an eye to self-regarding and other-regarding demands. For liberals, nonapologetical, nonethnocentric criticism—and the confident articulation of indignation in response to an injustice—are not expressions of disrespect. On the contrary: they are grounded in an account of human dignity that understands all of us as deserving equal respect for the security and liberty required to exercise our moral commitments and responsibilities.

APPENDIX 1

THE RIGHT TO WAR AND SELF-DEFENSE

Earlier I provided reasons for the idea that individuals have rights to life and security that justify resort to force in self-defense against certain acts of aggression. The right to life is based on the idea that arbitrary threats to existence fail to respect individuals as free and finite moral subjects who are responsible for ordering their lives toward their respective visions of the good. The right of security is based on the notion that each of us depends on social, political, and cultural conditions that aid and abet our pursuits of the good. Communities provide the intersubjective conditions on which we depend and within which we exercise our capacities to develop and revise our ends. We do not formulate our respective accounts of the good in isolation but in dialogue with others, an intergenerational dialogue that creates and presupposes social customs, political institutions, and cultural traditions. These practices have value insofar as they provide the ambient structures within which our lives are constituted over time, the horizon of meaning according to which we gain sense and direction in our pursuits of the good. On these terms, states have the right to go to war in response to unprovoked aggression in order to defend their citizens and to secure the conditions of their common life.

Yet here we face questions of justification that have been generally unexamined in the ethics of international conflict. Just-war doctrine, the chief framework for assessing the ethics of war, assigns states the right to go to war. But it is unclear in just-war doctrine how that right is to be understood. Specifically, it is unclear whether the right being defended belongs to individuals or to the state.

Consider the problem in this way. As I have noted, the right to self-defense is premised in part on the liberal idea that "we lead our life from the inside, in accordance with our beliefs about what gives value to life."[1] Having a common life provides individuals with cultural and moral resources for developing and revising their beliefs about what gives value to life. Citizens have rights to security in light of their interest in maintaining a common life, and states have the duty to protect such interests. On this account, we say that states have the right to go to war in response to a serious grievance, one that arises from the infringement of rights to life and security. States can have a just cause to act in defense of such rights. The problem with this line of thinking is that it appears to blur two sets of rights—individual and collective rights—and seems to equivocate about which is more fundamental.

In this appendix, I want argue that a state's right to resort to force in response to a serious grievance should be understood as permitting that state to defend individuals' rights, not some form of collective rights. With that point resolved, we can then turn in the next appendix to specific ethical questions about the resort to force against al Qaeda and the Taliban in response to the grievance of 9/11.

COLLECTIVE DEFENSE:
REDUCTIVE AND ANALOGICAL STRATEGIES

David Rodin's *War and Self-Defense* raises the problem of establishing the right to war in an especially perspicuous way and poses serious challenges to the concept. I want to focus on his argument in order to fix ideas about the right to war with an eye toward securing a basic claim in just-war doctrine and the ethics of international affairs more generally.

Rodin identifies two strategies for establishing a state's right to go to war: the "reductive strategy" and the "analogical strategy." To see how these work, consider the following problem: Suppose soldier-citizens in Country A assault Country B, either by villainously attacking Country B's infrastructure and citizens at home and abroad, or by invading uninhabited parts of Country B's territory. Just-war doctrine and international law typically allow states to use force in self-defense against all such actions. But that permission begs two questions: What sorts of rights are at stake for Country B? Is killing a proportionate way to defend such rights?

The reductive strategy goes about answering these questions in what I will call a *pure version* and a *complex version*. Both versions view Country B's right of national defense as a special case of the right of *personal self-defense*. On the pure account, national defense is simply an aggregated and coordinated exercise of personal self-defense—"an organized exercise of the right of self-defense by large numbers of individuals at one time."[2] Attacks by citizens in Country B against citizen-soldiers from Country A are justified as a defense against Country A's lethal assault. But citizens in Country B may *not* attack citizen-soldiers in Country A who are not posing a direct or immediate threat to them or to third parties in Country B. The aggression to be thwarted must be direct, interpersonal, and immediate.

Rodin observes that just-war doctrine typically grants soldiers far more permission to use force than provided by the right of self-defense against another's immediate threat to life or safety. Soldiers may attack uniformed soldiers who do not pose a threat. They may also attack even when retreat is a viable option for them, when the use of force might be unnecessary to defend their lives. They may kill in order to protect others—their fellow citizens—from threat or assault. And they may kill other soldiers whether they are aggressing or defending given the view that soldiers are "moral equals" on each side of a conflict.[3] These sorts of action indicate that "moral discourse of personal self-defense is too fine-grained to encompass the prosecution of war."[4]

Moreover, and most tellingly for Rodin, the idea of a personal right to self-defense cannot make sense of two forms of military action that just-war doctrine respectively permits to defend against or to perform: bloodless invasions and humanitarian interventions. Rodin understands these cases as posing special challenges to what I am calling a complex version of the reductive strategy. According to that idea, wars are not simply matters of aggregated versions of personal self-defense. Rather, wars are carried out by states that are viewed on the model of protective parents, responsible for defending the lives of their citizens at risk of death or serious injury.[5]

The first challenge to this account involves the case of defending against the annexation of territory or the violation of airspace—forms of bloodless aggression in which no lives are put at risk.[6] Here again, we see that a reductive strategy is more restrictive than standard accounts of a just war. Insofar as the complex reductive strategy connects the right of national self-defense to the end of protecting lives of individual citizens, it fails to justify military action in response to a bloodless invasion by an outside aggressor.

The second challenge involves the case of humanitarian intervention, in which one nation intrudes on another nation's territory to protect its citizens from widespread suffering or death. If a right to humanitarian intervention exists, Rodin observes, then "the moral basis of the right of national self-defense can in certain circumstances be justly overridden."[7] The right to intervene to defend individuals within another state means denying that state the right to war as a means of individual self-defense. Protecting one's own citizens, then, cannot suffice as a basis for permitting a nation to act in self-defense.

Taken together, the cases of bloodless invasion and humanitarian intervention appear to pose enormous problems for the complex reductive strategy—the idea that states can protect their citizens on the model of protective parents. The first case indicates that personal self-defense is not necessary to ground national self-defense; the second case indicates that personal self-defense is not sufficient to ground national self-defense.[8]

Consider, then, the analogical strategy. That strategy views Country B's right of national defense on the premise that states possess rights that are independent of, but on analogy with, the right of personal self-defense.[9] This analogy understands states to be the international equivalent of persons, with rights and duties vis-à-vis other states, just as persons possess rights and duties in personal and domestic relations. According to this view, states (or at least the communities that inhabit them) have a value independent of the rights of individuals. That is to say, there is a value attached to a common life that transcends individual rights. When a state uses force in self-defense, it is defending goods typically associated with a superpersonal value.

The question, again, is what can vindicate the right of national defense, now understood on analogy with personal rights? As Rodin understands it, the analogical strategy must connect the state to a superpersonal value that satisfies three criteria: the value must be minimal enough for many states to satisfy, it must be objective enough to provide a universal value, and it must have a sufficient measure of particularity for real people to recognize and "connect with."

One candidate for such a value is state legitimacy, understood in terms of Hobbesian contract theory. Here the idea is that states have value insofar as they provide security and order as an alternative to the rapacious competition that characterizes life in the state of nature. National defense would be justified in light of protecting the order and security that political association provides. This sort of value is minimal enough for many states to satisfy, is objective, and is one that persons can readily recognize and affirm.

Yet the problem with this claim, Rodin argues, is that the values of stability and order are not robust enough to ground a moral basis for national defense. A state may have better reason to capitulate to an aggressor than to resist insofar as that aggressor may bring greater stability and order to a nation by imposing its own brand of political ideology. That is to say, the status quo of order may be less stable and secure than the imposition of a new order by an outside regime. Moreover, armed resistance to an aggressor may produce more disorder than would capitulation. The value of political order may thus generate a duty not to go to war rather than a right to go to war. For these reasons, the value of order is insufficient for vindicating a state's right to use force.

Rather than relying on the value of a political order, then, we might think of national defense as defense of a particular kind of order, what might be called a community's shared understandings and its cultural identity. Herein lies a second possibility for grounding the analogical strategy for national defense: "Shared values and laws, language and literature, history and traditions" give a community its distinctive character.[10] On this premise, national defense is understood in terms of protecting a settled and established way of life.

The problem here, Rodin argues, is that this value is too subjective and relativistic, allowing for the defense of communities and their traditions regardless of the moral quality of those traditions. It would allow for the defense of communities that are corrupt and oppressive simply because they pass the test of having become a tradition and way of life. Appeals to the value of "shared understandings" thus generate a paradox: states have a transcultural right to defend a way of life that is exempt from moral scrutiny on transcultural terms. This paradox, Rodin holds, can hardly withstand rational scrutiny.[11]

A third option would be to think of the analogical strategy in light of autonomy and a community's right to self-determination. This value avoids the thinness of the value of security and order, and it avoids the relativism inherent in defending a shared way of life. It is the liberal value around which I have centered my discussion of the rights of life and security along with the grounds and limits of toleration. About this idea, Rodin observes: "Freedom, autonomy, and self-determination are objective trans-cultural goods. . . . In so far as each person pursues projects which they are committed to regarding as good, they are also committed to regarding the freedom necessary to the attainment of those projects as good. Humans cannot flourish or attain full well-being, without the ability to shape their own lives in accordance with their conception the good."[12]

Against this notion, Rodin registers three challenges. The first is to note that the argument seems to restrict itself to the defense of democratic states, for only those states have genuine processes of collective autonomy and self-determination. It would thus deny a right of self-defense to most of the political world.[13] The second is to note the mismatch between communities and states: there is no neat "fit" between the boundaries of discrete communities and the boundaries of states. Insofar as an appeal to collective autonomy and self-determination presupposes a sociology of discrete communities, it fails to generate a basis of national defense insofar as communities and states to not map onto each other. A community at risk in one state, say State B, hardly generates a right of State A to defend that community even if its traditions and practices provide meaningful resources to many citizens in State A.[14] Third, there are (again) challenges posed by the case of humanitarian intervention and the contradictory permissions that the values of autonomy and collective determination generate. The right of communities to autonomy and self-determination can produce a right for others to defend. Suppose that a minority in State A is at risk of expulsion or oppression. If State B possesses a right to defend a minority community in State A, then State A must lack the right of national defense against State B that the value of communal autonomy and self-determination allegedly provides.[15]

Taking these challenges together, it appears as if the reductive strategy and the analogical strategy fail to generate a right of national defense. That conclusion demolishes a key plank in the ethics of international affairs. What can be said in response?

THE RIGHT OF NATIONAL SECURITY

Consider first Rodin's main argument against what I have called the pure version of the reductive strategy. Recall that for Rodin, soldiers have the right to kill other soldiers only when their lives are immediately at risk. In Rodin's mind, that right generates the duty to retreat when their lives are not in immediate danger along with the duty not to kill uniformed soldiers who do not pose an immediate threat. But the idea that only an immediate threat to life can justify killing in self-defense is surely too strict. During war, soldiers have good reason to suspect that enemy soldiers have designs on their lives, even when they are not launching an attack. What may not be an immediate threat can become one, and acting preventively against such dangers is surely a reasonable precaution to take in war. Moreover, retreat in war is hardly a guarantor of personal safety and security. Opting to use force, on balance, may be in a soldier's basic interest.

Consider as well Rodin's two main arguments against what I have called the complex reductive strategy. For Rodin, the case of a bloodless invasion reveals that just-war doctrine allows for killing in nonlethal situations and this permission, he argues, is not justified by the complex reductive strategy because such an invasion does not require the state to act protectively on behalf of its citizens. In a bloodless invasion citizens are obviously not in need of protection. But Rodin's case of bloodless invasion is too abstract and atypical. The likelihood that such an invasion would remain genuinely bloodless or harmless is small. The presumption should rather be that a threat to territorial integrity is an imminent threat to the security rights of a political community's citizens. Citizens have legitimate interests, I have argued, not only with regard to their physical lives but also with regard to their general security. The right to security provides a shield behind which they can pursue their basic interests in personal growth and meaningful choices. Failure to resist such incursions, moreover, would embolden other states to do the same, further imperiling personal safety and well-being. Accordingly, the complex reductive strategy could easily justify using force to defend against bloodless territorial invasions or attempts at annexation.[16]

Rodin's attempt to confound the complex reductive strategy with the case of humanitarian intervention is likewise misleading. He is correct to say that a right of humanitarian intervention, assuming that it exists, stands in tension with the right of national defense. But that fact only points to hard cases rather than the weakness of a basic principle. States that open themselves up to humanitarian interventions may be understood to have forfeited their right of self-defense owing to how they treat their citizens. Their failure to protect their citizens renders moot their claim to have a rightful defense against intervening parties. This is not to say that the bar to humanitarian intervention is low, only that it is not insuperable.[17] What the case of humanitarian intervention reveals is that the right of national defense grounded in the defense of individual citizens must satisfy certain conditions. Absent satisfying those conditions, the right may be justifiably challenged.

Different problems haunt Rodin's arguments against versions of the analogical strategy: order, custom and tradition, and collective self-determination. Rodin is surely correct to say that the principle of order may generate the duty not to resist given that a better order may be imposed by an intruding state. But again, it is important not to confound basic principles with atypical cases. States rarely aggress upon another state or region altruistically—with pure motives that seek to improve the lives of citizens there. The historical record of states that have claimed to do so is discouraging. The presumption should rather be that a threat to a state is an imminent threat to its citizens' right of security, and that an invading state's military aims include some measure of self-interest.

Rodin is on more solid ground in his critique of custom and tradition as a basis for justifying the right of national defense. There is no question that certain traditions and ways of life are morally indefensible. But in his discussion of vindicating the right of national defense on these terms, Rodin misses an important transcultural value. What is arguably at stake in the second version of the analogical argument, and surely in the third version, is the value of respect for persons, or what might be called a nonpaternalistic principle. States have the right of self-defense against other nations on the premise that they and their citizens deserve, at a *prima facie* level, respect for their political communities and ways of life. Rodin overlooks the fact that states have the right of national defense on the premise that other states cannot generally presume to know what is better for them.

That oversight invites us to think more carefully about the ideas of autonomy and self-determination, the third version of the analogical strategy. Rodin's critique of those ideas misrepresents them and their connection to justified national defense. What Rodin overlooks is that autonomy and collective self-determination do not generate a superpersonal value that is independent of the rights of individuals. Recall that, at the heart of his discussion of the analogical strategy's possible connection to the values of autonomy and self-determination, we find the following claim: "In so far as each person pursues projects which they are committed to regarding as good, they are also committed to regarding the freedom necessary to the attainment of those projects as good. Humans cannot flourish or obtain full well-being, without the ability to shape their own lives in accordance with their own conception the good."[18] Rodin fails to see that the freedom necessary to the attainment of one's projects is an *individual* interest. States that use force to defend such liberty-interests are justified in defending individuals rather than an independent superpersonal value. That is to say, what Rodin identifies as a possibility for vindicating the analogical strategy is rather a possibility for vindicating the reductive strategy. Rodin's effort to undermine this basis for national self-defense—defending autonomy and self determination—misses the mark.

Of Rodin's two strategies and their variations, my argument comes closer to the complex reductive strategy insofar as it is premised on the defense of individual rights, not the rights of states as superpersonal agents. But the rights of individuals must be understood far more capaciously than Rodin's account presupposes in his analysis. My account avoids his critique of the complex reductive strategy in that it focuses not only on the right to life and its legitimate defense by states, but also on individuals' interest in security and the need to protect a common life. The right of national defense includes reference to the value of life along with other basic interests. It thus includes the importance of freedom necessary to the attainment and revision of our projects.

This value of freedom provides a mediating principle between individualist and collectivist groundings of the right of national defense and likely confounds a sharp distinction between reductive and analogical approaches to the rights of war. Aggressive nations endanger not only persons' lives but also their liberties and the security necessary to build a meaningful life. These ideas generate a value attached to a common life that has a derivative, not independent value—a value insofar as it enables persons to live life "from the inside" in a meaningful way.

My argument thus provides a basis for national defense not only as a form of personal self-defense but as a defense of the infrastructural conditions that aid and abet the exercise of commitment and choice. What Rodin misses is the idea that citizens have an interest not only in their lives now, but also in the persistence and development of their common life as a matter of meaning for them and for (their) future generations. There is the temptation in moral discourse about war to abstract from the lived realities and attractions of a common life understood, in Benedict Anderson's famous phrase, as "imagined communities."[19] The value of freedom and the infrastructural conditions that aid and abet the exercise of commitment and choice focus our attention not on the value of communities in the abstract or in a relativistic way, but on our interest in having a secure and common life—understood as having a temporal dimension. That idea constitutes a transcultural norm on which to anchor a defense of states' rights.

It bears repeating that the right of national defense, properly understood, is connected to individuals, not to communities as independent and superpersonal agents. This idea points to the fact that membership and belonging are of sufficient importance to fall within the parameters of human well-being, the defense of which is justified. Jeff McMahan puts the point well: Although Rodin may be correct to say that the idea of states as superpersonal rights-bearers cannot withstand scrutiny, "there is another possibility that is more plausible—namely, that membership in the collective and participation in collective self-determination are of sufficient importance to the well-being of *individuals* to come within the scope of those individuals' rights of self- and other-defense."[20] This is perhaps a more precise way to express the idea that individuals have an interest in the security of the intergenerational and infrastructural conditions that aid and abet the exercise of commitment and choice.

APPENDIX 2
IS ATTACKING THE TALIBAN AND AL QAEDA JUSTIFIED?

One thrust of this book is the idea that indignation in response to 9/11 is justified on terms that should matter to persons in addition to those who feel aggrieved by the atrocity. Seen in this way, indignation is a form of *address*, an appeal with moral authority. It stakes a claim on the consciences of others, including those implicated in, or supportive of, the wrongdoing. And it stakes that claim as a valid *moral* command, not one addressed to others' self-interest or expressed with an eye to outcome-based rationality.[1] Such an address, or a claim on another's conscience, works to transform a relationship from one of indifference, apathy, or disregard to one that has the potential for mutual respect. Indeed, moral indignation should matter in principle to any person when it implicates the values of human dignity and respect along with the rights to life and security. Clarifying the moral basis of indignation is important, moreover, because it provides the foundation for confidently articulating one's grievances and acting appropriately in response. In the wake of 9/11, the United States and Britain, along with several allies, deployed military force in Afghanistan and, later, Iraq. They rounded up, interrogated, and detained numerous terrorist suspects for prolonged periods of time in addition to increasing intelligence efforts around the globe to thwart the danger posed by Muslim extremists. Those actions were authorized to defend against future terrorist action and to respond to the grievances incurred by the attacks. One question that faces us in the wake of 9/11 is whether those actions are morally permissible.

In this appendix I want to address part of this question by defending the idea that attacking al Qaeda and the Taliban in Afghanistan is justified.[2] On the argument I have developed throughout these pages, the attack on 9/11 was an act of grievous injustice against persons who did nothing to forfeit their entitlement to rights of life and security. It destroyed property, political and social infrastructure, and the bases for personal livelihood—crucially important features of a common life. The use of force in response to such an injustice can be justified if it satisfies certain conditions. I will take up that idea as it bears on the war against al Qaeda and the Taliban in Afghanistan, a conflict that has continued (at this writing) for eight years. In particular, I want to turn to just-war doctrine given that doctrine's importance in guiding public debate and individual reflection about the ethics of war, focusing on how, and on what terms, just-war doctrine would shape moral judgments about the war in Afghanistan.

Just-war doctrine enables us to say that the United States had a solid justification for resorting to armed force in response to the 9/11 attacks. That is not to say that the war has been militarily or politically successful in any meaningful sense. Nor does it allow us to say that everything that has been done in response to the grievance of 9/11 is morally justified. At a minimum, the doctrine enables to us say that the United States has an unambiguous just cause for resort to force. It also allow us to say that the United States, especially during the Bush administration, appears to have assumed that the strength of its cause allows U.S. forces to relax moral restrictions on their conduct of war. This is especially true regarding the treatment of prisoners. The effect of this assumption is to situate U.S. policy in Afghanistan along a "sliding scale," one that permits policy planners, strategists, and the military to trade off means for ends in order to increase their chances of success.[3]

The background idea is that having a just cause provides a state or alliance some latitude about war's means. Otherwise we prejudice war's outcome by expecting the party defending a just cause to fight in a way that might cause it to lose.[4] Such an approach assigns a priority to war's ends at the risk of weakening just-war doctrine's rigorous attention to the morality of war's means. One aim of this chapter is to bring that rigorous attention into focus and to spell out its implications for judgments about U.S. military action, and its "sliding scale" rationality, in the wake of 9/11.

In order to pursue this aim and its bearing on moral discourse about the war in Afghanistan, I need to make several preliminary comments about the pattern of moral reasoning, some background assumptions, and the criteria of just-war doctrine.

JUST-WAR DOCTRINE

Just-war doctrine consists of two rubrics that structure how we are to assess political decision-making and military action in times of conflict. The first rubric, the *jus ad bellum*, assigns states and their leaders the basis for going to war. In legal terminology, *ad bellum* criteria call attention to "crimes against peace" that are committed by those who instigate acts of unjust aggression and against whom hostilities are justified. The second rubric, the *jus in bello*, assigns soldiers the right to kill persons who pose immediate or potential threats to their lives and well-being in war, and it allows for the destruction of military and related facilities that contribute directly to a war-effort. *In bello* criteria limit the permissions provided by *ad bellum* criteria by restricting what may be done to combatants and noncombatants in the course of war. Such restrictions place a metaphorical shield around innocent persons who may find themselves tragically in the path of battle, and they identify rights of captured combatants to proper treatment and medical care. In international law, *in bello* criteria call attention to "crimes against humanity" that are committed by military leaders and soldiers in battle. Let us turn to each rubric, the *jus ad bellum* and the *jus in bello*, in order.

Ad bellum criteria, governing the decision about resort to military force, address the morality of war's ends. They focus moral attention on the context, aim, and necessity of going to war. The first three criteria (more on these later) are anchored to basic principles of right, while the remaining criteria call attention to practical and political factors that should be weighed when considering resort to war. There are seven *ad bellum* criteria, which I will outline here.

JUST CAUSE

Just cause allows for wars of self-defense, law enforcement in cases of aggression, and rescue in cases of internal oppression and human rights abuses. This criterion holds that war is occasioned by another group's gross violation of justice. I say "*gross* violation" to distinguish just causes for war from other grievances between nations. Just cause thus includes proportionate considerations of the gravity of whatever offense may prompt a grievance. Grievances must meet a certain threshold: the actual or imminent use of force or oppression that violates rights to life, security, and law.

This criterion requires us to look to the initial reasons for going to war. Moreover, it specifies in general terms the goals toward which war should be aimed. War should be directed toward defending a people, enforcing international law, or defending human rights. But those terms (or aims) are general. Additional criteria are needed to inform judgments about a state's proper response to an injury or offense. It is conceivable for a state to have a legitimate grievance but to resort to war in pursuit of other goals. A state that acts on behalf of such goals lacks a right intention, another criterion of the *jus ad bellum*. Moreover, a state may have a just cause but decide, all things considered, that war's prospective destruction is a disproportionate response to an injury, however serious that injury might be. Just cause needs to be supplemented by additional considerations in judgments about the goals and stakes of war.

That said, the criterion of just cause sets the terms for much of what we should consider when applying many of the remaining *ad bellum* criteria. For that reason it is correct to say that it is the most important *ad bellum* principle;[5] other *ad bellum* criteria are constrained by it. For example, war's purpose (or *intention*) must be ordered toward addressing the grievances that underlie a just cause. *Last resort* can be satisfied only if war is necessary to achieve a just cause. If war is to satisfy the criterion of *proportionality*, moreover, then the relevant good effects that are balanced against the bad effects must be confined to those established by a war's cause.[6] (War cannot be justified, for example, by saying that the good effects of reducing international oil prices or easing trade arrangements should be weighed against war's deleterious effects.) And the *competent authority* that publicly authorizes war must do so by identifying the injuries defined by just cause. In these ways just cause guides and constrains the work that several other *ad bellum* criteria perform.

Typically, the grievance on which just cause focuses is the crime of interstate aggression. In the wake of the carnage of two world wars, the United Nations sought to severely restrict the just cause of war to cases of defense against interstate aggression. Henry Shue captures the context well:

> Partly in shock and revulsion that the attrition strategy imposed upon combatants in the trenches of the First World War had been succeeded in only a few decades by the terror bombing, nuclear and non-nuclear, visited upon civilians in Asia and Europe in the Second World War, in both cases by the self-proclaimed defenders of civilization, many concluded at the time that, with the conduct of war appearing to be out of control, the better hope was to control the resort to war.[7]

Hence the U.N. Charter of 1945 clearly and firmly limits the justifiable use of force to national self-defense.[8] In contrast, legal warrants for intervention to stop internal oppression remain unclear. As Michael Ignatieff observes, "While the U.N. Charter calls on states to proclaim human rights, it also prohibits the use of force against other states and forbids internal interference. The human rights covenants that states have signed since 1945 have implied that state sovereignty is conditional on adequate human rights observance, yet this conditionality has never been made explicit in international law, except in the human rights instruments of the European continent."[9]

RIGHT INTENTION

This criterion looks prospectively, not retrospectively—toward the aims and goals of war. As I noted above, fighting in response to a gross infringement of justice is not sufficient for having a just war; one must also be fighting for an end that is conditioned by the grievance itself. More generally, war should be subordinate to and directed toward the goods of peace and justice. For that reason, we must place the use of military force within a broader framework of interpretation and assessment. A just war aims not merely at success or victory but toward the re-establishment of peace and justice.

Just-war doctrine is thus distinct from other frameworks according to which war is often understood. We might view war as a catalyst for social change, as a symptom of native human aggression, as a form of divine punishment, as a form of economic and colonial expansion, or as an attempt to establish a balance of power in the international system. All of these are descriptive or explanatory accounts of war and its functions.[10] Just war, by contrast, assumes a normative framework according to which political bodies have the right to remedy the breakdown of justice and peace through recourse to lethal force. Such recourse is morally justified insofar as it aims to restore the *status quo ante bellum* and strengthen the conditions of peace in order to reduce future occasions of war as a means of settling disputes. The criterion of right intention thus implies that whatever political, economic, or social factors might explain the outbreak of war, its resolution must aim toward the moral goods of justice and peace.

COMPETENT AUTHORITY

Just war doctrine is a morality of political responsibility and decision-making. It is not a doctrine for private armies, gang wars, or the like. We assume that in the absence of a global authority it falls to established political rulers to adjudicate disputes about matters of rights and legality. Lacking an international body to settle differences impartially, states must take it upon themselves to defend against aggression, enforce international law, and protect human rights.

No doubt this is an imperfect arrangement given states' uneven commitment to justice within and outside their own borders. But that imperfect arrangement is moderated by the fact that the criterion of competent authority requires war to be a public matter. War must be publicly declared and marshaled by public officials who are responsible for representing a bona fide political community, sovereign state, or alliance of states and who must account for their actions before their own legislative bodies if not the court of world opinion.

Seen in this way, a just war must meet the criterion of what Rawls calls the condition of "publicity." The point of this condition, Rawls notes, is to enable parties to "evaluate conceptions of justice as publicly acknowledged and fully effective moral constitutions of social life."[11] Although Rawls makes these remarks in the context of crafting fair constraints on the concept of right in his construction of principles of social justice, the point intuitively commends itself as a condition for thinking about the ethics of war and international justice. As a doctrine of political responsibility—and as a constraint on the power of public officials—just-war doctrine constitutes a public charter, a moral constitution of sorts, to which those officials may be held accountable before the court of global opinion and to which they must address themselves when declaring war and marshaling a defense.

LAST RESORT

According to this criterion, effective means of settling disputes short of war must be tried before resort to force is justified. Of course, nonmilitary alternatives to war must be within reasonable reach of public officials charged with representing their communities and resolving differences with others. War cannot be entered rashly or in haste but in response to an actual or imminent danger to collective security, legal order, or human rights.

This criterion does not necessarily rule out the first use of military force, although it greatly restricts such use. By waiting to be attacked, a state may irreparably compromise its ability to uphold justice and defend its citizens. Preemptive uses of force in self-defense against a real and imminent threat can be justified according to just-war doctrine.[12] Otherwise states would be left at a great disadvantage against belligerent opponents who plan to attack, rendering their citizens vulnerable to the aggressive plans of their enemies. The right of security and the principle of proportionality, about which I will say more soon, justify the use of force in some cases of anticipatory self-defense.

PROPORTIONALITY

Deriving from the Latin *pro portione*—"according to each part"— proportionality means balance, symmetry, ratio, or corresponding in magnitude or degree. In the ethics of war, proportionality asks us to consider the means and ends of war—the risks and sacrifices that war asks us (and others) to assume in the service of its cause. Proportionality reminds us that war's ravages tend to metastasize insofar as adopting some means can lead to ends that may not be intended. With that fact in mind, we often say that not all threats or injustices should be countered with the use of armed force; the political and moral stakes of going to war must be carefully weighed. When we make that decision we are intuitively making a judgment about a war's potential for disproportionate harm.

Yet the principle of proportionality involves an ambiguity that has been overlooked in just-war theorizing. Proportionality requires (a) that we produce the best overall balance of benefits to risks or (b) that we use the most efficient way of achieving a goal. Equally important, this ambiguity haunts proportionality in either *ad bellum* or *in bello* terms—regarding the proportional recourse to war and the proportional conduct in war. The difference between these views of proportionality may seem overly subtle, but each view leads to a different kind of moral analysis.

Interpreters of just-war doctrine often take Thomas Aquinas's position about the ethics of killing as their point of departure for thinking about proportionality in war. But Aquinas's position deploys only the second account of proportionality. Arguing that killing in self-defense can be justified, Aquinas states:

> A single act may have two effects, of which one alone is intended, while the other is incidental to that intention. But the way a moral act is to be classified depends on what is intended, not on what goes beyond such an intention, since this is merely incidental thereto. . . . In light of this distinction we can see that an act of self-defense may have two effects: the saving of one's own life, and the killing of the attacker. Now such an act of self-defense is not illegitimate just because the agent intends to save his own life, because it is natural for anything to want to preserve itself in being as far as it can. An act that is properly motivated may, nevertheless, become vitiated if it is not proportionate to the end intended. And this is why somebody who uses more violence than is necessary to defend himself will be doing something wrong . . . according to the law it is legitimate to answer force with force provided it goes no further than due defense requires.[13]

On this view, an action's means must not exceed what is necessary for effective self-defense—what "due defense requires." Brian V. Johnstone rightly calls this the "act/end" account of proportionality.[14] The point is to focus on the relationship between means and ends and to constrain the harmful features of the means by restricting harm to what is necessary to produce the end. Violence that exceeds the minimal requirement for effective self-defense is disproportionate and therefore wrong. If I stab an attacker when it is obvious that I may effectively resist him with a push, then my action is disproportionate, even if the values at stake—his life and mine—are commensurate. The "act/end" account of proportion restricts harm according to the criterion of minimally necessary effectiveness. Since this view seeks to limit the harmful means with an eye to efficiency, let us call it the "economic" account of proportionality.

The other account of proportionality asks us to weigh the foreseen risks and benefits on the premise that the latter should outweigh the former to produce a justified action. Whether this assessment turns on qualitative or quantitative terms is less important than the fact that it focuses exclusively on outcomes. It does not focus on the relationship between means and ends according to the criterion of minimally necessary effectiveness. Johnstone calls this view the "effect/effect" account of proportionality because it attends exclusively to an act's consequences.[15] Here the emphasis is on the concept of balance: for an action to be justified, the beneficial effects must compensate for or outweigh the evil effects. Let us call this the "compensatory" account of proportionality.

These two ways of understanding proportionality are relevant to *ad bellum* considerations in the following way. According to the economic account, a war is disproportionate if less destructive but effective measures are available to resolve a dispute. War can be an inefficient use of public resources to achieve an end. According to the compensatory account, in contrast, a war is disproportionate if the risks outweigh the benefits. It does not ask us to consider whether we are more or less efficient in securing those benefits.

Each of these accounts informs proportionality as a criterion in the *jus ad bellum* and the *jus in bello,* but each does so in different ways. The compensatory account shapes *ad bellum* deliberations in political or macro-level decision-making. Political leaders are responsible for determining whether, on balance, the stakes in war outweigh the risks of taking it on. They are to think in comprehensive, not tactical, terms about those whose lives and welfare will likely suffer as a result of their decision. *Ad bellum* considerations of proportionality thus require deliberations of this sort: Is the war worth it, morally speaking, given the effects it likely poses to all involved? Here political leadership is thinking in compensatory terms. Yet it is also true that political leaders must consider matters of efficiency and risk—the relation of means and ends—at a comprehensive level. They must consider how many troops to deploy in order to accomplish a mission, and how to deploy them given their specialties and training. Strategic debates about how to balance the deployment of air and ground troops, for example, are shaped by such economic renditions of proportional judgment.

In bello considerations of proportionality focus not on political leaders but on military leaders and soldiers. At one level, they have us consider how to balance risks to soldiers and civilians in light of specific military goals in the course of war. The overriding question in such deliberations is whether the putative benefits of accomplishing a military mission compensate for the foreseeable risks imposed to noncombatants as well as one's own combatants. Yet here, too, it is necessary to consider matters of efficiency and risk—about how to use force economically. Obvious self-regarding considerations—concerns about wastefulness or needless risk-taking, for example—help shape economic rationality. Complicating the economic rendition of *in bello* proportionality, however, is the idea that military operations may be required to trade off some considerations of efficiency in order to reduce risks to noncombatants. I will return to these ideas below.

REASONABLE HOPE FOR SUCCESS

Another of just-war doctrine's practical considerations, this criterion holds that parties may not enter war against obviously insuperable odds or make decisions premised on irrational or futile recourse to force. This practical consideration is not without a moral core. Entering into a suicidal war violates a basic duty to the self or imposes risks on soldiers that require them to violate that duty. On the other hand, taking on enormous odds for symbolic reasons, however unlikely a successful military outcome, is not entirely ruled out by this criterion. Understood within a moral framework, success in war should not be measured in terms of military victory alone.

RELATIVE JUSTICE

This criterion invites us to think self-reflexively about moral claims during times of war, reminding us of the dangers of moral triumphalism and self-righteousness along with the moral complexities involved in defending a just cause. With Augustine as its progenitor, just-war doctrine resists a Manichaean cosmology, according to which war is conceived as a battle between powers of light and darkness—between saints and demons.[16]

This idea cuts in more than one direction. Against those who insist on moral purity as a condition for going to war, relative justice reminds us that states bear the burden of their political histories and have no mechanism for completely redeeming themselves of their past. Given the facts of human fallibility and vice, the historical dimensions of political community, and the multifaceted nature of political decision-making, moral purity is impossible. States that claim the mantle of self-righteousness deceive themselves. Against those who insist that all states are corrupt and have no basis for invoking moral claims as a basis for entering war, relative justice reminds us that there can be relative differences between imperfect regimes, just as there are relative differences between imperfect persons.

Against both of these extremes, the criterion of relative justice seeks a middle way. On the one hand, it eschews expectations of innocence in international politics. States are morally imperfect institutions given their many actors and complex political legacies. Relative justice also claims that to deny states with imperfect histories the idea of being unjustly treated would be to empty politics of any moral distinctions, since no state can claim moral perfection. It thereby prevents present and future generations from being fated by or shackled to the moral and political legacies of their past.

In bello criteria focus on the morality of war-fighting and remind us that just-war doctrine is an ethic of limited war, depending as it does on the ideas of individual rights, responsibilities, and protections. Just-war doctrine says that those who defend a just cause may not do certain things to prosecute a war more efficiently, that justice is prior to necessity. The central idea is that the justification for entering war does not extend to all possible methods of war: the ends do not justify the means. There are two *in bello* criteria.

DISCRIMINATION

According to this principle, soldiers and military planners must confine their aims to destroying legitimate targets. Typically, we understand this requirement to mean that the intentional killing of noncombatants is wrong. Known as the principle of *noncombatant immunity*, this criterion states that civilians have a right not to have war directly waged upon them regardless of their political affiliation, that noncombatants are illegitimate targets. Noncombatants, as nonparticipants in war, have done nothing to forfeit their claim to be left alone—a claim that falls to them as free and equal persons, endowed with dignity and deserving of respect. The intentional killing of noncombatants thus counts as murder, a violation of their rights to life and security. Instrumentalizing and deliberately terrorizing noncombatants is likewise prohibited as a violation of the right of security. The principle of discrimination is firmly embedded in the 1977 Geneva Protocol I, which states: "The civilian population as such, as well as individual civilians, shall not be the object of attack. Acts or threats of violence the primary purpose of which is to spread terror among the civilian population are prohibited."[17]

PROPORTIONALITY

Concerns about the proportional conduct of war are matters for military decisions by officers and their subordinates; they are not of the comprehensive sort about which political leaders are responsible. Yet *in bello* reasoning, like *ad bellum* reasoning, requires us to think about the ratio of disvalues to values in the pursuit of an end. As it informs moral deliberations in the tactics of war, *in bello* proportionality requires soldiers and military planners to weigh foreseeable risks against putative benefits. As Walzer notes, we ask whether "the good effect is sufficiently good to compensate for allowing the evil effect" as one condition for permitting acts in war.[18] In addition to such compensatory estimations, there is the question of means in relation to ends. *In bello* proportionality demands that we assess such matters in light of economic concerns. The point seems intuitively obvious; it is one we examined in my discussion of Islamic views of *in bello* restrictions in chapter 2. Military planners and soldiers have a clear interest in conserving their resources, and that interest provides a reason for condemning profligate killing and destruction of property and infrastructure.

Yet, as I mentioned earlier, the economic rendition of proportionality in Western just-war doctrine is complicated by the special status of noncombatants as immune from direct attack. Here we see one place where considerations of justice and efficiency can conflict in the ethics of war. More precisely, we see an instance in which the principle of discrimination places pressure on the economic rendition of proportionality in *in bello* reasoning. The core idea is that soldiers should *not intend* civilian casualties out of respect for noncombatants as persons. On some accounts of just-war doctrine, moreover, the principle of discrimination requires military planners and soldiers actively to reduce dangers to noncombatants, within the limits of self-protection. Walzer describes this as the right civilians have that "due care" be taken by soldiers who impose risks on them.[19] The claim is that soldiers should do more than *not intend* civilian casualties; they should also, as a "second intention," actively *intend not* to commit civilian casualties, even at some risk to themselves. Something like this idea has become enshrined in international law. According to the 1977 Geneva Protocol I, "constant care" must be taken in war to "refrain from deciding to launch any attack which may be expected to cause incidental loss of civilian life, injury to civilians, damage to civilian objects, or a combination thereof, which would be excessive in relation to the concrete and direct military advantage anticipated."[20]

In addition to focusing on the morality of imposing risks to noncombatants, *in bello* criteria include rules about the proper treatment of combatants. This fact is better known to international lawyers than to many just-war theorists, given the latter's penchant for concentrating on the rights of civilians along with the difficult cases that typically arise in the conduct of war. But the Geneva Conventions of 1949 and subsequent protocols amending those conventions provide guarantees to prisoner combatants that prohibit acts and threats of torture, corporal punishment, mutilation, enforced prostitution, and "outrages upon personal dignity."[21] One question facing the Bush and Obama administrations is whether they have acted within the framework of humanitarian law in their treatment of the hundreds of detainees at Guantanamo Bay and elsewhere. I will return to this issue before concluding.

When we consider 9/11 in light of just-war doctrine, immediately we meet a stumbling block. The relevance of the doctrine to 9/11 is unclear given that wars typically occur between sovereign states and no state launched an attack against the United States on 9/11. That fact suggests that the language of "just cause" and "war" fails to describe what ought to shape a response to that attack or to attacks from nonstate actors more generally. Political and moral discourse that brings together concepts of grievance, war, surrender, and resolution are typically premised on holding a state liable for its actions and having a state (or its political leaders) with whom to negotiate a settlement, ensure a cease-fire, and the like. It might seem more appropriate to describe 9/11 as a criminal act and to conceive of the proper response as a police action—to round up criminals and bring them to justice in a court of law. These facts suggest that the term *war* might be only metaphorically rather than literally applicable to what occurred.[22] As a practical matter, viewing the attacks of 9/11 in that way would mean that U.S. authorities should classify those who are captured as criminals rather than as prisoners of war, and to deny those against whom force is used the rights and protections that surround soldiers in traditional conflicts.

Put differently, one question raised by 9/11 is whether having a just cause depends on having suffered interstate aggression. According to just-war doctrine, the answer is no. A sovereign state may have a just cause for war in response to aggression from nonstate actors. In the previous appendix, I defended a point that is concretely at stake here: acts of aggression violate individuals' rights to life and security, which a state has the moral right to defend with the use of force. We do well to remember, moreover, that just-war doctrine predates the rise of the modern nation-state and rests on ideas that are not tied to the international state system. As Shue notes, "The doctrine of just war is centuries older than the doctrine of state sovereignty."[23] Basic to the idea of having a just cause is the permission to repel violence to defend the common life of a people in response to a serious grievance. In other words, the core moral idea is that individuals within a state can suffer unjust aggression from without, not that a state must be a victim of another state's aggression.

This conceptual anomaly raises the more basic question of what constitutes a war—about how to define *war* as a social practice. Focusing on fighting that occurs in battle, Barrie Paskins and Michael Dockrill enumerate four features of war:

1. The fighting is likely to be to the death, not merely to subdue the enemy. War may spare some who are injured, but the main goal is to produce fatalities among the opposition.
2. The fighting typically occurs between groups organized for such fighting, or organized groups and their organized or disorganized opponents. Individual combat occurs in war, but such combat happens within the wider orbit of conflict between armies, or between organized forces and other forces or civilian populations.
3. The fighting employs weapons that are designed for the purpose of killing and injuring.
4. The fighting typically proceeds from quarrels about issues that are fundamental to peoples' outlook toward their social, political, religious, and economic life.[24]

The attacks of 9/11 clearly meet Paskins and Dockrill's first, second, and fourth characteristics of war; they arguably meet the third as well. Muslim terrorists studied and trained in highly organized and well-disciplined groups before carrying out the attacks, and their aim was to kill a large number of persons whom they considered sinners and infidels. While the attacks did not involve conventional military weapons, such as bombers or machine guns, they did deploy weapons such as sharp instruments to highjack airplanes and turn those planes into weapons of devastating destruction. Using Paskins and Dockrill's criteria, we can say without hesitation that the attacks were an act of war.

Still, settling this conceptual matter leaves one important question unanswered: against whom may the U.S. direct its attack in response to 9/11? Assuming that an act of war was carried out on 9/11, who, specifically, is liable for the atrocity?

In response to this question, President Bush stated soon after the attacks, "From this day forward, any nation that continues to harbor or support terrorism will be regarded by the United States as a hostile regime."[25] According to that view, any nation that provides safe haven to terrorists, even if it does not authorize their conduct or fails to prevent their conduct, is liable to attack by the United States in self-defense. On the day when the United States launched attacks on Afghanistan, the U.S. representative to the United Nations sent a letter stating that the United States was asserting its right of self-defense because of "the decision of the Taliban regime to allow the parts of Afghanistan that it controls to be used by [al Qaeda] as a base of operation."[26] The United States justified its actions on the premise that it had a right to act in self-defense against a state that had been harboring terrorists.

One question is whether international law supports the "harboring theory" of the United States. Reviewing international legal doctrine and decisions by the International Court of Justice (ICJ), the International Criminal Tribunal for the Former Yugoslavia (ICTY), and the U.N. Charter, Steven R. Ratner observes that the legal grounds for holding Afghanistan liable for the attacks of 9/11 are not entirely obvious.[27] Ratner arrives at this conclusion in light of precedents provided by other cases in international law. In *Nicaragua v. United States*, the ICJ held that the acts of the Nicaraguan contras could not be imputed to the United States because no U.S officials had issued specific instructions to the contras. In *Prosecutor v. Tadic*, the ICTY held that acts of a Bosnian soldier accused of war crimes could be imputed to Serbia because Serbia had exercised "overall control" over him. The International Law Commission put forth its view of law based on a review of state practice in a draft on the responsibility of states for the wrongful acts of 2001, indicating that a state is responsible "if the person or group of persons is in fact acting on the instructions of, or under the direction or control of, that State in carrying out the conduct"; "if the person or group of persons is in fact exercising elements of the governmental authority in the absence or default of the official authorities;" and "if and to the extent that the State acknowledges and adopts the conduct in question as its own." None of these legal dicta supports the harboring theory alone; they presume a higher bar for determining a state's liability. Ratner concludes: "These apparently authoritative pronouncements suggest that normally states would not hold another state responsible per se for the actions of nonstate actors on its territory absent proof of a connection closer than harboring, and certainly not to justify the use of force against that state in self-defense."[28]

In the case of Afghanistan, considerable evidence indicates that Afghan officials, including the Taliban, worked with impunity to aid bin Laden and his lieutenants. For that reason, assigning charges of complicity and liability are warranted. The Taliban, a militant Muslim group of students (*taliban*), most of whom were schooled in madrassas, or Muslim schools, assumed control of Afghanistan in 1996. Driven by a desire to rid Afghani society of Western influences that they believe corrupt Islam, the Taliban secured power after a brutal two-year civil war and closed the country to non-Muslim religious, political, and cultural influences. After removing the *mujahideen* (the anti-Soviet resistance fighters) from power, the Taliban's chief opponent was the Northern Alliance, against whom they struggled to control the marketing and transport of drugs and commercial goods.

Within twenty-four hours of taking Kabul, the Taliban imposed the strictest system of Islam in the world. All women were banned from work; girls' schools were closed, affecting more than seventy thousand female students; and a strict dress code of head-to-toe coverings (known as *chadri* or *burqa*) for women was imposed. Under the watch of the newly established Department of the Promotion of Virtue and Prevention of Vice, citizens' conduct was strictly monitored. Television, movies, music, and games including soccer, chess, and kite-flying were banned. Non-Muslim images, including giant statutes of the Buddha, were defaced or destroyed. Punishment for alleged wrongdoing was swift and severe. Thieves had their hands and feet amputated, prostitutes were summarily shot in the back of the head, adulterers were stoned to death, and homosexuals were crushed under a wall of stone. None of those who were punished were tried in court, and many punishments took place before public gatherings that included children.[29]

Bin Laden had been in Afghanistan from 1989 to 1991, where he founded al Qaeda before he left for the Sudan. After the Taliban assumed control of Afghanistan in 1996, bin Laden returned to Afghanistan, where he enjoyed protection in exchange for his financial and military support. There he developed a dozen terrorist camps, at least four of which trained terrorists who boarded the planes of 9/11. Mullah Omar headed the Taliban and enjoyed a close relationship with bin Laden. Forces under bin Laden's control fought alongside the Taliban in Afghanistan's war against the Northern Alliance and rival factions in the south. Al Qaeda and the Taliban collaborated in the Afghan drug trade and stockpiled large stores of opium in order to finance their activities.

My point here is that sufficient data exist to establish a cooperative link between the Taliban and al Qaeda and to hold Afghanistan liable for the actions that bin Laden's terrorists carried out. The United States had an unambiguous *just cause* to wage war in Afghanistan against Taliban officials and soldiers along with al Qaeda terrorists.

Indeed, numerous governments and political organizations expressed support for the United States' cause. The day after the attacks, the U.N. Security Council affirmed "the inherent right of individual or collective self-defense in accordance with the [U.N.] Charter."[30] That same day, NATO's policymaking organ, the North American Council, invoked the "commitment to collective self-defense," and stated that "if it is determined that this attack was directed from abroad against the United States, it shall be regarded as an action covered by Article 5 of the Washington Treaty [1949]," which makes an attack against one NATO member an attack against all.[31] On September 21, the Organization of American States adopted a more expansive resolution, affirming "the inherent right of individual and collective self-defense in accordance with [OAS and U.N.] Charters," and added that "those responsible for aiding, supporting, or harboring the perpetrators ... [of the September 11] attacks are equally complicit in these acts."[32] These organizations stated in no ambiguous terms that the United States had a just cause to go to war against the Taliban and al Qaeda in Afghanistan.

Despite the clarity that surrounds this point, complications nonetheless exist. The just cause on behalf of which the United States may attack involves two separate conflicts. As George H. Aldrich writes,

> The first, the conflict with Al Qaeda, is not limited to the territory of Afghanistan. Al Qaeda is evidently a clandestine organization consisting of elements in many countries and apparently composed of people of various nationalities. . . . Al Qaeda does not in any respect resemble a state, is not subject to international law, and lacks international legal personality. It is not a party to the Geneva Conventions, and it could not be a party to them or to any international agreement. Its methods brand it as a criminal organization under national laws and as an international outlaw.[33]

The war against the Taliban, in contrast, is a separate attack "rendered necessary because the Taliban, as the effective government of Afghanistan, refused all requests to expel Al Qaeda and instead gave it sanctuary."[34] Aldrich adds: "While the United States . . . refused to extend diplomatic recognition to the Taliban, both Afghanistan and the United States are parties to the Geneva Conventions of 1949, and the armed attacks by the United States and other nations against the armed forces of the Taliban in Afghanistan clearly constitute an international armed conflict to which those Conventions, as well as customary international humanitarian law, apply."[35]

In launching this twofold attack, the president and Congress acted as representatives of American citizens to plan and carry out a response to terrorist aggression. They are assigned those responsibilities by the Constitution and, according to the framework of just-war doctrine, clearly constitute *competent authority* to act on the United States' behalf. On September 14, Congress gave President Bush sweeping authority to use force against any nation, organization, or person that he believed planned or assisted in the attacks. Given that the president was assigned this authority, what did political justice require or permit him to do?

Just-war doctrine requires political authorities to pursue justice in international conflict according to *right intention*. That criterion requires military action to aim at producing peace and justice. These of course are broad goals that invite specification. That fact requires us to ask: What should have been the special aims of politically orchestrated coercion and military force in response to the events of 9/11? In fact, there are four aims that guide United States policy. Those aims are:

- apprehending Osama bin Laden and his confederates, the chief suspects behind the 9/11 attacks;
- destroying bin Laden's terrorist bases in Afghanistan and weakening his material base of support;
- waging a "war on terrorism" more broadly;
- defeating the Taliban and helping to produce a new government and strengthened political institutions in Afghanistan.

Let's consider these aims in turn.

First, military forces rightly set out to capture those who planned and helped execute the terrorist bombings with the aim of bringing them to an international tribunal for prosecution under rules of war and treaties, such as that established in Nuremberg after the Second World War. Efforts at capture required on-the-ground elite forces and covert operations to apprehend those whom U.S. officials had probable cause to suspect as wrongdoers. As Aldrich notes, moreover, members of al Qaeda are subject to trial and punishment as criminal outlaws, not war criminals attached to a recognized political regime.[36]

Second, political action may justifiably be orchestrated to help eradicate global terrorism. Strategy here differs from the use of military force to eliminate global terrorism, about which I will say more soon. Here I want to address nonmilitary methods. Freezing the assets of individuals and companies that provide commercial and other support for terrorism, prohibiting uncooperative banks from doing business in the United States, and putting pressure on banks to disclose how they provide cover for the financial operations of terrorist groups and their supporters, is right and proper.[37]

If banks, companies, charities, or wealthy individuals are complicit with terrorism, then attempts should be made to limit their dealings with the financial world. Such efforts, organized with the cooperation of different nations, help to strengthen the world's collective stand against terrorist activity.

Drying up terrorism's financial resources is insufficient, however, because such terror also relies on weapons and impressionable young people who are manipulated into dying (and killing) for ignominious causes. Hence, military action that aims to destroy terrorist base camps and centers of operation, and to provide cover for ground forces that are deployed to find terrorists and destroy their network of operations in Afghanistan, is justified. That is not to say that *every* possible use of military force in Afghanistan is justified. Striking back against terrorism on its own terms is hypocritical, returning one injustice for another—fighting terrorism by imitating it. The United States and its allies undermine moral integrity and political credibility when they ignore principles they claim to defend. Air and ground forces are always required to focus their aims narrowly, guided by just-war doctrine's *in bello* requirements of discrimination and proportionality. Those criteria require military operations to target military sites and take special precautions to limit collateral damage to civilians and the conditions of everyday life in civil society.

As I noted earlier, Washington had grounds to hold the Taliban liable not only for harboring but for actively cooperating with al Qaeda. Given that fact, the attacks on Afghanistan are justified responses to prior hostilities insofar as those attacks seek to avoid civilian populations and seek to minimize collateral damage to civilian life. Such are *proportionate* acts that tell terrorists and their political supporters in Afghanistan that they will not go unpunished for their actions. Insofar as the benefits outweigh the risks, such acts are proportionate in a compensatory sense.

Potentially related to self-defense in the wake of 9/11 is the third goal I listed above, namely, fighting terrorism where it is nurtured beyond Afghanistan. In his address to the world after 9/11, President Bush stated: "Our war on terror begins with al Qaeda, but it does not end there. It will not end until every terrorist group of global reach has been found, stopped and defeated."[38]

Global terrorism poses a special challenge to just-war doctrine, or policy guided by it, because terrorism by nonstate actors lacks institutional mechanisms by which to negotiate a resolution. This fact likely makes terrorism difficult to assimilate into conventional political ethics and public policy. Right intention requires leaders to seek peace and justice. Clearly such aims rely on institutional arrangements that mediate interactions between leaders during disputes. Nonstate terrorists typically have no such arrangements, and that fact frustrates efforts to bring their disputes to some kind of resolution. Lacking a political infrastructure, they invite a ceaseless war against them, a politics with no other means but violence.

A war against terrorism is thus a dangerous position to embrace. It is not obviously warranted on just-war grounds, for it commits U.S. personnel and resources to conflicts across the globe. Within three months after initiating air strikes over Afghanistan, the U.S. began expanding its military operations into Southeast Asia on the pretext of eradicating global terrorism. In January 2002, 650 U.S. soldiers and "advisors" arrived in the Philippines on a mission to help oust the separatist Muslim group Abu Sayyaf from its main stronghold, Basilan Island. Abu Sayyaf appears to be loosely affiliated with bin Laden and other al Qaeda figures. Although U.S. personnel came at the invitation of Philippine government, it is unclear how such a large deployment is justified. Abu Sayyaf kidnapped an American missionary couple, but that hardly strengthens the case for deploying American troops and joining the effort to expunge terrorism from the Philippines.[39] The idea of fighting terrorism across the globe conflates one cause with another and pays little heed to facts around which particular grievances form.

The problems of a "war on terrorism" become more acute when we remember that terrorist organizations, al Qaeda and others, exist across the Middle East, the Saudi Peninsula, Central Asia, South Asia, and Southeast Asia. Stanley Hoffmann writes:

Some [terrorists] have limited missions and do not see the U.S. as their principal enemy. In Sri Lanka or Northern Ireland, in Corsica or Chechnya, in Palestine or in the Basque province, most terrorists see themselves, convincingly or not, as "freedom fighters."

It is hard to imagine U.S. forces acting directly against them. It is the groups that have declared war on America, or on the entire Judeo-Christian world, that the U.S. must respond to.[40]

Many terrorist groups have no interest in planning attacks against the United States or in endangering its interests. Yet the National Security Strategy of the United States (2002, 2006) identifies a wide array of terrorist threats against which the United States is developing military and political policy.[41] Of the forty-five entries on the U.S. State Department's list of foreign terrorist organizations, only six (all of them linked to al Qaeda) have ever attacked the United States. Many of the remaining groups, such as the Shining Path, the Real IRA, or the Liberation Tigers of Tamil Eelam, are engaged in local conflicts that have little if anything to do with the United States.[42] President Bush overstepped proper boundaries in using the just cause against al Qaeda to declare war against a broader swath of admittedly pernicious actors. No such mandate is justified by the cause and case of 9/11, for many terrorist organizations pose no threat to the United States or its interests. As I noted earlier, acts carried out in defense of a just cause must be constrained by the particulars of the grievance.

The widespread and diverse nature of global terrorism means that embarking a war on terrorism poses the danger of using a high level of military force, contrary to the *ad bellum* principle of proportionality. That criterion requires us to consider the level of risk appropriate to the moral stakes involved in war. Proportionality thus provides shorthand for those citizens and policy makers who worry about the escalation of war. In more general terms, proportionality is a principle that invites nations to weigh duties to themselves. It enables them to ask (among other things) what kinds of sacrifices they can demand of themselves in light of a particular war's ends.

One of the problems to which proportionality calls our attention is public officials' attempt to define the ends of war in order to permissibly broaden a military's means. By using the language of a war on terrorism, the U.S. administration opened the door to an improperly expansive set of American initiatives. A war on terrorism imposes grave risks on military service personnel and the citizens of Central Asia. It also means high costs to U.S. taxpayers with no obvious moral or other benefit to the United States.

The fourth and final aim of military action in immediate response to 9/11 was to foment civil war with the aim of toppling the regime in Afghanistan and helping to install a democratic government there. This feature of the conflict moves U.S. policy toward the aims of *regime change*, which is different from self-defense. Toward the end of producing such change, allied forces waged a proxy war that assimilated itself to the Northern Alliance's fight against the Taliban, a policy that carried many dangers. It was never clear that the Northern Alliance would be any less despotic or ruthless than its predecessors. A month after the war began, reports indicated that members of the Northern Alliance were killing Taliban prisoners of war in cold blood, raising questions about whether soldiers in the alliance would be easy to control should they rout the Taliban and take Kabul.[43] Subsequent reports allege that the Bush administration worked hard to discourage an investigation into allegations that General Abdul Rashid Dostum, a Northern Alliance warlord on the CIA's payroll during the early months of the war, authorized the killings of up to 1,500 Taliban prisoners of war.[44]

Nor was it clear that any new group of rulers would shift the country's economic priorities. Much of the past rivalry between the Northern Alliance and the Taliban focused on acquiring and exporting opium for heroin production. The Northern Alliance seemed no more committed than the Taliban to ending Afghanistan's reliance on poppy farming, which underwent a rapid resurgence after a brief ban imposed by Mullah Omar. Afghanistan feeds much of Europe's drug habit, and has expanded its market into Russia, Pakistan, Iran, and Central Asia. In 2000, opium production in Afghanistan surged to 4042 tons, amounting for 70 percent of the opium produced in the world.[45] After a brief decline in growth resulting from Omar's ban, poppy production quickly resumed. Cheap, relatively easy to grow, and extremely lucrative, poppy farming has clear market incentives. In 2005, more than two million Afghan farmers were growing poppy as their primary cash crop.[46] In 2006, opium production was at 6,100 tons; it rose to

8,200 tons the following year, when Afghanistan produced 93 percent of the world's opium. The revenue from trafficking in opium contributed to approximately half of the country's gross national product in 2006.[47] Seeking a transition to a new government, even a democratic one, is gnarled by enormous economic challenges.

The Bush administration did not adequately address all the dimensions of right intention, for the endgame of their war against al Qaeda and the Taliban was not even remotely apparent when the war began. A robust view of right intention asks policy makers to aim for a resolution that builds on peace and justice, not one that merely ends further threats of immediate aggression. Stated differently, a robust rendition of right intention involves political as well as military dimensions of war, especially the significance of political decisions made in the aftermath of war. Such an understanding of right intention requires us to ask, What political arrangements will emerge in the wake of war, and to what extent can such arrangements mark an improvement for justice and peace? Public officials in the United States—especially during the Bush administration—said little to address that question.[48]

One concern in the ethics of war is whether nations act precipitously when they anticipate or respond to aggression with military force. Nations that appear eager to enter war seem to care less about fairness than about advancing their interests. Hence one component of just-war doctrine is the criterion of *last resort*. Summarizing that idea, editors of the Catholic newsweekly *America* write: "The just war theory emphasizes that waging war is a last resort, not a first option. Diplomatic efforts are to be preferred, not only because they are less violent, but also because, in the long run, only with the cooperation of other nations will we make the world safe from terrorism."[49] When the United States began launching air strikes against Afghanistan on October 7, 2001, did political and military leaders act in undue haste? Lying behind the notion of last resort is the idea of necessity and an attitude of reluctance. Those who think that war is necessary believe that nothing short of military force can serve the ends of capturing bin Laden and destroying his network of terrorist operations along with the support provided by the Taliban. Are they correct?

The answer is clearly yes. Consider the following facts about bin Laden and his terrorist network.

In 1989 bin Laden left his country of Saudi Arabia, wealthy, disaffected, and aggrieved about U.S. presence in and around the Arabian Peninsula. He first traveled to Afghanistan where he founded al Qaeda. From 1989 to 1991 he was based in Afghanistan and Pakistan before he moved to Sudan until 1996. Bin Laden's network developed links to other terrorist organizations, including the Egyptian Islamic Jihad and other jihadi groups in Sudan, Yemen, Somalia, Pakistan, and India. As I noted in previous chapters, he has regularly disseminated statements calling for all Muslims to kill Christians, Americans, and Jews.

During the 1990s, bin Laden and al Qaeda orchestrated a series of attacks against the United States. Bin Laden has claimed credit for an attack that killed eighteen U.S. soldiers in Somalia in 1993, and for the attacks on the U.S. Embassies in Kenya and Tanzania in 1998, which killed 224 and injured nearly five thousand. He has been linked to the attack on the U.S.S. Cole in 2000, which killed seventeen crew members and injured forty others. Al Qaeda trained Ahmed Ressam, who was stopped in December 1999 at the U.S.-Canada border while carrying numerous explosives on his way to Los Angeles, where he was planning to set off a large bomb at the Los Angeles International Airport on New Year's Day.

Considerable evidence links bin Laden and his terrorist network to the airline hijackings and attacks on the Pentagon and the World Trade Center on 9/11. Three of the hijackers have been identified as associates of al Qaeda, and one of those played a key role in the East African embassy attacks. No other organization had both the motivation and the ability to carry out the attacks of 9/11. Those attacks replicate the pattern that occurred in 1993, 1998, and 2000. They all involved meticulous, long-term planning, simultaneous attacks, a desire to inflict massive casualties, and the use of suicide bombers.

In a message sent via Pakistani authorities to Afghanistan on September 2001, President Bush demanded that the Taliban turn over bin Laden to U.S. authorities or face military action.[50] Soon after Bush's ultimatum, Prime Minister Tony Blair presented evidence that linked bin Laden and al Qaeda to the 9/11 attacks.[51] In early October, the United States and the United Kingdom began a series of air assaults over Afghanistan. Given the pattern of attacks against the United States by bin Laden and his conspirators, the criterion of last resort was clearly met.

Yet if the timing of the U.S. response was sound, another moral and practical question must be considered. Was it wise to enter into war in the inhospitable environment of Afghanistan? Was—or is—there a *reasonable hope for success*?

President Bush said little on this point that was encouraging. In an address to the nation soon after 9/11, the president indicated that the war against bin Laden, his associates, and the Taliban would be long and unconventional. Some successes, he added, would not be revealed to the public. Recent history is instructive: the Soviets fought Afghanistan for a decade with no success. Given the challenges of establishing a stable government in Afghanistan, moreover, it is unclear whether success in achieving a peaceful resolution to the problems in the region is possible. How one measures "success" is a function of the ends that are sought, none of which President Bush made clear in his public speeches.

But even a scaled-down account of "success" leaves much to be desired when we consider the war in Afghanistan. At this writing, none of the four aims I have listed has been achieved. The Afghanistan Study Group Report, released in January 2008, provides little reason to be hopeful about the prospects for succeeding in what has become known as the "forgotten war." The report makes the damning charge that the United States' effort has been crippled by "too few military forces and insufficient economic aid, and without a clear and consistent comprehensive strategy to fill the power vacuum outside Kabul and to counter the combined challenges of reconstituted Taliban and al-Qaeda forces in Afghanistan and Pakistan, a runaway opium economy, and the stark poverty faced by most Afghans."[52] Among other recommendations is to detach the war in Afghanistan from the war in Iraq, to invest more vigorously in infrastructural development, and to create a regional plan that addresses threats along the border region between Afghanistan and Pakistan. That these recommendations come from a group of conservative consultants and advisors, more than six years after the conflict began, is disturbing in the extreme. In the six years prior to the report's release, the United States had spent over six billion dollars and deployed over thirty thousand troops in the region. Bin Laden has not been captured or killed, and he continues to communicate and arouse antipathy toward the United States. The Taliban has reestablished its control over much of Afghanistan and its lucrative marketing of opium, especially in the southern region of that country. Although terrorist bases in Afghanistan were destroyed by early attacks and al Qaeda was initially routed, evidence indicates that the Taliban and al Qaeda continue to provide mutual support.[53] However much the war in Afghanistan might have appeared winnable at the outset, the Bush administration's lack of coordinated planning and its diversion of resources to Iraq and elsewhere have left this conflict orphaned to a patchwork of policies and sources of support.

In March 2009, newly elected President Obama presented a revised foreign policy for the United States in Afghanistan and Pakistan, one that provided a more focused set of aims and a commitment to greater financial support to the region.[54] Obama added four thousand new troops to the seventeen thousand troops he deployed to Afghanistan immediately upon assuming office. The additional troops, Obama added, would be deployed to train Afghan security forces. In December 2009, in response to a request by General McChrystal, Obama pledged to send an additional thirty thousand troops to Afghanistan between the end of the year and May 2010 while also vowing to begin bringing American forces home by the middle of 2011. He also signed off on a plan by the CIA to expand that agency's activities in Pakistan, which will include more strikes by drone aircraft and sending additional spies to Pakistan.[55] Those decisions are part of a mission that has several prongs: to defeat al Qaeda in Pakistan and Afghanistan, to help finance the building of infrastructure in Pakistan and Afghanistan, to develop economic initiatives that provide viable alternatives to the lucrative drug trade in the region, to oversee a crackdown on governmental corruption in Afghanistan, and to train Afghan security forces so that they can eventually take responsibility for securing their country. Obama made it clear in his

December 2009 decision that he was not offering President Karzai a "blank check" of support from the United States. Obama's strategy entails shifting resources away from the war in Iraq, focusing military action on dismantling the enemy that attacked the United States, and concentrating financial and diplomatic resources in order to create alliances and strengthen democratic institutions in the region. It also entails linking security problems in Afghanistan to its border region with Pakistan, which now provides safe haven to the Taliban and al Qaeda—including, it is believed, Osama bin Laden and Ayman al Zawahiri. Shifting away from the unilateralism of the Bush administration, moreover, Obama made explicit a commitment to secure greater military and financial support from U.S. allies. All of those aims, however difficult they may be to achieve, are long overdue.

Taking these considerations together, we can say that the just-war tenets of *just cause, legitimate authority, right intention,* and *last resort,* shoulder the burden of proof to justify using military force against the Taliban and bin Laden's terrorist camps in Afghanistan. Considerations of *proportionality* leave a mixed verdict: attacking Afghanistan was indeed a proportionate response to 9/11, but declaring a full scale "war against terrorism" is clearly not. And considerations of success, or lack thereof, invite social critics to visit and revisit questions about the war's overall proportionality and the morality of its means on a regular basis.

Given that several just-war criteria have been met, it may seem incongruous to consider the criterion of *relative justice*—the idea that one side cannot claim a monopoly on justice or righteousness in international conflict. Relative justice calls attention to the conditions of finitude within which political actors operate and demands ongoing self-reflexivity about the morality of one's cause and conduct. Yet it would seem wise to dismiss the idea of relative justice for a variety of reasons. Among other things, that idea might open the door to excessive self-criticism and dissent, thereby undermining political motivation and allegiance in times of national crisis. And there are crises that demand clear and committed action, when the suffering of injustice is indisputable. When terrorism occurs on one's own soil, as it did on 9/11, the case for going to war seems unambiguously (not relatively) clear. As I have been arguing throughout this book, indignation felt in response to those attacks is unequivocally justified.

That said, the criterion of relative justice remains pertinent to the United States and its allies' resort to armed force. It is important to remember that the foes in Afghanistan—the Taliban—were supported by the United States during Afghanistan's fight with the Soviets in the 1980s. During this period, the United States was also concerned about neutralizing the influence of Iran and was wary of Pakistan's influence in Afghanistan. For a while, the Taliban appeared to provide a hedge against Iran's presence in Central Asia. But once the Taliban's atrocities in Afghanistan became clear to the world, the United States found itself having to reverse its policies regarding a regime that it had been complicit in supporting. Herein lies one merit to the criterion of relative justice: it counsels us to consider, with humility, the burdens of history and the morally complex contexts in which wars often arise.

What about questions regarding the war's means and restrictions imposed by the *jus in bello*? Here our focus turns to the risks posed to noncombatants and the treatment of combatants and terrorist suspects rounded up in the wake of 9/11. Over the past seven years, the war in Afghanistan has taken thousands of lives and has left many thousands of Afghan citizens wounded, sick, displaced, and at risk of crime, exposure, and further violence. Civilian casualties resulting from U.S. and allied military missions raised concerns within a week of President Bush's authorization to use force in Afghanistan in October 2001. Mosques, hospitals, news bureaus, bazaars, wedding parties, and entire villages have been damaged or destroyed by American air strikes. Moreover, coalition forces have been implicated in mortar and rocket attacks, house raids, and ground combat in which local police and civilians have been killed or wounded.[56] Many casualties were caused by U.S. air troops, especially air troops called in to provide protection for underresourced ground troops under heavy attack. As a report by Human Rights Watch observes, "The combination of light ground forces and overwhelming airpower has become the dominant doctrine of war for the U.S. in Afghanistan."[57]

Numbers hardly tell the entire story, but they do offer a picture, however incomplete, that raises concerns. In 2002 the *Los Angeles Times* found that between 1,067 and 1,201 civilian deaths from the bombing campaign were reported in the U.S., British, Pakistani, and international news services during the first five months of war.[58] Professor Marc Herold of the University of New Hampshire estimates that between October 2001 and June 2003, 3,100 to 3,600 civilians lost their lives in U.S. airstrikes and ground attacks in Afghanistan.[59] Herold estimates that from June 2003 to June 2004, 412 to 437 Afghan civilians died, and that in 2005, 408 to 478 Afghan civilians died due to U.S. and NATO actions.[60] In 2006, Human Rights Watch estimated that at least 230 Afghan civilians were killed by U.S. or NATO attacks; Herold's estimations increase that number threefold.[61] In 2007, at least 434 civilians died during U.S. or NATO attacks, and another fifty-seven civilians were killed in crossfire. The number of civilian casualties resulting from U.S. or NATO airstrikes tripled from 2006 to 2007, from 116 to 321.[62] In August of 2007, a British senior commander asked U.S. Special Forces to leave his area of operations because of the high number of civilian casualties they had caused.[63] According to a U.N. survey, in 2008 there were 828 civilian deaths caused by U.S. and NATO air and ground attacks in Afghanistan, a 39 percent increase over the previous year.[64] Several of those attacks generated a storm of protest among Afghan citizens, whose grievances were communicated by President Karzai to the United States. In one incident in November 2008, a U.S. airstrike hit an Afghan wedding, killing forty civilians and wounding twenty-eight others. That attack followed a previous tragedy in August 2008, also involving a wedding party, in which forty-seven civilians were killed, including the bride.[65] Another bombing in August 2008, at midnight, killed ninety civilians, including sixty children.[66] In February 2009, U.S.-led attacks killed thirteen civilians in western Afghanistan;[67] that same month, the commander of Special Operations Forces (SOF) ordered a halt to most commando missions after several nighttime raids by SOF killed women and children.[68] In May 2009, a B-1B plane dropped five five-hundred-pound bombs and two two-ton bombs in a village in the Afghan village of Granai, killing between twenty-six and 140 civilians.[69]

These facts do not include information about injuries and fatalities caused by the Taliban. According to the U.N. survey of civilian casualties in 2008, 55 percent of the total number resulted from the Taliban's and al Qaeda's actions. Indeed, over the past three years civilian injuries and fatalities caused by the Taliban have greatly increased, owing largely to a rise in suicide attacks and use of roadside bombs.[70] Civilian deaths at the hands of the Taliban and al Qaeda have received little coverage in the Western press.[71] Failure to report these facts and subject them to critical scrutiny encourages the view that the insurgents are beyond the pale of moral accountability, paradoxically beyond and beneath reproach. The entire thrust of this book is to have us understand that such silence is scarcely to be commended. It is to deny the insurgents their standing as moral subjects, free and accountable for their actions. Stated differently, the norm of respect for persons, grounded in moral subjectivity and understood in terms of human freedom and accountability, urges against that paradoxical attitude. That the Taliban and al Qaeda are engaged in acts of injustice cannot be gainsaid. U.S. and NATO forces are fighting against ruthless defenders of an unjust regime.

When it comes to assessing U.S. and NATO actions, we should begin by saying that civilian casualties are terrible and tragic, and at times reprehensible.[72] How to assess such losses, however, is rarely simple or straightforward. We don't always know whether they are the result of human error, negligence, or intentional design. The loss of innocent life owing to intentional design or culpable negligence is morally unacceptable according to any doctrine that values human dignity. The loss of innocent life owing to miscalculation, the imprecision of weaponry, or collateral damage is more difficult to judge. In just-war doctrine, such tragedies are assessed in terms of the principle of proportionality, which requires us to weigh risks to noncombatant life against potential benefits of a military action. Even if such events do appear proportionate from a military point of view, there is still the fact of political fallout. The loss of civilian life in the war against the Taliban and al Qaeda undermines the

U.S. effort to win the minds and hearts of Afghan citizens, a key component in securing good will, intelligence, and other forms of assistance in the ongoing counterinsurgency.

The Obama administration shows promising signs of prudence and sensitivity in this regard. In the wake of the May 2009 tragedy in the Fatah province, President Obama appointed a new commander, General Stanley A. McChrystal, who quickly announced a tightened airstrike policy in Afghanistan. McChrystal soon followed up that directive with orders to ground troops to back down in their pursuit of Taliban fighters whenever they think that civilians might be at risk, even if Taliban forces are thereby enabled to escape.[73]

Captured combatants present other challenges. During the first six years of war, the Bush administration carried out numerous actions against combatants and terrorist suspects that showed little respect for justice. In the first few months after 9/11, the United States and its allies rounded up and detained more than ten thousand people on suspicion of terrorism, denying them access to legal counsel or rights of due process and transporting some of them to prisons and secret locations for indefinite periods of time, including locations where torture is practiced.[74] The United States introduced at least six systems of holding prisoners: the main holding area at Guantanamo Bay, Cuba; jails in Bagram and Kandahar in Afghanistan; a dozen secret jails on U.S. firebases in the Afghan mountains; and jails run by Afghan warlords and the secret services of Afghanistan and Pakistan.[75] The CIA "rendered" an untold number of terrorist suspects—abducting and transporting them to allied countries, including Azerbaijan, Egypt, Jordan, Morocco, Pakistan, Poland, Syria, Thailand, and Uzbekistan, where they could be secretly interrogated and tortured by local intelligence agencies.[76] Persons rendered by the CIA have been denied all access by the International Committee of the Red Cross. Generally the treatment of suspects was ignored by the public until the sadistic abuse of prisoners at Abu Ghraib, Iraq, was revealed in 2004.[77] There, prisoners were raped, sodomized, urinated upon, scalded with phosphoric liquid or cold water, forced to form human pyramids in the nude, made to masturbate in the presence of a female soldier and toward the mouth of a kneeling prisoner, intimidated by military dogs with threats of attack, and subjected to extensive physical deprivation, brutal bodily violence, and psychological harassment—including insults to Islamic faith. To compound the prisoners' humiliation, photographs of many of these events were taken by the soldiers carrying them out. Those incidents constitute only one piece of a larger picture of extreme interrogation and torture at detention centers in Kandahar, Bagram, and Guantanamo Bay. Since 2002 at least eight Afghan prisoners have died in U.S. custody in Afghanistan. By 2005, the Afghan Independent Human Rights Commission recorded eight hundred cases of abuse against prisoners at over thirty U.S. bases.[78] In January 2007, hundreds of prisoners marked their five-year stay at Guantanamo without any high-level suspect being brought to trial. These incidents undermine any effort by the United States and its allies to assume the high moral ground in the face of terrorism and injustice. When Barack Obama campaigned for the presidency he vowed to close the Guantanamo prison immediately if he was elected. One year into his first term, that prison remained in operation.

Questions surrounding the proper treatment of prisoners are seemingly complicated by the twofold nature of the conflict—the fact that the Taliban and al Qaeda are proper objects of hostilities. Official U.S. policy toward captured Taliban or al Qaeda personnel is that they are not entitled to be prisoners of war under the Geneva Convention of 1949 and the Protocols of 1977. This policy has been defended on the argument that captured members of the Taliban and al Qaeda are "unlawful combatants" and thus not entitled to the protections owed to prisoners of war (POWs) according to the Convention. (Classifying prisoners as unlawful combatants turns on the fact that they are not fighting a conventional war, one that is authorized by a political authority and in which they fight with military insignia.) But it is unclear why captured Taliban prisoners may be denied POW status or denied a tribunal to clarify their status given that the Taliban regime is considered liable for the 9/11 attacks. One plank of the Bush administration's position on this matter is that the Taliban is fighting a war of terror. According to the Geneva Convention and its protocols, however, the fact that prisoners are considered unjust by their opponents in war does not entail their forfeiture of war rights. Captured members of the Taliban are legal combatants and are entitled to POW status.

U.S. policy toward captured members of al Qaeda with respect to POW status arguably stands on firmer legal ground. Al Qaeda members lack any formal connection to an internationally recognized personality and are therefore "outlaw combatants." Nevertheless, under customary international law, those combatants are entitled to humane treatment as outlined by Article 3 in the Geneva Conventions of 1949 and in Protocol I of 1977, the latter of which the United States has not joined as a signatory. As Adam Roberts observes, "the fact that certain prisoners may be viewed as unlawful combatants . . . does not mean that they have no legal rights at all."[79] Roberts notes that the United States could explicitly accept rights guaranteed by the 1977 Geneva Protocol I, Article 75. That article, Roberts observes, "is designed to provide basic protection for arrested and detained people who do not qualify for POW status. The United States is not party to Protocol I but has long viewed Article 75 as customary law."[80] According to that article, prisoners "under the power of a Party to the conflict and who do not benefit from more favorable treatment under the Conventions or under this Protocol shall be treated humanely in all circumstances." Article 75 goes on to specify acts that are prohibited, including "violence to the life, health, or physical or mental well-being of persons," including murder, physical or mental torture, corporal punishment, mutilation, humiliating and degrading treatment, forced prostitution, denial of information of the reasons of his or her arrest, and the denial of the presumption of innocence until proven guilty.[81] To date the United States has refused to offer these fundamental guarantees to the unlawful combatants captured in the war.

Resort to force in Afghanistan in response to the attacks of 9/11 is, on balance, justified. U.S. officials in the Bush administration failed, however, to outline their endgame and their aims for a just and peaceful resolution of the conflict. That fact is made no better by the Bush administration's commitment to a broad range of antiterrorist activity around the world, raising questions of proportion-ality. The Bush administration also deployed means that raise questions about its commitment to the principle of respect for persons and international law. Obama's more focused, constructive, and multilateral policy marks a clear improvement. But at this writing, the verdict on that policy is still out.

In terms of the policies and practices of the Bush administration, the overall picture is one in which the United States embraced an expansive justification for resorting to war and a weak understanding of war's proper limits. U.S. policy in Afghanistan proceeded along a sliding scale according to which policy makers and strategists traded off means for ends at the expense of fundamental respect for persons. Political officials must now contend with the cruel irony that, in response to the grievance of 9/11, hostilities in Afghanistan have generated countless individual grievances and moral indignation against the United States. American leaders during the Bush administration squandered their initial moral high ground by failing to articulate and honor the terms that permit the use of limited force in response to a grievous injustice. Now the Obama administration, and the American people, must deal with the wreckage.

NOTES

1. THE PROBLEM OF RELIGIOUS VIOLENCE

1. I say "regimes" to note their plurality. For a discussion of regimes that range across multinational empires, (multinational) consociations, republican nation-states, immigrant societies, and, of course, international society itself, see Michael Walzer, *On Toleration* (New Haven: Yale University Press, 1997).

2. Http://www.state.gov/s/ct/rls/other/des/123085.htm. Accessed on July 10, 2009.

3. For discussions of these and other religious groups, see Mark Juergensmeyer, *Terror in the Mind of God: The Global Rise of Religious Violence*, updated edition with a new preface (Berkeley: University of California Press, 2000); Juergensmeyer, *Global Rebellion: Religious Challenges to the Secular State, from Christian Militias to al Qaeda* (Berkeley: University of California Press, 2008); Jessica Stern, *Terror in the Name of God: Why Religious Militants Kill* (New York: HarperCollins, 2003); Ahmed Rashid, *Descent into Chaos: The U.S. and the Disaster in Pakistan, Afghanistan, and Central Asia* (New York: Penguin, 2008).

4. Definitions of terrorism are contested. Throughout this work I understand *terrorism* to designate a random attack on innocent persons or property in order to express a grievance or to foment terror for political ends. Terrorists murder some innocent victims randomly in order to hold others hostage to fear. "Random" does not mean "unplanned" or "aimless"; it rather means that the attack's perpetrators seek not to target specified persons in order to succeed in their efforts. Indeed, not specifying one's victims beyond general political, demographic, or religious identifiers often appears integral to a terrorist's act.

5. Michael Walzer, *Interpretation and Social Criticism* (Cambridge, Mass.: Harvard University Press, 1987), 35.

6. Will Kymlicka, *Multicultural Citizenship: A Liberal Theory of Minority Rights* (Oxford: Clarendon Press, 1995), 81.

7. John Rawls, "Kantian Constructivism in Moral Theory," *Journal of Philosophy* 77, no. 9 (September 1980): 544.

8. Michael Walzer, *Arguing about War* (New Haven: Yale University Press, 2004), 51–55.

9. Ibid., 140–41.

10. My views regarding indignation and the general inability to conceive of injustice are informed by Judith N. Shklar, *The Faces of Injustice* (New Haven: Yale University Press, 1990).

11. Peter Strawson, "Freedom and Resentment," in *Free Will*, ed. Gary Watson (Oxford: Oxford University Press, 1982), 59–80.

12. Ibid., 70–72.

13. My remarks here are informed by Charles Taylor, *Sources of the Self: The Making of the Modern Identity* (Cambridge, Mass.: Harvard University Press, 1989), chap. 3.

14. World Islamic Front, *Jihad against Jews and Crusaders* at http://fas.org/irp/world/para/docs/980223-fatwa.htm. Bin Laden reiterated this individual duty in an interview in December of 1998. See Osama bin Laden, "A Muslim Bomb," in *Messages to the World: The Statements of Osama bin Laden*, ed. Bruce Lawrence, trans. James Howarth (London: Verso, 2005), 65–94.

15. Bin Laden's putative grievances for orchestrating the attacks of 9/11 are inconstant. Three years after 9/11 he stated that his grievances were in response to American support for Israel's invasion of Lebanon in 1982. See Bin Laden's "Message to the American People," in *Al Qaeda in Its Own Words*, ed. Gilles Kepel and Jean-Pierre Milelli, trans. Pascale

Ghazaleh (Cambridge, Mass.: Harvard/Belknap University Press, 2008), 71–77.

16. World Islamic Front, *Jihad against Jews and Crusaders*.

17. Osama bin Laden, in a statement faxed to al-Jazeera, "To Our Brothers in Pakistan," in *Messages to the World*, 102.

18. World Islamic Front, *Jihad against Jews and Crusaders*.

19. Yousef H. Aboul-Enin, "Ayman Al-Zawahiri's Knights under the Prophet's Banner: The al-Qaeda Manifesto," at http://findarticles .com/p/articles/mi_moPBZ/is_1_85/ai_n14695417. Accessed on February 14, 2008.

20. Nimrod Raphaeli, "Radical Islamist Profiles (3): "Ayman Muhammad Rabi' Al-Zawahiri: The Making of an Arch Terrorist," at www .memri.org, Special Dispatches Series, no. 127, March 13, 2003. Accessed on February 14, 2008.

21. I owe this distinction between religion as a *warrant* for resort to force and as providing the basis for *identifying targets* in the use of force to David Little, "Studying 'Religious Human Rights': Methodological Foundations," in *Religious Human Rights in Global Perspective: Legal Perspectives*, ed. Johan D. van der Vyver and John Witte Jr. (The Hague: Martinus Nijhoff, 1996), 45–77, at 54–55.

22. Atta's instructions to the 9/11 hijackers are saturated with references to Islamic tradition. For an analysis, see Bruce Lincoln, *Holy Terrors: Thinking about Religion After September 11* (Chicago: University of Chicago Press, 2003), chap. 1. Atta's instructions are included as appendix A in Lincoln's book.

23. Ibid., 11.

24. I count the attacks of 9/11 as "terrorism" on the understanding of terrorism as defined in n. 4: a random attack on innocent persons or property in order to express a grievance or to foment terror for political ends. Occasionally I will use the term "extremism" to capture a more general worldview or set of sentiments that gives birth to terrorism, and occasionally I will refer to Muslim extremists, radical Muslims, and radical Islamists interchangeably.

25. Cited in David Sanger, "A Nation Challenged: The President; Bin Laden is Wanted in Attacks, 'Dead or Alive,' President Says," *New York Times*, September 18, 2001.

26. Cited in Malise Ruthven, "How to Understand Islam," *New York Review of Books* 54 (November 8, 2007): 66.

27. John L. Esposito, *Unholy War: Terror in the Name of Islam* (New York: Oxford University Press, 2002), xii.

28. The phrase is Esposito's. See ibid.

29. Ahmet Rashid, *Taliban: Militant Islam, Oil, and Fundamentalism in Central Asia* (New Haven: Yale University Press, 2000), 211–12.

30. I say "one mood" cognizant of other moods, e.g., those of antireligionists. See, e.g., Richard Dawkins, *The God Delusion* (Boston: Houghton Mifflin, 2006); Christopher Hitchens, *God Is Not Great: How Religion Poisons Everything* (New York: Hachette, 2007).

31. Editors, *New York Review of Books* 54 (November 8, 2007): 1.

32. Stephen L. Darwall, "Two Kinds of Respect," *Ethics* 88, no. 1 (October 1977): 36–49; John Rawls, *Political Liberalism, with a New Introduction and the "Reply to Habermas"* (New York: Columbia University Press, 1996), 54–66.

33. By "ethics of belief" I mean, as I will make clear in chapter 7, the idea that beliefs come with moral responsibilities toward oneself and others. I do not mean "ethics of belief" as understood by W. K. Clifford in his essay "The Ethics of Belief." Clifford coined the phrase "ethics of belief" to refer to the moral obligation to hold beliefs only after careful testing and investigation. My view, in contrast, refers to the moral obligation to refrain from holding beliefs that violate basic principles of human dignity. See W. K. Clifford, "The Ethics of Belief," in *Religion from Tolstoy to Camus*, ed. Walter Kaufmann (New York: Harper, 1961), 201–20. Clifford's essay famously sparked a response by William James, "The Will to Believe," in *Essays on Faith and Morals* (New York: New American Library, 1974 [1962]), 32–62. For a reassessment of Clifford's views, see Van A. Harvey, "The Ethics of Belief Reconsidered," *Journal of Religion* 59, no. 4 (October 1979): 406–20.

34. See, e.g., Rawls, *Political Liberalism*, xxiv–xxxii.

35. Charles Taylor, *Multiculturalism: Examining The Politics of Recognition*, ed. Amy Gutmann (Princeton: Princeton University Press, 1994), 70.

36. Ellen Willis, "Bringing the Holy War Home," *The Nation* 273, no. 20 (December 17, 2001): 15–18, at 15.

2. 9/11 AND VARIETIES OF SOCIAL CRITICISM

1. Jonathan Z. Smith, *Imagining Religion: From Babylon to Jonestown* (Chicago: University of Chicago Press, 1982). Smith relies on

the Enlightenment premise that (in his words) "nothing human is foreign to me" to address incomprehension surrounding the mass suicide at Jonestown, Guyana, drawing parallels between the utopia of Jonestown and the *Bacchae* in *Imagining Religion*, chap. 7.

2. Ibid, chap. 6.

3. The phrase is from Michael Walzer, *The Company of Critics: Social Criticism and Political Commitment in the Twentieth Century* (New York: Basic Books, 1988), 28; see Walzer, *Interpretation and Social Criticism* (Cambridge, Mass.: Harvard University Press, 1987).

4. James Turner Johnson, *The War to Oust Saddam Hussein: Just War and the New Face of Conflict* (Lanham, Md.: Rowman and Littlefield, 2005); John Kelsay, *Arguing the Just War in Islam* (Cambridge, Mass.: Harvard University Press, 2007). See also Bernard Lewis, "License to Kill: Usama bin Ladin's Declaration of Jihad," *Foreign Affairs* 77 (November–December 1998): 14–19; Ladan Boroumand and Roya Boroumand, "Terror, Islam, and Democracy," *Journal of Democracy* 13 (April 2002): 5–20; Zayn Kassam, "Can a Muslim be a Terrorist?" in *Terrorism and International Justice*, ed. James P. Sterba (New York: Oxford University Press, 2003), 114–31; Sohail Hashmi, "9/11 and the Jihad Tradition," in *Terror, Culture, Politics: Rethinking 9/11*, ed. Terry Nardin and Daniel J. Sherman (Bloomington: Indiana University Press, 2006), 149–64. For a useful survey of the topic of Islam and terrorism, see John L. Esposito, *Unholy War: Terror in the Name of Islam* (New York: Oxford University Press, 2002). For an ethnographic account of religious terrorists and their motives, including but going beyond Muslim terrorists, see Jessica Stern, *Terror in the Name of God: Why Religious Militants Kill* (New York: HarperCollins, 2003).

5. John Kelsay, "Osama bin Laden and the Just Conduct of War," *America* (October 8, 2001): 25–27, at 27. See also Kelsay, "Armed Force and Political Responsibility: Justification and Resort to War in Abrahamic Traditions," in *Humanity Before God: Contemporary Faces of Jewish, Christian, and Islamic Ethics*, ed. William Schweiker, Michael A. Johnson, and Kevin Jung (Minneapolis: Fortress Press, 2006), 284–98.

6. John Kelsay, *Islam and War: A Study in Comparative Ethics* (Louisville, Ky.: Westminster/John Knox, 1993).

7. Kelsay, "Osama bin Laden," 27.

8. Ibid.

9. Johnson, *The War to Oust Saddam Hussein*, 13.

10. Ibid., 14.

11. Ibid.

12. Ibid.

13. Ibid., 16.

14. Kelsay, *Arguing the Just War*, 4.

15. Ibid., 5.

16. Ibid., 129.

17. Ibid., 144.

18. Ibid., 150.

19. John P. Reeder Jr. connects neopragmatism to this kind of cross-cultural analysis and contrasts a neopragmatist's openness to such opportunities with attitudes of relativists. "The relativist," Reeder writes, "sees the inevitability of intractable moral disagreement from the top down due to divergences in basic criteria. But the neopragmatist has discarded the very idea of 'basic' criteria on which a moral system 'rests.' Thus the neopragmatist argues that we can work to try to discover convergences or *overlaps* in our moral, valuational, and factual beliefs—on the basis of which we can perhaps come to moral agreement." See Reeder, "Foundations without Foundationalism," in *Prospects for a Common Morality*, ed. Gene Outka and John P. Reeder Jr. (Princeton: Princeton University Press, 1993), 191–214, at 194. In chapter 6 I will embark on the kind of inquiry that Reeder's description of neopragmatism might call for, although that discussion is not grounded in uniquely neopragmatist terms.

20. By "just-war doctrine" I am referring to the body of reflection in Western theology and ethics regarding the morality of resort to war (*jus ad bellum*) and the conduct of participants in war (*jus in bello*). Contemporary works developing this general body of ideas include Paul Ramsey, *War and the Christian Conscience: How Shall Modern War Be Conducted Justly?* (Durham: Duke University Press, 1961); Ramsey, *The Just War: Force and Political Responsibility* (New York: Charles Scribner's Sons, 1968); Michael Walzer, *Just and Unjust Wars: A Moral Argument with Historical Illustrations*, 4th ed. (New York: Basic Books, 2006[1977]); James Turner Johnson, *Just War Tradition and the Restraint of War: A Moral and Historical Inquiry* (Princeton: Princeton University Press, 1981); James F. Childress, *Moral Responsibility in Conflicts: Essays on Nonviolence, War, and Conscience* (Baton Rouge: Louisiana State University Press, 1982); U.S. Catholic Bishops, *The Challenge of Peace: God's Promise and Our Response* (Washington, D.C.: National Conference of Catholic Bishops, 1983);

Richard B. Miller, *Interpretations of Conflict: Ethics, Pacifism, and the Just-War Tradition* (Chicago: University of Chicago Press, 1991); Lisa Sowle Cahill, *Love Your Enemies: Discipleship, Pacifism, and Just War Theory* (Minneapolis: Fortress Press, 1994); A. J. Coates, *The Ethics of War* (Manchester: Manchester University Press, 1997); Jean Bethke Elshtain, *Just War against Terror: The Burden of American Power in a Violent World* (New York: Basic Books, 2003); Brian Orend, *The Morality of War* (Orchard Park, N.Y.: Broadview Press, 2006); Jeff McMahan, *Killing in War* (Oxford: Clarendon Press, 2009).

21. Johnson, "Jihad and Just War," *First Things: A Journal of Religion and Public Life* 124 (June/July 2002): 12–14, at 14.

22. Kelsay *Arguing the Just War,* 97–154; cf. Kelsay, *Islam and War,* 43–76.

23. Kelsay, *Arguing the Just War,* 146.

24. Ibid., 106.

25. Ibid., 114.

26. Ibid., 117.

27. Ibid., 118.

28. Suggested by John Kelsay in personal correspondence.

29. Just-war theorists would say that such uses of force are disproportionate, not that they are indiscriminate.

30. Walzer, *Just and Unjust Wars,* 135; see also 219. During the Second World War, John C. Ford condemned the obliteration bombing of German cities on the basis of noncombatants' "natural law right of immunity from violent repression." See John C. Ford, S. J., "The Morality of Obliteration Bombing," *Theological Studies* 5 (September 1944): 261–309. G. E. M. Anscombe articulates immunity as one implication of natural law rights, which shield innocent persons from direct attack. Paul Ramsey articulates the idea of noncombatant immunity as one implication of agape, or Christian charity. The U.S. Catholic bishops organize their account of the ethics of war around a theological rendition of human dignity, viz., the idea that "each human life is sacred" (1983, par. 15). Today contemporary theorists are engaged in a lively debate about the basis for assigning liability (or immunity): forfeiture based on moral fault (David Rodin); material noninnocence (Michael Walzer); objectively unjust danger (G. E. M. Anscombe, John Reeder). For a clarifying discussion, see David R. Mapel, "Innocent Attackers and Rights of Self-Defense," *Ethics and International Affairs* 18, no. 1 (2004): 81–86. See also Richard B. Miller, "Killing, Self-Defense,

and Bad Luck," *Journal of Religious Ethics* 37, no. 1 (March 2009): 131–58. Jeff McMahan argues in a different vein, focusing on matters of what he calls responsibility. All of these authors proffer moral, not practical, reasons for shielding certain persons from direct attack. In addition to the works cited above, see G. E. M. Anscombe, *The Collected Philosophical Papers of G. E. M. Anscombe*, vol. 3, *Ethics, Religion, and Politics* (Oxford: Basil Blackwell, 1981); chaps. 6–8; John P. Reeder Jr., *Killing and Saving: Abortion, Hunger, and War* (University Park: Pennsylvania State University Press, 1996); David Rodin, *War and Self-Defense* (Oxford: Clarendon, 2002); Jeff McMahan, "The Ethics of Killing in War," *Ethics* 114, no. 4 (July 2004): 693–733; McMahan, *Killing in War*.

31. I say "accounts" to mark a plurality of discussion in modern just-war theorizing. It may very well be the case, as James Turner Johnson has argued, that the genesis of noncombatant in Western just-war doctrine can be explained as materializing from various religious, legal, and customary sources rather than from a deontic principle or entitlement conceived in the abstract. For a discussion, see Johnson, *Just War Tradition and the Restraint of War*, 44–49, 131–50. I believe that the mainstream contemporary interpretation is grounded in a general philosophical principle. One formulation of that principle is summarized by Henry Shue who writes: "Non-combatant immunity says one ought, most emphatically, not to harm others who are themselves not harming anyone. This is as fundamental, and as straightforward, and as nearly non-controversial, as moral principles can get." See Henry Shue, "War," in *The Oxford Handbook of Practical Ethics*, ed. Hugh Lafollette (New York: Oxford University Press, 2003), 734–61, at 742.

32. Thanks to Cheryl Cottine, Faraz Sheikh, and Jae Chung for seeking clarification on this point.

33. Kelsay, *Islam and War*, 76.

34. Ahmet Rashid, *Taliban: Militant Islam, Oil, and Fundamentalism in Central Asia* (New Haven: Yale University Press, 2000), 211–12.

35. See World Islamic Front, *Jihad against Jews and Crusaders*.

36. Anthony Lewis, "The Inescapable World," *New York Times*, October 20, 2001.

37. Ellen Willis, "Bringing the Holy War Home," *The Nation* 273, no. 20 (December 17, 2001): 15–18, at 16.

38. Mashood Rivzi, "Intolerable Injustices." In *The Place of Tolerance in Islam*. With essays by Khaled Abou El fadl, Tariq Ali, Milton

Viorst, John Esposito, and others. Edited by Joshua Cohen and Ian Lague (Boston: Beacon Press, 2002), 67–69.

39. Alan B. Krueger and Jitka Malečková, "Does Poverty Cause Terrorism?" *The New Republic* 226, no. 24 (June 24, 2002): 27–33.

40. Rashid, *Taliban*, 107.

41. Ibid.

42. Ibid., 207.

43. Stern, *Terror in the Name of God*, 188–236.

44. United Nations, *Arab Human Development Report* at http://arabstates.undp.org/subpage.php?spid=14.

45. Jane Mayer, "The House of bin Laden," *New Yorker*, November, 12, 2001.

46. Ibid.; Steve Coll, *The Bin Ladens: An Arabian Family in the American Century* (New York: Penguin, 2008), 493.

47. Coll, *The Bin Ladens*, 14–15.

48. Ibid., 15.

49. Mayer, "The House of bin Laden," 65.

50. In addition to the references I provided in chapter 1, see, "*Jihad, Martyrdom, and the Killing of Innocents*," in *The Al Qaeda Reader*, ed. and trans. Raymond Ibrahim, introduction by Victor Davis Hanson (New York: Broadway Books, 2007), 141–71. The text is described as "Prepared for the Council of the Jihad Organization under the Supervision of Dr. Ayman al-Zawahira."

51. Stanley Fish, "Condemnation without Absolutes," *New York Times*, October 15, 2001.

52. See Edward Rothstein, "Attacks on U.S. Challenge the Perspectives of Postmodern True Believers," *New York Times*, September 22, 2001.

53. Fish, "Condemnation without Absolutes."

54. Ibid.

55. Ibid.

56. Stanley Fish, *The Trouble with Principle* (Cambridge, Mass.: Harvard University Press, 1999), 287.

57. Ibid., 288.

58. Ibid., 289.

59. Ibid., 287.

60. Ibid., 209.

61. Ibid., 289.

62. Ibid.

63. Such will be my task in the next chapter.

64. I will address these issues in chap. 4

65. Transcript from "PFAW President, Ralph G. Neas, Addresses Divisive Comments by Religious Right Leaders," at http://www.pfaw.org/pfaw/general/default.aspx?oid=1817. Accessed on September 15, 2001. For the full transcript, see Bruce Lincoln, *Holy Terrors: Thinking about Religion after September 11* (Chicago: University of Chicago Press, 2003), 104–7. See also Gustav Niebuhr, "U.S. 'Secular Groups' Set Tone for U.S. Attacks, Falwell Says," *New York Times*, September 14, 2001.

66. For an analysis of the religious and political layers of the conversation between Falwell and Robertson, along with the conversation's cultural and political fallout, see Lincoln, *Holy Terrors*, 36–50.

67. Sontag's comments were published as one among several reflections in "From Our Correspondents: September 11, 2001," *New Yorker*, September 24, 2001.

68. Ibid.

69. Aristotle identifies rashness as an extreme that the virtue of courage avoids in *Nicomachean Ethics*, ed. Richard McKeon, trans. W. D. Ross (New York: Random House, 1941), 1115b30–16a10.

70. Benjamin R. Barber, "The War of All Against All: Terror and the Politics of Fear," in *War after September 11*, ed. Verna V. Gehring (Lanham, Md.: Rowman and Littlefield, 2003), 75–91, at 78.

71. Ibid., 85.

72. Ibid., 84.

73. Ibid., 85.

74. Ibid., 91.

75. Ibid., 88.

76. Ibid., 90.

3. RIGHTS TO LIFE AND SECURITY

1. The broader theoretical frameworks shaping the direction of these lines of inquiry are, of course, those of Weber and Marx, respectively.

2. Consider, for example, the theory of natural selection. We could hardly say that natural selection is a parochial idea of the Victorian era whose veracity is intelligible only to scientific researchers in England.

3. I make this comment in light of Freud's distinction between mourning and melancholia. On his account, mourning is a feeling of sadness and distress upon the experience of loss, of unwanted dis-

connection. Melancholia is more: it is a pathological expression of mourning—the internalization of mourning so that the grieving person experiences a radical, punishing loss of self-esteem. "The distinguishing mental features of melancholia," Freud writes, "are a profoundly painful dejection, abrogation of interest in the outside world, loss of the capacity to love, inhibition of all activity, and a lowering of the self-regarding feelings to a degree that finds utterance in self-reproaches and self-revilings, and culminates in a delusional expectation of punishment" (165). Melancholia for Freud is mourning transformed into punitive self-reproach. Melancholics believe that they deserve the grievous state they are in. They blame the victim—themselves.

For Freud, the root cause of melancholia turns on the relationship of the ego and the superego. He writes: "In this condition one part of the ego sets itself over against the other, judges it critically, and, as it were, looks upon it as an object. . . . It is the mental faculty commonly called conscience that we are thus recognizing; we shall count it, along with the censorship of consciousness and the testing of reality, among the great institutions of the ego and shall also find evidence elsewhere showing that it can become diseased independently"(168–69). On this account, melancholics suffer from an excess of prohibition and internalized self-judgment. The remedy for the melancholic would be a lifting of the conscience, liberating the ego from the moral realm. We can properly mourn, Freud suggests, when the overbearing voice of conscience is silenced and the ego can adjust to the reality of loss.

But mourning understood in this way is misguided, and this for two reasons. Freud speaks of an overly strong superego as the culprit in melancholia, but he fails to consider whether or how the conscience might assist in the proper mediation of memory and grief. Freud speaks of the problems of the superego tout court, suggesting that any moral claim accompanying the experience of mourning is an unhealthy one. In my view, grief that is mediated by a sense of justice need not be subject to pathology—to weak self-esteem, excessive self-pity, or self-punishment. Such grief would be accompanied not by melancholia in Freud's sense, but by indignation. As I indicated in chapter 1, indignation is a morally reactive emotion in response to wrongdoing. It can be the feeling of grief informed by justice. The properly grieving conscience is not turned narcissistically within; it is structured by an active judgment regarding another's action and an affirmation of oneself and others as deserving respect, as having dignity and inherent worth. I shall develop the moral core of these ideas in this chapter. See Sigmund Freud, "Mourning and Melancholia," in *General Psychological Theory*, ed. Philip Rieff (New York: Touchstone Books, 1991), 164–79.

4. We could likewise test a moral theory against its potential for prohibiting transparently desirable actions. For the sake of this discussion, I will confine my analysis to how a theory would test itself against transparently wrongful actions.

5. David Little, "The Nature and Basis of Human Rights," in *Prospects for a Common Morality*, ed. Gene Outka and John P. Reeder Jr. (Princeton: Princeton University Press, 1993), 73–92. On Moore's intuitionism, see p. 91n27.

. 6. Ibid., 84.

7. Ibid., 81.

8. Ibid.

9. David Little, "On Behalf of Rights," *Journal of Religious Ethics* 34, no. 2 (June 2006): 287–310 at 298n14; see also 302.

10. Albert R. Jonsen and Stephen Toulmin, *The Abuse of Casuistry: A History of Moral Reasoning* (Berkeley: University of California Press, 1988), 16–20.

11. Stanley Fish, *The Trouble with Principle* (Cambridge, Mass.: Harvard University Press, 1999), 288.

12. Ibid., 287.

13. Ibid.

14. Little, "The Nature and Basis of Human Rights," 85–86.

15. Ibid., 86.

16. Ibid., 87.

17. Ibid.

18. Alasdair MacIntyre, *After Virtue: A Study in Moral Theory* (Notre Dame, Ind.: University of Notre Dame Press, 1981), 10.

19. Ibid., 2.

20. Ibid.

21. Little, "The Nature and Basis of Human Rights," 76.

22. Ibid., 82.

23. Ibid., 83.

24. David Little, "Response to Terrorism," *Bulletin of the Boston Theological Institute* 1, no. 2 (Spring 2002): 1, 6–7, at 1.

25. Ibid., 6.

26. Little, "The Nature and Basis of Human Rights," 85.

27. G. Scott Davis, "Comment," *Journal of Religious Ethics* 35, no. 1 (March 2007): 165–70.

28. David Little, "The Author Replies," *Journal of Religious Ethics* 35, no. 1 (March 2007): 171–75, at 173.

29. I have elaborated on such ideas in *Casuistry and Modern Ethics: A Poetics of Practical Reasoning* (Chicago: University of Chicago Press, 1996), chaps. 1 and 9 and in "Rules," in *The Oxford Handbook of Theological Ethics*, ed. Gilbert Meilaender and William Werphehowski (New York: Oxford University Press, 2005), 220–36.

30. Nancy Davis, "Abortion and Self-Defense," *Philosophy and Public Affairs* 13 (1984): 175–207.

31. Ibid., 192.

32. Ibid.

33. Ibid., 193.

34. In a similar vein, Henry Shue defends security rights as necessary for the exercise of other rights. See Henry Shue, *Basic Rights: Subsistence, Affluence, and U.S. Foreign Policy*, 2nd ed. (Princeton: Princeton University Press, 1996 [1980]).

35. Stephen L. Darwall, "Peace as Politics," in *Religion, Politics, and Peace*, ed. Leroy Rouner (Notre Dame, Ind.: University of Notre Dame Press, 1999), 85–103, at 98.

36. Will Kymlicka, *Multicultural Citizenship: A Liberal Theory of Minority Rights* (Oxford: Clarendon Press, 1995), 81.

37. The language of first- and second-order desires draws from Harry G. Frankfurt, "Freedom of the Will and the Concept of the Person," *Journal of Philosophy* 67, no. 1 (January 1971): 5–20; Charles Taylor, "What is Human Agency?" in Taylor, *Human Agency and Language, Philosophical Papers* (Cambridge: Cambridge University Press, 1985), 1:15–44.

38. David A. J. Richards, "Rights and Autonomy," *Ethics* 92, no. 1 (October 1981), 3–20, at 13.

39. Of course, viewing rights in this way becomes complicated when we think of nonautonomous persons, such as fetuses or the irreversibly dying, whose grasp on life is precarious. For now I wish to focus on clear rather than penumbral cases according to which the rights to life and security establish an immunity from serious danger.

40. Fish could say that there are "local" grounds for rendering an absolute condemnation of the 9/11 attacks. But Fish might be relying

on an understanding of "absolutism" to describe not the weight of a moral norm but one strand of philosophy understood to be in pursuit of what Richard Rorty calls "one right answer." We will turn to those ideas in chapter 4.

41. Reinhold Niebuhr, *The Nature and Destiny of Man,* (New York: Charles Scribner's Sons, 1941), 1:208–40.

42. The idea that collective security is a value justifying the use of force is overlooked in Richard Norman's critique of just-war doctrine's idea of just cause in his discussion of killing, war, and political sovereignty. See Richard Norman, *Ethics, Killing, and War* (Cambridge: Cambridge University Press, 1995), 132–58.

43. See Michael Walzer, *Just and Unjust Wars: A Moral Argument with Historical Illustrations,* 4th ed. (New York: Basic Books, 2006 [1977]), 54.

44. On justice and legitimate expectations, see John Rawls, *A Theory of Justice* (Cambridge, Mass.: Harvard/Belknap, 1971), 310–15.

45. James Turner Johnson, *The War to Oust Saddam Hussein: Just War and the New Face of Conflict* (Lanham, Md.: Rowman and Littlefield, 2005), 13.

46. Alan Gewirth, "The Basis and Content of Human Rights," in Gewirth, *Human Rights: Essays on Justification and Applications* (Chicago: University of Chicago Press, 1982), 41–78. See as well, Gewirth, *Reason and Morality* (Chicago: University of Chicago Press, 1978), chap. 2; Gewirth, "Common Morality and the Community of Rights," in *Prospects for a Common Morality,* 29–52.

47. Gewirth, "The Basis and Content of Human Rights," 47.

48. Ibid.

49. Ibid., 49–50.

50. Ibid., 53.

51. Ibid., emphasis in the original.

52. Ibid.

53. Ibid., 48.

54. Kymlicka, *Multicultural Citizenship,* 81.

55. Gewirth, "The Basis and Content of Human Rights," 51.

4. TOLERATION, EQUALITY, AND THE BURDENS OF JUDGMENT

1. See Andrew Jason Cohen, "What Toleration Is," *Ethics* 115, no. 1 (October 2004): 68–95.

2. Stephen L. Darwall, "Peace as Politics," in *Religion, Politics, and Peace*, ed. Leroy Rouner (Notre Dame, Ind.: University of Notre Dame Press, 1999), 98.

3. In the next chapter I will clarify this notion of respect in light of Darwall's concept of recognition respect.

4. World Islamic Front, *Jihad against Jews and Crusaders*.

5. Nimrod Raphaeli, "Radical Islamist Profiles (3): Ayman Muhammad Rabi' Al-Zawahiri: The Making of an Arch Terrorist," at www.memri.org, Special Dispatches Series, no. 127, March 13, 2003. Accessed on February 14, 2008.

6. Osama bin Laden, "A Muslim Bomb," in *Messages to the World: The Statements of Osama bin Laden*, ed. Bruce Lawrence, trans. James Howarth (London: Verso, 2005), 65–94.

7. That is to say, bin Laden's statements threaten the *forum externum* (security) as well as the *forum internum* (conscience). Liberal grievances attached to threats to each forum are connected, as I stated in chapter 1, by the concept of respect for persons.

8. Richard Rorty, *Objectivity, Relativism, and Truth: Philosophical Papers I* (Cambridge: Cambridge University Press, 1991).

9. Ibid., 176.

10. Ibid., 198.

11. Ibid., 176.

12. Ibid., 176–77.

13. John Rawls, *Political Liberalism, with a new Introduction and the "Reply to Habermas"* (New York: Columbia University Press, 1996), 54–58.

14. John Rawls, *The Law of Peoples, with "The Idea of Public Reason Revisited"* (Cambridge, Mass.: Harvard University Press, 1999), 16n8.

15. See J. M. Brennan, *The Open-Texture of Moral Concepts* (New York: Barnes and Noble, 1977).

16. Rawls, *Political Liberalism*, 57.

17. Ibid.

18. Ibid., 56–58.

19. Ibid., 61.

20. Ibid., 58.

21. Rawls, *A Theory of Justice*, 217.

22. Darwall, "Peace as Politics," 89.

23. Ibid., 90.

24. Martin Luther, "The Bondage of the Will," in *Martin Luther: Selections from His Writings*, ed. John Dillenberger (New York: Doubleday, 1961), 196.

25. Martin Luther, "Secular Authority," in *Martin Luther: Selections*, 366.

26. Ibid., 367.

27. Ibid., 383.

28. Luther, quoted in Joseph Lecler, *Toleration and the Reformation* (New York: Association Press, 1960), 147–64, cited in Darwall, "Peace as Politics," 96.

29. John Calvin, *Institutes of the Christian Religion*, ed. John T. McNeill and trans. Ford Lewis Battles (Philadelphia: Westminster Press, 1960), book IV, chap. 20, par. 2, 1487–88.

30. Darwall, "Peace as Politics," 95.

31. Ibid., 101.

32. Ibid., 96.

33. Ibid., 98.

34. Ibid.

35. Ibid.

36. John Rawls, *A Theory of Justice* (Cambridge, Mass., Harvard/Belknap, 1971), 206–15. Rawls reiterates this contractualist line of argument for liberty of conscience in *Political Liberalism*, 310–13. He then proceeds to supplement that argument with a defense of liberty much along the lines I articulate here. See ibid., 313–15.

37. Rawls, *Law of Peoples*, 78–81.

38. See Will Kymlicka, "Two Models of Pluralism and Tolerance," in *Toleration: An Elusive Virtue*, ed. David Heyd (Princeton: Princeton University Press, 1996), 81–105, at 99n11.

39. David A. J. Richards, "Rights and Autonomy," *Ethics* 92, no. 1 (October 1981): 3–20, at 14.

40. Ibid., 13.

41. John Stuart Mill, *On Liberty*, ed. Currin V. Shields (Indianapolis: Bobbs-Merrill, 1956), 70.

42. See also Allen Buchanan, "Revisability and Rational Choice," *Canadian Journal of Philosophy* 5, no. 3 (1975): 395–408.

43. Rawls, *Political Liberalism*, 72.

44. John Rawls, "Kantian Constructivism in Moral Theory," *Journal of Philosophy* 77, no. 9 (September 1980): 515–72, at 544.

45. Darwall, "Peace as Politics," 98.

46. Rawls, *Law of Peoples*, 14, 27, 121.

47. Ibid., 122.

5. RESPECT AND RECOGNITION

1. See p. 14.

2. Stephen Darwall, "Two Kinds of Respect," *Ethics* 88, no. 1 (October 1977): 36–49, at 38.

3. Ibid.

4. Ibid.

5. As David Miller observes, demands for recognition are gnarled by the fact that "it may simply be impossible for some groups to recognise and endorse certain other groups in the way that is required without violating their own identities. Toleration may be possible, but recognition is not" (117). For a discussion of tensions between toleration and recognition, see David Miller, "Group Identities, National Identities, and Democratic Politics," in *Toleration, Identity, and Difference*, ed. John Horton and Susan Mendus (New York: St. Martin's Press, 1999), 103–25.

6. Darwall, "Two Kinds of Respect," 38.

7. Ibid.

8. Ibid., 45.

9. Ibid., 38.

10. Ibid., 42.

11. By saying "in appropriate contexts" I mean to indicate that, in some instances, appraisal respect may be context-dependent in complex ways. We may assign esteem owing to considerations that may permissibly bracket questions of recognition respect. For example, we might esteem a politician or a celebrity for her admirable public persona while disapproving of her personal lifestyle.

12. Darwall, "Two Kinds of Respect," 47.

13. Charles Taylor, *Multiculturalism: Examining the Politics of Recognition*, ed. Amy Gutmann (Princeton: Princeton University Press, 1994), 25.

14. Ibid., 30–31.; cf. Charles Taylor, *The Ethics of Authenticity* (Cambridge, Mass.: Harvard University Press, 1992).

15. For example, Makah Indians in the state of Washington secured an exemption from U.S. law banning whale hunting. Robert Sullivan, "Permission Granted to Kill a Whale. Now What?" *New York Times*

Magazine, August 9, 1998; Sam Howe Verhovek, "Protesters Shadow a Tribe's Pursuit of Whales and Past," *New York Times,* October 2, 1998; Sam Howe Verhovek, "Reviving Tradition, Tribe Kills a Whale," *New York Times,* May 18, 1999. The Makah's exemption is premised on an 1855 federal treaty granting them the legal right to hunt gray whales.

16. A special electoral list is reserved for Maori citizens in New Zealand so that some legislators in the New Zealand parliament are elected solely by Maori voters. This is one mechanism for providing group representation. Another would be drawing constituency boundaries that largely coincide with particular groups that need representatives who voice, and perhaps mirror, those groups' interests and/or identity. For discussions, see Will Kymlicka, *Multicultural Citizenship: A Liberal Theory of Minority Rights* (Oxford: Clarendon Press, 1995), 133–34, 147–49; Amy Gutmann and Dennis Thompson, *Democracy and Disagreement* (Cambridge, Mass.: Harvard University Press, 1996), 151–55.

17. Native American groups in the United States and Canada exercise self-government in various areas of each country. For example, in 1998 Canada assigned liberal sovereignty rights to the Nisga Indians in British Columbia. See Anthony DePalma, "Canada Pact Gives a Tribe Self-Rule for the First Time," *New York Times,* August 5, 1998.

18. Taylor, *Multiculturalism,* 59.

19. Thanks to Lisa Sideris for helping me clarify this point here and in chapter 1.

20. Taylor, *Multiculturalism,* 72.

21. Ibid., 72–73.

22. Ibid., 66.

23. Ibid., 72–73.

24. Ibid., 66–67.

25. Ibid., 70. See Hans-Georg Gadamer, *Truth and Method,* 2nd rev. ed., trans. Joel Weinsheimer and Donald G. Marshall (New York: Crossroad, 1991), 306–7, 374–75, 397, 576.

26. Taylor, *Multiculturalism,* 67.

27. Ibid.

28. Ibid.

· 29. I develop a similar line of criticism in "On Making a Cultural Turn in Religious Ethics," *Journal of Religious Ethics* 33 (September 2005): 409–43.

30. The questions I raise about Taylor's (and, by implication, Gadamer's) account of a "fusion of horizons" are not of the sort posed by Jürgen Habermas. Habermas is concerned about asymmetries of power between interlocutors in the dialogical situation presumed by the idea of a fusion of horizons. The effect of his critique is to propose extraconversational norms to overcome imbalances in the distribution of power. Those norms cohere with the general line of inquiry I am developing in this work, focusing as they do on freedom and equality. However, my questions about Taylor's account of a fusion of horizons proceed independently of whether a power differential between interlocutors has been equalized. See Jürgen Habermas, "On Systemically Distorted Communication," *Inquiry* 13 (Autumn 1970): 205–18.

31. The last of these examples comes from Indiana. See "Charges Unlikely against Parents Who Allowed 12-year-old Boy To Die," *Herald Times* (Bloomington, Ind.), February 2, 1999. Cases involving members of the Church of the Firstborn who refuse medical treatment for their children have also cropped up in Oklahoma and Colorado. See, e.g., "Girl's Life in Limbo, DHS Feud," Associated Press, January 24, 1999; Nancy Lofholm, "Baby Dies after Medical Care Withheld," *Denver Post*, March 3, 1999.

32. Taylor, *Multiculturalism*, 70.

33. Ibid., 72–73.

34. For a discussion from a feminist perspective, see Susan Moller Okin, *Is Multiculturalism Bad for Women?*, ed. Joshua Cohen, Matthew Howard, and Martha C. Nussbaum (Princeton: Princeton University Press, 1999).

35. Taylor, *Multiculturalism*, 66–67.

36. Darwall, "Two Kinds of Respect," 38.

6. RELIGION, DIALOGUE, AND HUMAN RIGHTS

1. Taking these first two paragraphs together, we see how the norm for respect for persons underwrites what are known as the "external" and "internal" fora—the right of security against (external) infringement and the (internal) right of religious freedom. See also chapter 4, n7.

2. Michael Ignatieff, *Human Rights as Politics and Idolatry*, ed. Amy Gutmann (Princeton: Princeton University Press, 2001), 85. Es-

chewing religious and philosophical foundations, Ignatieff defends the idea of human rights on the basis of reciprocity and "shared human capacities—empathy, conscience and free will." For Ignatieff, "we judge human actions by the simple test of whether we would wish to be on the receiving end." Ignatieff's argument invokes intuitions of the sort I evaluated in chapter 3, "intuitions [that] derive simply from our own experience of pain and our capacity to imagine the pain of others." Although his view claims to have the advantage "that it cannot justify inhumanity on foundational grounds," it fails to answer this obvious question: On what grounds can we say that "shared human capacities—empathy, conscience, and free will" have the advantage of preventing inhumanity? Clearly, the record of barbarity in the twentieth century indicates that such capacities and corresponding intuitions are not reliably and widely shared. See Ignatieff, *Human Rights*, 88–89.

3. I do not mean by this to suggest that identifying common ground can strengthen the *justification* of basic rights. I speak rather to the question of the *legitimation* of such rights, the prospect of securing agreements according to which individuals or groups would bind themselves to human rights. The project of legitimation, as Ignatieff suggests, diminishes the problem of human rights imperialism. See Ignatieff, *Human Rights as Politics and Idolatry*, 18–20.

4. See Robert Traer, *Faith in Human Rights: Support in Religious Traditions for a Global Struggle* (Washington, D.C.: Georgetown University Press, 1991), which surveys major world religions and their bases for supporting human rights doctrine.

5. Barbara Herman, "Pluralism and the Community of Moral Judgment," in *Toleration: An Elusive Virtue*, ed. David Heyd (Princeton: Princeton University Press, 1996), 60–80, at 61.

6. For a discussion of the positive obligation of respect to keep conversations going in contexts of disagreement, see Charles E. Larmore, *Patterns of Moral Complexity* (Cambridge: Cambridge University Press, 1987), 59–68.

7. For useful discussions, see Traer, *Faith in Human Rights*, chap. 7; John Kelsay, *Arguing the Just War in Islam* (Cambridge, Mass.: Harvard University Press, 2007), chap. 5; David Little, John Kelsay, and Abdulaziz A. Sachedina, *Human Rights and the Conflict of Cultures: Western and Islamic Perspectives on Religious Liberty* (Columbia: University of South Carolina Press, 1988); Irene Bloom, J. Paul

Martin, and Wayne Proudfoot, eds., *Religious Diversity and Human Rights* (New York: Columbia University Press, 1996).

8. For an essay written in the same spirit, see David Little, "Religion, Human Rights, and Secularism: Preliminary Clarifications and Some Islamic, Jewish, and Christian Responses," in *Humanity Before God: Contemporary Faces of Jewish, Christian, and Islamic Ethics*, ed. William Schweiker, Michael A. Johnson, and Kevin Jung (Minneapolis: Fortress Press, 2006), 256–83.

9. John Esposito, *Unholy War: Terror in the Name of Islam* (New York: Oxford University Press, 2002), 16.

10. See Miriam Cooke and Bruce Lawrence, "Muslim Women Between Human Rights and Islamic Norms," in *Religious Diversity and Human Rights*, 313–31.

11. Abul A'la Maududi, *Human Rights in Islam* (Lahore, Pakistan: Islamic Publications, 1977; original presentation in 1948).

12. In addition to the works above and below, see Maulana Maududi, *Selected Speeches and Writings of Maulana Maududi*, trans. S. Zakir Aijaz (Karachi, Pakistan: International Islamic Publishers, 1981, 1982); Abul A'la Maududi, *Let Us Be Muslims*, ed. Khurram Murad (London: The Islamic Foundation, 1985).

13. Maududi, *Human Rights in Islam*, 6. See also Abul A'la Maududi, *Islamic Law and Constitution*, ed. and trans. Khurshid Ahmad (Lahore, Pakistan: Islamic Publications, 1960), chaps. 4–8.

14. Maududi, *Human Rights in Islam*, 6.

15. Ibid., 8.

16. Ibid., 14–21.

17. Ibid., 22–34.

18. Ibid., 20.

19. Ibid., 35–39.

20. Ibid., 12.

21. Abul A'la Maududi, "Fallacy of Rationalism," in *Contemporary Debates in Islam: An Anthology of Modernist and Fundamentalist Thought*, ed. Mansoor Moaddel and Kamran Talattof (New York: St. Martin's Press, 2000), 210.

22. Maududi, *Human Rights in Islam*, 9.

23. Ibid.

24. As reported in Cooke and Lawrence, "Muslim Women Between Human Rights and Islamic Norms," 313–31.

25. Maududi, *Human Rights in Islam*, 12.

26. Ibid., 39.

27. United Nations, "Universal Declaration of Human Rights," at http://www.un.org/Overview/rights.html.

28. For a discussion, see Heiner Bielefeldt, "Muslim Voices in the Human Rights Debate," *Human Rights Quarterly* 17 (1995): 587–617. Irene Oh examines Maududi's ideas in a comparative way, endorsing the idea of a "fusion of horizons" along the lines that I question in chapter 5. See Irene Oh, *The Rights of God: Islam, Human Rights, and Comparative Ethics* (Washington, D.C.: Georgetown University Press, 2007).

29. Maududi, *Human Rights in Islam,* 39.

30. Abdulaziz Sachedina, *The Islamic Roots of Democratic Pluralism* (New York: Oxford University Press, 2001).

31. Ibid., 68, see also 49.

32. Ibid., 20–21.

33. Ibid., 43.

34. Ibid.

35. Ibid., 70.

36. Ibid., 43.

37. Ibid.

38. Ibid., 83: "Natural law in Islam is ontologically related to the Koranic notion of *fitra* and its essential function in perceiving God, the source of both natural law and the revelation." For a discussion of parallels between *fitra* and natural law ethics in Christianity, along with implications for religious toleration, see David Little, John Kelsay, and Abulaziz Sachedina, "Christianity, Islam, and Religious Liberty," in *Religious Diversity and Human Rights,* 213–39.

39. Sachedina, *The Islamic Roots of Democratic Pluralism,* 82.

40. Ibid., 57–58.

41. Ibid., 23–35.

42. Ibid., 52.

43. Ibid., 58–60.

44. Ibid., 71.

45. Ibid., 33.

46. Ibid., 83.

47. Ibid., 88.

48. Ibid., 71, 102, 112.

49. Ibid., 71. See also Abdulaziz Sachedina, "Human Vicegerency: A Blessing or a Curse? The Challenge to Be God's Caliph in the Qur'an," in *Humanity Before God,* 41–42.

50. Sachedina, *Islamic Roots of Democratic Pluralism*, 82.

51. Ibid., 25.

52. Ibid., 84.

53. Ibid.

54. Ibid., 82.

55. Ibid., 64.

56. Ibid., 83.

57. Ibid., 70.

58. Ibid., 64–65.

59. Ibid., 31.

60. Ibid., 138.

61. Ibid., 50.

62. Ibid., 50–51.

63. Ibid., 14.

64. Ibid., 111.

65. Ibid., 112.

66. Ibid., 109–12.

67. Robert Merrihew Adams, "Religious Ethics in a Pluralistic Society," in *Prospects for a Common Morality*, ed. Gene Outka and John P. Reeder Jr. (Princeton: Princeton University Press, 1993), 93–113, at 100.

68. Ibid.

69. Ibid.

70. Ibid., 101.

71. Ibid.

72. See, e.g., Stephen L. Carter, *The Culture of Disbelief: How American Law and Politics Trivialize Religious Devotion* (New York: Basic Books, 1993). Carter favorably quotes David Tracy who states, "The religions, at their best, always bear extraordinary powers of resistance. When not domesticated as sacred canopies for the status quo nor wasted by their own self-contradictory grasps at power, the religions live by resisting" (cited on p. 37; see David Tracy, *Plurality and Ambiguity: Hermeneutics, Religion, Hope* [New York: Seabury, 1987], 83–84). However agreeable this statement might be to apologists of religion, it obviously begs these questions: What does it mean to say—and on what basis may one say—that a religion is acting at its "best"? Are *all* forms of religious resistance to be commended? These questions open up inquiry into the ethics of belief.

1. I am invoking the categories *religion* and *ethics* as shorthand, in an abstract rather than historical way. In talking about the priority of religion to ethics, what I mean to capture is the notion that moral norms are always relative to wider webs of belief. On the phrase "ethics of belief," see chapter 1, n33.

2. By "respect" here I obviously mean recognition respect, as spelled out in chapter 5.

3. This latter locution is from Gene Outka, *Agape: An Ethical Analysis* (New Haven: Yale University Press, 1972), 9.

4. Michael Walzer, *Thick and Thin: Moral Argument at Home and Abroad* (Notre Dame, Ind.: University of Notre Dame Press, 1994), 1–19.

5. Ibid.

6. Ibid., 3.

7. Ibid., 11. Yet Walzer seems to equivocate. Contrary to the holist (or antidualist) interpretation that his argument invites, he speaks of maximal and minimal morality as involving a moral dualism (3–4). It is not clear if this dualism marks a difference of degree (thin versus thick) or whether it assigns to thin and thick morality respective forms of work that might at times occur at cross-purposes—say, when (thin) claims of procedural fairness constrain (thick) aspirations to advance particular cultural legacies and traditional practices. Moreover, he claims that a morality "whose practitioners could not respond to other people's pain and oppression or march (sometimes) in other people's parades, would be a deficient morality" (10). To this point Walzer adds that when we criticize other societies with a minimum morality "that can't be all that we are doing" (ibid.). It is not clear, however, what more we are doing, or how doing something "more" would challenge the defense of minimalism, focusing on moral subjectivity, that I have offered in this book.

8. On "side constraints," see Robert Nozick, *Anarchy, State, and Utopia* (New York: Basic Books, 1974), 28–35.

9. Jeremy Waldron discusses indirect and direct ways of connecting first- and second-generation human rights (civil and socioeconomic rights). One account views socioeconomic rights as necessary for the exercise of agency: "If one is really concerned to secure civil or political liberty for a person, that commitment should be accompanied by

a further concern about the conditions of the person's life that make it possible for him to enjoy and exercise that liberty" (7). Waldron continues: "The rights that are most familiar to us, rights to civil and political liberty, evoke images of autonomy, rational agency, and independence. It is our interest in those underlying ideas that explains our allegiance to first-generation rights, but we know that things like malnutrition, epidemic disease, and exposure can debilitate and finally destroy all the human faculties that such rights presuppose" (7–8). Another, more straightforward account grounds socioeconomic rights on the notion that "socioeconomic needs are as important as any other interests, and that a moral theory of individual dignity is plainly inadequate if it does not take them into account" (11). This second line of thought would assign dignity presumably on terms other than that of moral subjectivity. Where predicaments such as death, disease, and malnutrition "are plainly unavoidable, a refusal to do anything to address them is evidently an insult to human dignity and a failure to take seriously the unconditional worth of each individual" (ibid.). The thrust of Waldon's discussion is to note reasons available to liberals for affirming second-generation rights. See Jeremy Waldron, "Two Sides of the Coin," in his *Liberal Rights: Collected Papers 1981–1991* (Cambridge: Cambridge University Press, 1993), 1–34, esp. 7–13. In a similar vein, Shue defends the idea of subsistence rights alongside security rights in *Basic Rights: Subsistence, Affluence, and U.S. Foreign Policy*, 2nd ed. (Princeton: Princeton University Press, 1996 [1980]), chap. 1.

10. I draw this insight from Charles Larmore, "History and Truth," in his *The Autonomy of Morality* (Cambridge: Cambridge University Press, 2008), chap. 1.

11. *Dignitas Humanae (Declaration on Religious Freedom)*, in *Renewing the Earth: Catholic Documents on Peace, Justice, and Liberation*, ed. David J. O'Brien and Thomas Shannon (New York: Doubleday, 1977), par. 2, 293.

12. Ibid., par. 1, 290.

13. Ibid., par. 11, 299.

14. For an effort to bring Augustinian thinking into dialogue with liberal democratic theory, broadly conceived, see Edmund Santurri, "Rawlsian Liberalism, Moral Truth, and Augustinian Politics," *Journal for Peace and Justice Studies* 8, no. 2 (1997): 1–36; Paul Weithman, "Toward and Augustinian Liberalism," in *The Augustinian Tradition*,

ed. Gareth Matthews (Berkeley: University of California Press, 1999), 304–22; Eric Gregory, *Politics and the Order of Love: An Augustinian Ethic of Democratic Citizenship* (Chicago: University of Chicago Press, 2008). For Gregory, "the dignity of a particular human person is grounded in participation with something other than what that person privately possesses or determines. The person is a creature of God and to be loved as such" (43). Gregory draws on Augustine's idea of love, which "has fostered compelling commitments to the equal dignity of persons and the creation of civic institutions that manifest this commitment" (45). Gregory distinguishes his Augustinian view of neighbor-love from "liberal respect" (43–45).

15. Clifford Geertz, *Local Knowledge: Further Essays in Interpretive Anthropology* (New York: Basic Books, 1983), 57.

16. Ibid.

APPENDIX 1

1. Will Kymlicka, *Multicultural Citizenship: A Liberal Defense of Minority Rights* (Oxford: Clarendon Press, 1995), 81.

2. David Rodin, *War and Self-Defense* (Oxford: Clarendon Press, 2002), 127.

3. Rodin has in mind the argument in Michael Walzer's *Just and Unjust Wars: A Moral Argument with Historical Illustrations,* 4th ed. (New York: Basic Books, 2006 [1977]), 34; see also 41–44; 144–47.

4. Rodin, *War and Self-Defense,* 129.

5. Ibid., 129–30.

6. Consider the Falklands War of 1982.

7. Rodin, *War and Self-Defense,* 131.

8. Ibid.

9. Ibid., 123.

10. Ibid., 149.

11. Ibid., 153.

12. Ibid., 155.

13. Ibid., 156.

14. Ibid., 159.

15. Ibid., 159–60.

16. Arguments against such actions would rest on the principle of proportionality, which are easily accommodated by just-war reasoning.

17. For one argument along these lines, see David Luban, "Just War and Human Rights," *Philosophy and Public Affairs* 9, no. 2 (Winter 1980): 160–81.

18. Rodin, *War and Self-Defense*, 155.

19. Benedict Anderson, *Imagined Communities: Reflections on the Origin and Spread of Nationalism*, rev. ed. (New York: Verso, 1983).

20. Jeff McMahan, "War as Self-Defense," *Ethics and International Affairs* 18, no. 1 (March 2004): 75–80, at 78. Emphasis in the original.

APPENDIX 2

1. For an extended discussion, see Stephen L. Darwall, *The Second Person Standpoint: Morality, Respect, and Accountability* (Cambridge, Mass.: Harvard University Press, 2006).

2. I address questions regarding the ethics of the war in Iraq in "Justifications of the Iraq War Examined," *Ethics and International Affairs* 22, no. 1 (Spring 2008): 43–67.

3. For a discussion, see Michael Walzer, *Just and Unjust Wars: A Moral Argument with Historical Illustrations*, 4th ed. (New York: Basic Books, 2006 [1977]), 229–32, 246–47, 264. As this idea helps to explain the Bush administration's approach to international law in the wake of 9/11, see Steven R. Ratner, "*Jus ad Bellum* and *Jus in Bello* after September 11," *American Journal of International Law* 96, no. 4 (October 2002): 905–21, at 913.

4. The point is put aptly by Ian Clark in *Waging War: A Philosophical Introduction* (Oxford: Clarendon Press, 1990), 36.

5. See Jeff McMahan, "The Ethics of Killing in War," *Ethics* 114, no. 4 (July 2004): 693–733, at 708–9.

6. Ibid., 709.

7. Henry Shue, "War," in *The Oxford Handbook of Practical Ethics*, ed. Hugh LaFollette (New York: Oxford University Press, 2003), 734–72, at 752–53.

8. *Charter of the United Nations*, Chapter 7, Article 51, at http://www.un.org/aboutun/charter/.

9. Michael Ignatieff, *Human Rights as Politics and Idolatry*, ed. Amy Gutmann (Princeton: Princeton University Press, 2001), 37.

10. Several of these alternatives are discussed in Clark, *Waging War*, 18–23.

11. John Rawls, *A Theory of Justice* (Cambridge, Mass.: Harvard/ Belknap, 1971), 133.

12. For one such defense, see Walzer, *Just and Unjust Wars*, 80– 85.

13. Thomas Aquinas, *Summa Theologiae*, trans. Marcus Lefébure (Cambridge: Cambridge University Press, 2006), 2a–2ae Q. 64, art. 7.

14. Brian V. Johnstone, "The Meaning of Proportionate Reasoning in Contemporary Moral Theology," *Thomist* 49 (1985): 223–47.

15. Ibid., 232.

16. A.J. Coates defends the idea of "bilateral" or "comparative" justice as providing a check against total war ideology. See A.J. Coates, *The Ethics of War* (Manchester: Manchester University Press, 1997), 147, 150–51, 154, 201, and passim.

17. 1977 Geneva Protocol I, Additional to the Geneva Conventions of 12 August 1949, in *Documents on the Laws of War,* ed. Adam Roberts and Richard Geulff (New York: Oxford University Press, 2001), 448.

18. Walzer, *Just and Unjust Wars*, 153.

19. Ibid., 156.

20. 1977 Geneva Protocol I, Additional to the Geneva Conventions of 12 August 1949, in *Documents on the Laws of War,* 453.

21. See 1949 Geneva Convention III, Art. 3; 1977 Geneva Protocol I, Additional to the Geneva Conventions of 12 August 1949, Art. 75, in *Documents on the Law of War,* 245, 464.

22. Michael Walzer, "First, Define the Battlefield," *New York Times*, September 21, 2001; Walzer, "After 9/11: Five Questions about Terrorism," in *Arguing about War* (New Haven: Yale University Press, 2004), 130–42.

23. Henry Shue, "Eroding Sovereignty: The Advance of Principle," in *The Morality of Nationalism*, ed. Robert McKim and Jeff McMahan (New York: Oxford University Press, 1997), 340–59, at 342.

24. Barrie Paskins and Michael Dockrill, *The Ethics of War* (Minneapolis: University of Minnesota Press, 1979), 105–6.

25. President George W. Bush, "Address before a Joint Session of Congress on the United States Response to the Terrorist Attacks of September 11" (September 20, 2001), at http://www.whitehouse. gov/news/releases/2002/0920010920–8.html. Accessed on September 21, 2001.

26. U.N. Document S/2001/946, available at http://www2.kobe-u.ac-jp/~shotaro/kogi/2005/s-2001–946e.pdf. Accessed on August 17, 2009.

27. Ratner, "*Jus ad Bellum* and *Jus in Bello* after September 11," 906–910.

28. Ibid., 908–9. Similar doubts are expressed by Michael Byers, "Terrorism, the Use of Force and International Law after 11 September," *International and Comparative Law Quarterly* 51, no. 2 (April 2002): 401–14.

29. Ahmed Rashid, *Taliban: Militant Islam, Oil, and Fundamentalism in Central Asia* (New Haven: Yale University Press, 2000), 105–16.

30. U.N. Security Council Resolution 1368 (September 12, 2001), available at http://www.un.org/News/Press/docs/2001/SC7143.doc.htm.

31. Statement by the North American Council, available at http://www.nato.int/docu/pr/2001/p01–124e.htm. Accessed on October 8, 2001.

32. Organization of American States Resolution RC24/RES.1/01, 21 September 2001, at http://www.cicte.oas.org/Rev/en/Documents/Resolutions/doc_rc_23_res_1_01_eng.pdf.

33. George H. Aldrich, "The Taliban, Al Qaeda, and the Determination of Illegal Combatants," *American Journal of International Law* 96 (October 2002): 891–98, at 893.

34. Ibid.

35. Ibid.

36. Ibid.

37. David E. Sanger and Joseph Kahn, "Bush Freezes Assets Linked to Terror Net; Banks 'On Notice,'" *New York Times*, September 25, 2001; Joseph Kahn and Judith Miller, "U.S. Freezes More Accounts; Saudi and Pakistani Assets Cited for Ties to Bin Laden," *New York Times*, October 13, 2001.

38. President George W. Bush, "Address before a Joint Session of Congress on the United States Response to the Terrorist Attacks of September 11."

39. James Brooke, "Unease Grows in Philippines on U.S. Forces," *New York Times*, January 19, 2002.

40. Stanley Hoffmann, "On the War," *New York Review of Books*, November 1, 2001, at http://www.nybooks.com/articles/14660.

41. See http://www.globalsecurity.org/military/library/policy/national/ nss-020920.pdf; http://georgewbush-whitehouse.archives.gov/nsc/nss/ 2006/.

42. See http://www.state.gov/s/ct/rls/other/des/123085.htm.

43. David Rhode, "Executions of P.O.W.'s Cast Doubts on Alliance," *New York Times*, November 13, 2001.

44. James Risen, "U.S. Said to Have Averted Inquiry Into '01 Afghan Killings," *New York Times*, July 11, 2009.

45. Tim Golden, "Afghan Ban on Growing of Opium Is Unraveling," *New York Times*, October 22, 2001.

46. Ahmed Rashid, *Descent into Chaos: The U.S. and the Disaster in Pakistan, Afghanistan, and Central Asia* (New York: Penguin, 2008), 318.

47. Ibid., 329.

48. See, e.g., David E. Sanger, "President Weighs Who Will Follow Taliban in Power," *New York Times*, October 14, 2001.

49. Editorial, "A Just War?" at http://www.americamagazine.org/ content/article.cfm?article_id=1068.

50. During the Clinton administration, the United States tried to mobilize the international community against bin Laden through a series of U.N. resolutions before 9/11. In 1999, the U.N. Security Council passed Resolution 1267, demanding that the Taliban hand over bin Laden. The United States had taken military action against al Qaeda the previous year. In retaliation for the bombing of U.S. embassies in Africa in August 1998, the U.S. launched cruise missiles on al Qaeda training camps in eastern Afghanistan. See Rashid, *Descent into Chaos*, 16, 18; *The 9/11 Commission Report* (New York: W. W. Norton, 2004), chap. 4.

51. Tony Blair, "Responsibility for the Terrorist Atrocities in the United States, 11 September 2001," at http://www.fas.org/irp/news/2001/ 11/ukreport.html. Accessed October 5, 2001.

52. *Afghanistan Study Group Report*, page 7, at http://www.the-presidency.org/pubs/Afghan_Study_Group_Report.pdf. Accessed February 14, 2008.

53. Ibid., 18.

54. "Remarks by the President on a New Strategy for Afghanistan and Pakistan," at http://www.whitehouse .gov/the_press_office/Remarks-by-the-President-on-a-New-Strategy-for-Afghanistan-and-Pakistan/.Accessed on March 29, 2009.

55. Sheryl Gay Strolberg and Helene Cooper, "Obama Adds Troops, but Maps Exit Plan," *New York Times*, December 2, 2009.

56. *"Troops in Contact"*: *Airstrikes and Civilian Deaths in Afghanistan*, a report by Human Rights Watch at http://www.hrw.org/en/reports/2008/09/08/troops-contact-0, p. 2. Accessed on July 2, 2009.

57. Ibid., 2–36.

58. David Zucchino, " 'The Americans . . . They Just Drop Their Bombs and Leave,' " *Los Angeles Times*, June 2, 2002.

59. "A Dossier on Civilian Victims of United States' Aerial Bombing of Afghanistan: A Comprehensive Accounting," at http://pubpages.unh/~mwherold/dossier.htm. Accessed on July 5, 2009.

60. Ibid.

61. Marc W. Herold, "The Matrix of Death: (Im)Precision of U.S. Bombing and the (Under)Valuation of an Afghan Life," at http://www.rawa.org/temp/runews/2008/10/06/the-imprecision-ofus-bombing-and-the-under-valuation-of-an-afghan-life.html. Accessed on July 5, 2009.

62. "Afghanistan: Civilian Deaths from Airstrikes," by Human Rights Watch, September 7, 2008, at http://www.hrw.org/en/news/2008/09/07/afghanistan-civilian-deaths-airstrikes. Accessed on July 2, 2009.

63. Carlotta Gall, "British Criticize Air Attacks in Afghan Region," *New York Times*, August 9, 2007.

64. Dexter Filkins, "Afghan Civilian Deaths Rose 40 Percent in 2008," *New York Times*, February 19, 2009.

65. Abdul Waheed Wafa and John F. Burns, "U.S. Airstrike Reported to Hit Afghan Wedding," *New York Times*, November 5, 2008.

66. Carlotta Gall, "U.S. Killed 90, Including 60 Children, in Afghan Village, U.N. Finds," *New York Times*, August 27, 2008.

67. Richard A. Oppel, Jr., "U.S. Concedes Afghan Attack Mainly Killed Civilians," *New York Times*, February 22, 2009.

68. Mark Mazzetti and Eric Schmitt, "U.S. Halted Some Raids in Afghanistan," *New York Times*, March 10, 2009.

69. Dexter Filkins, "U.S. Tightens Airstrike Policy in Afghanistan," *New York Times*, June 21, 2009.

70. *"Troops in Contact*," a report by Human Rights Watch (see n56).

71. For an exception, see *"Troops in Contact*," 2–36. At this writing, news reports are beginning to include data about civilian casualties caused by the Taliban. See, e.g., Abdul Waheed Wafa and Alan

Cowell, "Truck Blast in Afghanistan Leaves at Least 24 Dead," *New York Times*, July 10, 2009.

72. I say "U.S. and NATO forces" rather than "all sides in this war" owing to a disputed point in just-war doctrine. On the account of the doctrine espoused by G. E. M. Anscombe, the Taliban and al Qaeda are fighting an unjust war and all the deaths they cause—combatant and noncombatant—count as murder. U.S. and NATO forces, as defenders of a just cause, commit wrongdoing only when they violate principles of the *jus in bello*. For Anscombe, there is a moral asymmetry between the threats to life posed by the just side and the threats to life posed by the unjust side in a conflict. On her view, the deaths of civilians caused by an unjust aggressor should not be sorted out in terms of intended and unintended and regrettable deaths, the latter of which would be evaluated in terms of the principle of proportionality. All deaths caused by an unjust side are impermissible. On the account of the doctrine espoused by Walzer, soldiers on each side of battle are "moral equals." On that view, we are not to draw an asymmetry between soldiers fighting a just cause and an unjust cause because all soldiers are coerced into war and become, by virtue of that coercion, "dangerous men." The deaths of civilians caused by either side, on Walzer's view, would be sorted out into two classes, those that are intended and those that are foreseen but unintended. Some unintended, foreseen deaths caused by either side may be permissible, however regrettable, if they are proportionate to a relevant military goal. Whether fighters for Taliban and al Qaeda can plausibly claim to be coerced into fighting—one of Walzer's premises for defending the idea that soldiers are "moral equals"—is an empirical matter that I cannot take up here. Rashid offers one example of a farmer forcibly conscripted into the Taliban to fight in Afghanistan. For the purposes of this discussion, I will focus on U.S. and NATO actions on the view that they are not fighting in defense of an unjust cause. That is not to suggest that all U.S and NATO actions are justified, as I hope to make plain. That soldiers fighting on a just side must be judged according to *in bello* criteria is a point on which Anscombe and Walzer would agree. See G. E. M. Anscombe, "The Justice of the Present War Examined," in *The Collected Philosophical Papers of G. E. M. Anscombe*, vol. 3: *Ethics, Religion and Politics* (Oxford: Basil Blackwell, 1981), 72–81; Walzer, *Just and Unjust Wars*, chap. 3; Ahmed Rashid, *Descent into Chaos*, 299.

73. Dexter Filkins, "U.S. Tightens Airstrike Policy in Afghanistan," Nancy A. Youssef, "U.S. Troops Told to Stop Taliban Pursuit if Civilians Are at Risk," *Miami Herald*, July 1, 2009; Julian E. Barnes, "U.S. Report on Afghan Civilian Deaths Urges Caution," *Los Angeles Times*, June 20, 2009

74. Rashid, *Descent into Chaos*, 296. See also Matthew Evangelista, *Law, Ethics, and the War on Terror* (Cambridge: Polity Press, 2008), chap. 3.

75. Rashid, *Descent into Chaos*, 298.

76. Ibid., 305.

77. Seymour M. Hersh, "Annals of National Security: Torture at Abu Ghraib," *New Yorker*, May 10, 2004; see Mark Danner, *Torture and Truth: America, Abu Ghraib, and the War on Terror* (New York: New York Review Books, 2004); Karen Greenberg, ed., *The Torture Debate in America* (Cambridge: Cambridge University Press, 2006).

78. Rashid, *Descent into Chaos*, 303.

79. Adam Roberts, "The Prisoner Question: If the U.S. Has Acted Lawfully, What's the Furor About?" *Washington Post*, February 3, 2002.

80. Ibid.

81. 1977 Geneva Protocol I, Additional to the Geneva Conventions of 12 August 1949, in *Documents on the Laws of War*, 464–65.

SELECT BIBLIOGRAPHY

The 9/11 Commission Report. New York: W.W. Norton, 2004.

Adams, Robert Merrihew. "Religious Ethics in a Pluralistic Society." In *Prospects for a Common Morality*, edited by Gene Outka and John P. Reeder Jr., 93–113. Princeton: Princeton University Press, 1993.

Afghanistan Study Group. *Afghanistan Study Group Report* (January 30, 2008), at http://thepresidency.org/pubs/Afghan_Study_Group.final.pdf.

Aldrich, George H. "The Taliban, Al Qaeda, and the Determination of Illegal Combatants," *American Journal of International Law* 96 (October 2002): 891–98.

Anderson, Benedict. *Imagined Communities: Reflections on the Origin and Spread of Nationalism.* Rev. ed. New York: Verso, 1983.

Anscombe, G.E.M. *The Collected Philosophical Papers of G.E.M. Anscombe*, vol. 3, *Ethics, Religion, and Politics.* Oxford: Blackwell, 1981.

Barber, Benjamin R. "The War of All Against All: Terror and the Politics of Fear." In *War After September 11*, edited by Verna V. Gehring, 75–91. Lanham, Md.: Rowman and Littlefield, 2003.

Bielefeldt, Heiner. "Muslim Voices in the Human Rights Debate." *Human Rights Quarterly* 17 (1995): 587–617.

Bin Laden, Osama. "Letter to the American People" at http://www.observer.co.uk/worldview/story/0,11581,84525,00.htm.

Blair, Tony. "Evidence against Bin Laden" at http://www.pm.gov.uk/text/evidence.htm.

Bloom, Irene, J. Paul Martin, and Wayne Proudfoot, eds. *Religious Diversity and Human Rights*. New York: Columbia University Press, 1996.

Bush, George W. "Address before a Joint Session of Congress on the United States Response to the Terrorist Attacks of September 11" (September 20, 2001), at http://www.whitehouse.gov/news/releases/2002/09200109 20-8.html.

Calvin, John. *Institutes of the Christian Religion*. Edited by John T. McNeill, translated by Ford Lewis Battles. 2 vols. Philadelphia: Westminster Press, 1960.

Clark, Ian. *Waging War: A Philosophical Introduction*. Oxford: Clarendon Press, 1990.

Clifford, W.K. "The Ethics of Belief." In *Religion from Tolstoy to Camus*, edited by Walter Kaufmann. New York: Harper and Row, 1961.

Cohen, Andrew Jason. "What Toleration Is." *Ethics* 115 (October 2004): 68–95.

Cohen, Joshua, and Ian Lague, eds. *The Place of Tolerance in Islam*. Boston: Beacon Press, 2002.

Darwall, Stephen L. "Peace as Politics." In *Religion, Politics, and Peace*, 85–103, edited by Leroy S. Rouner. Notre Dame, Ind.: University of Notre Dame Press, 1999.

——. *The Second-Person Standpoint: Morality, Respect, and Accountability*. Cambridge, Mass.: Harvard University Press, 2006.

——. "Two Kinds of Respect." *Ethics* 88, no. 1 (October 1977): 36–49.

Davis, Nancy. "Abortion and Self-Defense." *Philosophy and Public Affairs* 13 (Summer 1984): 175–207.

Elshtain, Jean Bethke. *Just War against Terror: The Burden of American Power in a Violent World*. New York: Basic Books, 2003.

Esposito, John L. *Unholy War: Terror in the Name of Islam*. New York: Oxford University Press, 2002.

Evangelista, Matthew. *Law, Ethics, and the War on Terror*. Cambridge: Polity Press, 2008.

Fish, Stanley. "Condemnation Without Absolutes." *New York Times*, 15 October, 2001.

———. *The Trouble with Principle*. Cambridge, Mass.: Harvard University Press, 1999.

Geertz, Clifford. *Local Knowledge: Further Essays in Interpretive Anthropology*. New York: Basic Books, 1983.

Gewirth, Alan. "Common Morality and the Community of Rights." In *Prospects for a Common Morality*, edited by Outka and Reeder, 114–48. Princeton: Princeton University Press, 1993.

———. *Human Rights: Essays on Justification and Applications*. Chicago: University of Chicago Press, 1982.

———. *Reason and Morality*. Chicago: University of Chicago Press, 1978.

Heyd, David., ed. *Toleration: An Elusive Virtue*. Princeton: Princeton University Press, 1996.

Hoffmann, Stanley. "On the War." *New York Review of Books*, November 1, 2001, http://www.nybooks.com/articles/14660.

———. "What Is to Be Done?" *New York Review of Books*, May 20, 1999.

Horton, John, and Susan Mendus, eds. *Aspects of Toleration: Philosophical Studies*. London: Metheun, 1985.

———, eds. *Toleration, Identity, and Difference*. New York: St. Martin's Press, 1999.

Ibrahim, Raymond, ed. *The Al Qaeda Reader*. Translated by Raymond Ibrahim, with an introduction by Victor Davis Hanson. New York: Broadway Books, 2007.

Ignatieff, Michael. *Human Rights as Politics and Idolatry*. Edited with an introduction by Amy Gutmann. Princeton: Princeton University Press, 2001.

Johnson, James Turner. "Jihad and Just War." *First Things: A Journal of Religion and Public Life* 124 (June/July 2002): 12–14.

———. *Just War Tradition and the Restraint of War: A Moral and Historical Inquiry*. Princeton: Princeton University Press, 1981.

Johnstone, Brian V. "The Meaning of Proportionate Reasoning in Contemporary Moral Theology." *Thomist* 49 (1985): 223–47.

Juergensmeyer, Mark. *Terror in the Mind of God: The Global Rise of Religious Violence*. Updated edition with a new preface. Berkeley: University of California Press, 2000.

Kelsay, John. *Arguing the Just War in Islam*. Cambridge, Mass.: Harvard University Press, 2007.

———. *Islam and War: A Study in Comparative Ethics*. Louisville: Westminster/John Knox, 1993.

———. "Osama bin Laden and the Just Conduct of War." *America* (October 8, 2001): 25–27.

Kelsay, John, and James Turner Johnson, eds. *Just War and Jihad: Historical and Theoretical Perspectives on War and Peace in Western and Islamic Traditions*. New York: Greenwood Press, 1991.

Kepel, Gilles, and Jean-Pierre Milelli, eds. *Al Qaeda in Its Own Words*. Translated by Pascale Ghazaleh. Cambridge, Mass.: Harvard/Belknap Press, 2008.

Krueger, Alan B., and Jitka Malečková. "Does Poverty Cause Terrorism?" *The New Republic* (June 24, 2002): 27–33.

Kymlicka, Will. *Multicultural Citizenship: A Liberal Theory of Minority Rights*. Oxford: Clarendon Press, 1995.

———. "Two Types of Pluralism and Tolerance." In *Toleration: An Elusive Virtue*, edited by David Heyd (Princeton: Princeton University Press, 1996).

Larmore, Charles. *The Autonomy of Morality*. Cambridge: Cambridge University Press, 2008.

———. "Respect for Persons." *Hedgehog Review* 7, no. 2 (Summer 2005): 66–76.

Lawrence, Bruce, ed. *Messages to the World: The Statements of Osama bin Laden*. With an introduction by Bruce Lawrence, translated by James Howarth. London: Verso, 2005.

Lewis, Anthony. "The Inescapable World." *New York Times*, October 20, 2001.

Lewis, Bernard. "License to Kill: Usama bin Ladin's Declaration of Jihad." *Foreign Affairs* 77 (November/December 1998): 14–19.

Lincoln, Bruce. *Holy Terrors: Thinking about Religion after September 11* (Chicago: University of Chicago Press, 2003).

Little, David. "On Behalf of Rights." *Journal of Religious Ethics* 34 (June 2006): 287–310.

———. "The Nature and Basis of Human Rights." In *Prospects for a Common Morality*, edited by Outka and Reeder, 73–92. Princeton: Princeton University Press, 1993.

———. "Response to Terrorism." *Bulletin of the Boston Theological Institute* 1 (Spring 2002): 1, 6, 7.

Little, David, John Kelsay, and Abdulaziz A. Sachedina. *Human Rights and the Conflict of Cultures: Western and Islamic Perspectives on*

Religious Liberty. Columbia, S.C.: University of South Carolina Press, 1988.

Luther, Martin. *Martin Luther: Selections from His Writings.* Edited with an introduction by John Dillenberger. New York: Doubleday, 1961.

MacIntyre, Alasdair. *After Virtue: A Study in Moral Theory.* Notre Dame, Ind.: University of Notre Dame Press, 1981.

Maududi, Abul A'la. "Fallacy of Rationalism." In *Contemporary Debates in Islam: An Anthology of Modernist and Fundamentalist Thought,* edited by Mansoor Moaddel and Kamran Talatoff.

——. *Human Rights in Islam.* Lahore, Pakistan: Islamic Publications, 1977.

——. *Islamic Law and Constitution.* Translated and edited by Khurshid Ahmad. Lahore, Pakistan: Islamic Publications, 1955.

——. *Selected Speeches and Writings of Maulana Maududi.* Translated by S. Zakir Aijaz. Karachi, Pakistan: International Islamic Publishers, 1981.

Mayer, Jane. "The House of bin Laden." *New Yorker,* November 12, 2001.

McMahan, Jeff. "The Ethics of Killing in War." *Ethics* 114, no. 4 (July 2004): 693–733.

——. *Killing in War.* Oxford: Clarendon Press, 2009.

——. "War as Self-Defense." *Ethics and International Affairs* 18, no. 1 (Winter 2004): 75–80.

Mill, John Stuart. *On Liberty.* Edited with an introduction by Currin V. Shields. Indianapolis: Bobbs-Merrill Educational Publishing, 1956.

Miller, Richard B. *Casuistry and Modern Ethics: A Poetics of Practical Reasoning.* Chicago: University of Chicago Press, 1996.

——. *Interpretations of Conflict: Ethics, Pacifism, and the Just-War Tradition.* Chicago: University of Chicago Press, 1991.

——. "On Making a Cultural Turn in Religious Ethics." *Journal of Religious Ethics* 33 (September 2005): 409–43.

Nardin, Terry, ed. *The Ethics of War: Secular and Religious Perspectives.* Princeton: Princeton University Press, 1996.

Nardin, Terry, and Daniel J. Sherman, eds. *Terror, Culture, Politics: Rethinking 9/11.* Bloomington: Indiana University Press, 2006.

Niebuhr, Reinhold. *The Nature and Destiny of Man,* 2 vols. New York: Charles Scribner's Sons, 1941.

Okin, Susan Moller. *Is Multiculturalism Bad for Women?* Edited by Joshua Cohen, Matthew Howard, and Martha Nussbaum. Princeton: Princeton University Press, 1999.

Paskins, Barrie, and Michael Dockrill. *The Ethics of War.* Minneapolis: University of Minnesota Press, 1979.

Rashid, Ahmed. *Descent into Chaos: The U.S. and the Disaster in Pakistan, Afghanistan, and Central Asia.* New York: Penguin, 2008.

——. *Jihad: The Rise of Militant Islam in Central Asia.* New Haven: Yale University Press, 2002.

——. *Taliban: Militant Islam, Oil, and Fundamentalism in Central Asia.* New Haven: Yale University Press, 2000.

Ramsey, Paul. *The Just War: Force and Political Responsibility.* New York: Charles Scribner's Sons, 1968.

Ratner, Steven R. "*Jus ad Bellum* and *Jus in Bello* after September 11." *American Journal of International Law* 96, no. 4 (October 2002): 905–21.

Rawls, John. *The Law of Peoples, with "The Idea of Public Reason Revisited."* Cambridge, Mass.: Harvard University Press, 1999.

——. *Political Liberalism, with a new Introduction and the "Reply to Habermas."* New York: Columbia University Press, 1996.

——. *A Theory of Justice.* Cambridge, Mass.: Harvard/Belknap Press, 1971.

Richards, David A. J. "Rights and Autonomy." *Ethics* 92, no. 1 (October 1981): 3–20.

Rivzi, Mashood. "Intolerable Injustices." In *The Place of Tolerance in Islam*, edited by Joshua Cohen and Ian Lague, 67–71. Boston: Beacon Press, 2002.

Roberts, Adam, and Richard Guelff, eds. *Documents on the Laws of War.* 3rd ed. New York: Oxford, 2000.

Rodin, David. *War and Self-Defense.* Oxford: Clarendon Press, 2002.

Rorty, Richard. *Objectivity, Relativism, and Truth: Philosophical Papers, I.* Cambridge: Cambridge University Press, 1991.

Sachedina, Abdulaziz. *The Islamic Roots of Democratic Pluralism.* New York: Oxford, 2001.

Shklar, Judith N. *The Faces of Injustice.* New Haven: Yale University Press, 1990.

Shue, Henry. *Basic Rights: Subsistence, Affluence, and U.S. Foreign Policy.* 2nd ed. Princeton: Princeton University Press, 1996 [1980].

———. "War," in *The Oxford Handbook of Practical Ethics*, edited by Hugh Lafollette. New York: Oxford University Press, 2003.

Sontag, Susan. "September 11, 2001," *New Yorker*, September 24, 2001.

Smith, Jonathan Z. *Imagining Religion: From Babylon to Jonestown*. Chicago: University of Chicago Press, 1982.

Stern, Jessica. *Terror in the Name of God: Why Religious Militants Kill*. New York: HarperCollins, 2003.

Strawson, Peter. "Freedom and Resentment." In *Free Will*, edited by Gary Watson. Oxford: Oxford University Press, 1982.

Taylor, Charles. *Multiculturalism: Examining the Politics of Recognition*. Edited with an introduction by Amy Gutmann. Princeton: Princeton University Press, 1994.

———. *Sources of the Self: The Making of the Modern Identity*. Cambridge, Mass.: Harvard University Press, 1989.

Thomas Aquinas, St. *Summa Theologiae*. Translated by Blackfriars. London: Eyre & Spottiswoode, 1964–80.

Traer, Robert. *Faith in Human Rights: Support in Religious Traditions for a Global Struggle*. Washington, D.C.: Georgetown University Press, 1991.

United Nations, "Universal Declaration of Human Rights," at http://www.un.org/Overview/rights.html.

U.S. Catholic Bishops. *The Challenge of Peace: God's Promise and Our Response*. Washington, D.C.: National Conference of Catholic Bishops, 1983.

Walzer, Michael. *Arguing About War*. New Haven: Yale University Press, 2004.

———. *Interpretation and Social Criticism*. Cambridge, Mass.: Harvard University Press, 1987.

———. *Just and Unjust Wars: A Moral Argument with Historical Illustrations*. 4th ed. New York: Basic Books, 2006 [1977].

———. *On Toleration*. New Haven: Yale University Press, 1999.

———. *Thick and Thin: Moral Argument at Home and Abroad*. Notre Dame, Ind.: University of Notre Dame Press, 1994.

Willis, Ellen. "Bringing the Holy War Home." *The Nation* (December 17, 2001): 15–18.

World Islamic Front. *Jihad Against Jews and Crusaders* at http://ww.fas.org/irp/paradocs/980223-fatwa.htm.

INDEX